#justpassingthrough

A Pilgrim's Journeys Home

Matthew Mueller

Copyright © 2019 by Matthew Mueller

All rights reserved. No part of this book may be reproduced or transmitted in any form or by any means without written permission of the author. For permissions, please contact the author via email at mattmueller95@hotmail.com.

First Edition

Library of Congresss Cataloging-in-Publication Data

Name: Mueller, Matthew, author

Title: #justpassingthrough: A Pilgrim's Journeys Home

Description: First edition. Independently published.

Identifiers: ISBN 9781710519013 (paperback)

Subjects: Nonfiction – Travel – Essays and Travelogues. Nonfiction – Religion – Christianity – Catholic

Cover design and photography: The author

For those who've been harmed by wolves in shepherds' clothing,
in the fervent hope that they, too, may get safely home.

Acknowledgments

This may be a collection of memoirs about trips I took alone, but neither the trips nor the book could have happened without the support, assistance, and involvement of a great many individuals. This list of acknowledgements is by definition incomplete, but I'll try to include as many as possible of the people who deserve to be mentioned here.

First, I am grateful to those of my family, friends, colleagues, and employers who, in some way small or large, are part of the stories I've told here. That list includes but is not limited to Fr. Mel Ayala, Janet and Jeff Bates and family, Paul Campbell, Greg DeStefano, Msgr. Paul Dudziak, Meghan Elliott and companions, Fr. Blake Evans, the late Joseph Flummerfelt, Jeff Freuler, Greg Gallagher, Peggy Gregory, Paul Hardy, Crossley Hawn, Jerry Kavinski, Christine Lane, Emily Lyons, Fitz Lyons, Grier Lyons, Michael Lyons, Peden Lyons, Scott McKinley, Andrew Megill, Fr. James Moore, O.P., Paul Murray, Esther Nyberg, Gretchen and the late Wilford Oakes, Fr. Jerry Pokorsky, Fr. Christopher Pollard, Anthony Rafaniello, Sarah Reyes, Kathy Sawyer, Teresa Schultz, Thomas Stehle, Lauren Tompkins, Neil Weston, Matthew Yost, and Bryan Zaros.

On a different level, thanks are due to the many people around the world who work in the transportation, hospitality, tourism, public safety, law enforcement, and pilgrimage sectors. Without them, we couldn't get much of anywhere.

Concerning the actual writing of this book, I thank Erin Bullock, Meghan Elliott, Sara Rennekamp, and Julie Zarukin for reading chapters or portions of the story from various angles and providing helpful suggestions. I'm especially indebted to Michael Lyons for his role as an advisor during the revision process; while the flaws of this book are all mine, a number of its improvements and potential successes are due to Michael's thoughtful review and feedback.

I'm also grateful to all the others who – knowingly or not – have encouraged me in this effort and/or been patient with my absence from other endeavors during its creation, including but not limited to Laurie and

Markus Bischof, Elizabeth and Patrick Carr and family, Constance Fee, Carol Jenkins, Jon Laird, Brodie Lyons, Steven Magnusen, Arthur Mueller, Brian Mueller, Elisha Mueller, Evan Mueller, Anthony and Sara Rennekamp and family, Clark Sawyer, and Andrew Weaver.

And as in all things, Soli Deo Gloria.

Table of Contents

Around the World By Accident 1

The East Coast's Main Street 39

The Sandbox 59

Visa Waiver 87

Misericordes Sicut Pater 121

Mistakes 163

Atlas Roads 183

The Americas 209

To Invade Normandy 227

Denouement 269

Around the World By Accident

With a few buzzes, vibrations, flashes, dings, and chimes, the smart phone woke me up, just as I'd programmed it. Stretching my arms and legs, I opened my eyes and adjusted to its faint light and the reflections of some street lights outside.

My own mental operating system was booting itself, taking note of my surroundings: first the location of the pillows and covers, next the layout of the room and the location of the bathroom. This wasn't my bed, so I must be in a hotel someplace. I yawned to feed oxygen to my Global Positioning System as it calibrated itself step by step.

It was 3:30 on Friday morning, and I needed to get from here to there by Saturday evening. "There" was (home sweet) Little Rome, the neighborhood in Northeast Washington, DC, where I'd lived for nearly seven years. "Here", I eventually remembered, was the Rex Hotel in Ho Chi Minh City, Vietnam. It was a business hotel in the center of the former South Vietnamese capital, made famous during the American War because the "Five O'clock Follies" military press conferences were held at the rooftop bar-restaurant where I'd dined a couple nights before.

Between my pillow in Ho Chi Minh City and my pillow in Little Rome lay 10873 miles of air travel, on four segments touching three countries. Plans called for a quick visit to central Hong Kong, a shower in southern California, and then Saturday breakfast on New York's Upper West Side with two college buddies. It would be a long journey home (about forty-eight hours) but my business class upgrade was confirmed across the Pacific, so getting adequate food, drink, and rest would be easy. Flipping my body clock upside down for the second time in a week wouldn't be much fun, but there was nothing to be done about that now except to get it over with.

With the alarm still ringing on the other side of the room (an inconvenience designed to make sure I got out of bed before I can hit the

#justpassingthrough

"snooze" and mess up the day's plans), my feet hit the floor. Gingerly, I stood up. I remembered that my right ankle was a little iffy: I'd jammed it in the tunnel at Cu Chi yesterday, after spending seven hours in a cramped Japanese airliner Tuesday afternoon. Relief came as I shifted my weight more onto the left foot.

No matter whether I'm at home or someplace else, these moments before I turn on my phone are blissful for the rare privilege of being truly alone. My geographical and bodily reorientation reaching completion, I prayed a "Glory be…" to re-place myself in proper relationship with God. This prayer is a quick reminder that all gifts come from God whether or not I'm inclined to view them as gifts.

But today would not be a day for lots of reflection. It was a day for action, and facing a 6:25 a.m. flight departure, I had talked myself into setting the alarm to wake me as late as 3:30 a.m. on the condition that I would not hit the snooze, but would immediately get in the shower. I found the light switch and then made my way to my phone, resting next to the television. Sad that my peace and quiet were about to come to an end, I turned off the alarm and tapped the little airplane icon. Quickly, my phone went through the same mental process I had just finished, first checking the local time, then reaching for a wi-fi signal to connect to its higher authority and locate itself. As I flipped on the bathroom light, there was some buzzing and rattling: apparently lots of people had responded to the photos I'd put on Facebook the previous day. This kind of human interaction was mildly disorienting, since I was an American traveling solo in a totalitarian Communist country and I didn't speak the local language. Maybe aloneness wasn't so hard to come by, after all, and maybe that was okay.

I was about to turn on the water, but for some reason I went back to the phone to see who had sent me so many e-mails, and that's when it started: the airline had delayed my Hong Kong-Los Angeles flight by a couple hours. Taking mental stock of the damage, I knew this would mean I couldn't take a shower at LAX without missing my onward flight to JFK. How horrible for my friends in New York. My mind put this squarely in the "first-world problems" category, so I showered, shaved, and dressed. If this was going to be my last opportunity to shower for ten thousand miles, I wanted to make the most of it!

Getting dressed proved to be interesting: when I tried to fasten my belt, the buckle finally fell off.

Letting the offending accessory fall onto the unmade bed, I looked at my phone and learned I had another gift to enjoy: while I was in the shower, the airline had now cancelled my flight from Hong Kong to Los Angeles.

#

That awkward moment was the product of a gestation period nearly nine months long. My first visit to Vietnam was conceived in a few frenzied moments amidst my snowbound boredom just after the Great Blizzard of 2016. In late January, Washington had been shut down by a storm that dumped two feet of snow. That week I'd been planning to fly to Trinidad. Owning no snow shovel, having paid to park my car in the public garage a block away, and seeing no opportunity to work, I lamented from the safety of my recliner that a flight cancellation would keep me from arriving in Port-of-Spain before I was scheduled to return.

Listening to my neighbors' snow-removal efforts had been rather like reading the expletives from a "Batman" fight scene on TV: Bam! Pow!! Whack!!! Slam!!!!! Biff!!!!!! Crack!!!!!!! As shovels reverberated from their collisions with automotive metal, neighbors argued about where they were allowed to pile the removed snow. The $60 I'd paid for a few days of underground parking seemed like a really competent investment choice.

I was due to visit my niblings that morning. They were snowed into their place in the suburbs with my sister and brother-in-law, and mildly ill health prevented them from going to play in the snow (holy cabin fever,

Batman!). This was all the excuse Uncle Matt needed to get his car out of the garage and go someplace.

Even though I wouldn't have to shovel and scrape, I was still delaying the time when I'd leave the warm safety of my apartment to walk through the winter wonderland, so I courageously took one more scroll through Facebook, finding that a travel blogger had published a notice for cheap fares to southeast Asia on my airline of choice.

I was a top-level frequent flyer with that particular airline, possessing a number of certificates I could use to upgrade any paid fare to the next class of service, one-way. Since I'm more tall-ish than skinny-ish, the prospect of taking long flights in flat-bed business class instead of cramped economy seats puts the world-traveling lifestyle within my reach. It's not just a matter of in-flight comfort: since my work as a liturgical musician means I usually can't be away on a Sunday, my trips are brief. Crossing time zones will always be the cause of jet lag, but flying in the part of the plane with flat-bed seats, together with having access to showers in lounges at many world airports, means I can usually arrive at my destination, and back at home, reasonably well-rested and refreshed.

I found an itinerary that would allow me three days in Ho Chi Minh City without missing a Sunday at home. After checking the visa requirements for Vietnam, I bought the ticket for a grand total of $412.26 and requested those business-class upgrades.

#

There's tons not to like about travel, if you're inclined toward seeing the glass as half-empty. Obnoxious fellow airline travelers, bad weather, not being able to communicate in the local language, avoiding germs in the local tap water, pickpocketing, rental car shenanigans, and mix-ups at the border crossing are all on my list of annoyances and hazards.

But if there's one thing I'd abolish entirely, it's the Transportation Security Administration. That's not because of the time they mistook my travel carrier full of CDs for a hazard to aviation and made me wait a half hour while they investigated it, nor because they so often seem to be standing around doing nothing while thousands of travelers stand around worried about missing their flights, nor because they are one of the Bush (43) administration's most visible additions to big government. The reason I detest the TSA is that some of their officers spend so much of their time on power trips, berating and belittling innocent travelers for breaking rules that aren't really rules, hiding behind the veneer of providing safety.

Were you selected for secondary screening? It's not because your behavior fit the profile of a terrorist, but because you packed the wrong size battery for your laptop. Where was that rule posted, protests the traveler? It's new, says the Blueshirt, and you're really dumb for not knowing about it when you packed your bag, says the look on his face.

Anyway, that Monday morning in October, the TSA checkpoint at Ronald Reagan Washington National Airport was crowded, as usual. As a frequent traveler, I take steps to avoid the most common pitfalls: the shoes and belt come off before I even reach the roller table, and my toothpaste and shaving cream practically live in little plastic bags. I thought this part of the trip was going to be annoying but uneventful, and that's where my thinking went wrong. See, when I finally got my stuff out of the scanning machine and tried to put myself back together, my belt buckle was a bit of a challenge. Examining it closely, I determined the buckle was coming loose from the strap of the belt. It probably had limited life left in it, so I'd need to be careful when fastening and unfastening it throughout my Vietnamese odyssey. Maybe I could even pick up a new belt at my next stop, Dallas-Fort Worth International Airport.

Or not: the shops at DFW would have been happy to sell me belts setting me back a third of what my ticket to Vietnam had cost. No matter; I would be seated for most of the next 20 hours, so I'd just have the adventure of finding a new belt in Ho Chi Minh City.

#justpassingthrough

\#

After takeoff from Texas, it was time to select a movie. I opted for "Beauty and the Beast", the good old animated version, because it's always fun to revisit a childhood classic to see if there's something there that wasn't there before. That, and a delicious Penang duck curry, lasted me across the Rockies, over Vancouver, and up to the southern coast of Alaska.

At that point, not tired enough to go to sleep because it was still afternoon at home but too restless to commit to another movie, I splurged on the in-flight wi-fi. (How else was I going to upload photos of my Penang duck curry to Facebook?) Having been persuaded by some well-meaning friends to sign up for a Catholic dating website, I found that I had a message from someone new, featuring complete sentences. In my reply, I mentioned that I was a few hundred miles south of Anchorage, and that I was on an airplane over the Pacific Ocean using the in-flight wi-fi.

\#

After the wonders of transpacific business class (in addition to the Penang duck curry, I'd tasted my first sake, some Japanese plum liqueur, and udon noodles) and crossing the International Date Line (thereby turning Monday magically into Tuesday without the hassle of sunset and sunrise), I found myself in Japan, waiting in the world's most orderly gate area to board a 787 Dreamliner to Ho Chi Minh City. This would be a quick evening hop from Narita Airport to Vietnam, so I didn't mind in theory that my upgrade certificate didn't apply. I'd selected a window seat next to an aisle seat in the middle of the economy cabin, and planned to doze a little bit since my body now thought it was approaching time for sunrise.

Around the World By Accident

The average Japanese man in 5' 7" tall, compared with 5' 10" for American men and 5' 11" for German men (relevant because of my genetic heritage). Also, the economy window seat on a Dreamliner is affected by the shape of the cabin wall and the presence of the in-flight entertainment control box under the seat in front of you. To translate, that means there was enough space for my whole body on this flight as long as I stored my detachable feet in the overhead bin.

#

There are first-rate cities around the globe with convenient mass transit options from the airport to downtown, and even a good many second-rate cities with such arrangements. Ho Chi Minh City isn't one of them, so after retrieving a couple million dong from the ATM (a process far less exotic or enriching than that sounds, since $1 US equaled over 20,000 VND), I was assigned to a taxi that got me to the Rex Hotel without costing me an arm, a de-cramping leg, or more than a few hundred thousand dong.

#

Ho Chi Minh City has been called the Paris of the East, an appellation that's not fair to the real Paris of the East, Beirut, nor to Paris itself, of which there's only one. It was called Saigon until 1976, but now that portraits of Ho are enshrined all over town, the new name fits; of course, by that measure, every town in Vietnam should be called Ho Chi Minh City. In the former Saigon, the pattern is most obvious in the central post office, where Ho silently presides over commerce even though (shh!) he died in 1969. He's remembered in a song whose lyrics begin with "You're still marching with us, Uncle Ho!" When, in 1975 the People's Army of Vietnam finally took over Saigon, an Australian journalist wrote that "they were led by a man who wasn't there".

#justpassingthrough

As it stands today, aside from Uncle Ho's presence nearly everywhere, Ho Chi Minh City doesn't have a whole lot of visual reminders that the country is one of the five Communist dictatorships remaining in the world nearly three decades after the fall of the Berlin Wall. (To save you the trouble of looking it up, the other such countries are China, Laos, North Korea, and Cuba.) Having been a child when Communism fell as the major world antagonist to my own country, I'm fascinated by these places where Red isn't dead. But, again, wandering around Ho Chi Minh City, I might not have guessed that I wasn't in a "free" country. Among my eating choices were McDonald's, Popeye's, Burger King, and Carl's Jr.; Beijing isn't much like that. In every shopping center I visited, stores were full of merchandise; Havana isn't at all like that.

Yes, wandering central Ho Chi Minh City is like wandering through any other city – London, New York, Chicago, Rio de Janeiro – except for the motorbikes. Oh, the motorbikes. Please save me from the motorbikes. In most European cities, and definitely in Tokyo or Melbourne or Princeton, you walk up to the edge of the intersection and wait until it's your turn to cross, indicated by some variation of the "Walk/Don't Walk" signs I learned to ignore as a kid in Grove City, Pennsylvania. So, having spent a refreshing first night in the Rex Hotel and consumed a sumptuous breakfast involving eggs, breads, and exotic fruits (papaya and passion fruit, y'all?), I set out on foot for the Vietnam History Museum, about a mile and a half away.

To a map nerd like me, there's little so thrilling as exploring a new city. In the case of this trip, I studied maps, descriptions, and photographs of Ho Chi Minh City for nine months before I ever set foot to pavement. With my visit being brief so I would make it home in time to work on Sunday, it was imperative to have plans, know how to accomplish them, and then be ready to make the most of the limited time on the ground. Getting disoriented or lost is just not something a respectable traveler does, least of all in a large city that's well-mapped and well-labeled. Ho Chi Minh City struck me as being a place that should be moderately easy to navigate on foot: it's laid out in a grid-like way, but with enough oddities and variations (a traffic circle here, a grid-interrupting park there, the river over yonder) to make up for the fact I wouldn't be able to speak the language or even translate the words on whatever signage might be present.

And there I was, confidently striding out the front door of the Rex Hotel, Google map on my phone screen, having memorized the general way to the museum. But my study hadn't prepared me for the motorbikes. Oh, the motorbikes. Please save me from the motorbikes!

It turns out there's a technique to crossing the street in Vietnam. Most intersections, even those involving major thoroughfares, don't have signals. Well, maybe they do, but nobody cares which bulb is currently illuminated, least of all Uncle Ho's police. And while the main streets are striped with lanes that fit your average Ford or Nissan, most of the traffic isn't Fords or Nissans. Most of the traffic is motorbikes. Oh, the motorbikes. Please save me from the motorbikes! It makes sense that the Vietnamese would choose to get around primarily on bikes, as the height of the average male is a mere 5' 4", making the Japanese look like giants (and making Vietnamese women, averaging at 5' flat, still look tiny), so it's not hard to fit both a person and his briefcase/satchel/lunchbox on a bike. When street traffic gets congested, those bike riders who are most in a hurry can ride on the sidewalk, a possibility for which the wise pedestrian accounts at all times. Best of all, it's seriously easier to park a bike than to park a car, again, with the sidewalk becoming useful for more than just walking.

If it seems like I'm avoiding the topic of crossing the street, it's because any sane person avoids trying to cross the street in Vietnam. That's because of the motorbikes. Oh, the motorbikes. PLEASE save me from the motorbikes! At some point, though, you just have to do it, and as with so many new skills, simple observation shows you the technique. Since there's rarely a lull in the stream of motorbikes, and since standing on the corner breathing the exhaust fumes is only a slightly slower way to die than crossing the street, you don't wait for a lull. You wait until there's no bike riding immediately next to the curb, and then you step off. Whatever pace you happen to set, you maintain it. The bikers, being human, don't want to hit you, so by observing your speed and trajectory, they adjust their path to avoid hitting you. This isn't really a case of strength in numbers; since no two people occupy the same space, a group of pedestrians crossing the street together is just a bigger area to hit, thus a harder area for the bikers to avoid hitting. Actually, it's to your advantage not to stop at all before crossing the street, if you can avoid it, simply because the biker has more time and distance data with which to avoid hitting you.

Now you know how to cross the street in Vietnam, but please don't try it at home.

Incidentally, I was proud of myself for figuring out this technique on the first try. Of course, I had to get it right on the first try, or else I'd have been run over by a dozen motorbikes before their drivers could adjust to the location of the imported roadkill in front of them. I continued to be proud of myself until I reached the Saigon River, which was in exactly the opposite direction from the museum toward which I had meant to walk. Oops.

#

Our minds are junkies for word association games. When I say "Vietnam", you probably say "War", and that history is a big part of why I'd come to Vietnam. Much has been written about America's involvement here; on its face, the idea that any country could have a military interest so far from home seems absurd. That such a country could be involved for a decade and half, with 60,000 dead and 150,000 wounded, achieving little net gain in the process, defies comprehension. Of course, that synopsis blithely ignores that over a million Vietnamese people, military and civilians, died in the conflagration, too.

Now, I'm no dove. It makes sense that a superpower needs to maintain a strong military force with advanced capabilities, that a nation known for being willing to use that force will have a much easier time securing justice diplomatically and economically, and that there is such a thing as a just war. I have little doubt that global Communism was an evil that needed to be opposed, contained, and in some cases defeated. And I'm sympathetic to the view that, despite the incompetence with which it may sometimes be carried out, trying to save Vietnamese or Poles or Afghanis or French or Iraqis from oppressive dictatorial regimes can actually be a noble goal. If the tables were turned and America were threatened by totalitarianism from within or from without, maybe I'd be glad somebody came to try to help. And whatever may have gone wrong later, I'm certainly not going to be so brazen as to suggest that Dwight Eisenhower or John Kennedy didn't understand the dangers of war when they sent troops to Vietnam. History is subtler than that.

But the fact is, as the saying goes, armies exist to kill people and break things. It follows that when military action starts, people will die and things will be destroyed. Vietnam has some museums dedicated to telling the horror of the American War; the War Remnants Museum was worth the price of admission and then some. Outside are some tanks, aircraft, and other war remnants too big to fit inside the building. Inside, you see pictures, letters, and so forth. It's not for the faint of heart. War may not literally be hell, but it has to be the closest we've come to imitating hell on a large scale in this life.

#

Let's play word association again. When I say "Saigon", you say "fall", or maybe "Miss". And once you've gone either of those places, the next word just might be "helicopter". In fact, the Fall of Saigon is seared in memories by the image of the last helicopter leaving what is now known as the Independence Palace.

#justpassingthrough

Until 1975, it was the presidential palace of South Vietnam. Though insulated from the surrounding streets by some welcome green space (did I mention Ho Chi Minh City has lots of noisy, smelly motorbikes?), the palace is in the same ugly Stalinist style that can be found in Beijing or (East) Berlin or Southwest DC. In that green space are some noteworthy exhibits from 1975, including the two tanks that first breached the fence. Also present is a South Vietnamese war plane that dropped a bomb on the palace; its pilot that fateful day was a North Vietnamese man who had infiltrated the South Vietnamese air force.

The basement levels of the palace are preserved with some of the communication equipment and maps used by South Vietnam's leaders and their American allies as they fought their losing battle against the Communists. The main floors include some impressive state gathering rooms, and the color red figures prominently.

I was on the walk back to my hotel from the Independence Palace, confidently dodging motorbikes on my second full day in-country, when I encountered that other universal hazard of life in Ho Chi Minh City: the rain. My philosophy of travel involves a healthy dose of "keep it simple" with a good amount of "be prepared". That's why I nearly always bring an umbrella. I skip it entirely when I go someplace like Morocco or Bahrain, and I even once spent six days in London without needing to open it, but everything I'd read about Vietnam mentioned the heavy rains that can come up with little warning, so my umbrella went everywhere with me on this visit.

I was mid-block, keeping an eye out for motorbikes, when the rain started. I don't mean Seattle rain, the kind that falls lightly. I don't even mean American midwestern thunderstorm rain that might eventually be heavy but usually starts with a few sprinkles. I mean that by the time my eyes and my ears and my touch receptors told my brain it was raining, and my brain decided it was time to activate the umbrella in my hand, it was too late. I was drenched. I put up the umbrella anyway, and maybe the top two-thirds of my American-size body stayed reasonably dry. That might sound like a partial win, but remember, the bottom third of my body was completely drenched. That included my shoes (the only pair I'd brought) and, crucially, the blue jeans I was wearing (I'd brought three pairs of these).

Do you know how heavy denim gets when it's wet? You need a small horse to transport your wet jeans from washer to dryer. Now, imagine that you've been walking miles and miles in a humid climate and you've been eating less because the food is unfamiliar and smaller-portioned. When those loose jeans get wet, you'd better hope you have a good belt.

And that brings us back to one of this trip's ongoing problems, my disintegrating belt. Yes, it's the only one I brought. Why would I carry an extra belt for a six-day trip in which nobody cares how I look? Somehow, I managed to make the mile walk back to the Rex Hotel without my pants falling down, involving constant tugs upward on the belt loops, all while holding the umbrella above my head. (At this point, the belt was still holding together, but in order to avoid straining the tenuously-attached buckle, I'd fastened it one notch looser than usual, rendering it nearly useless.)

It's not like I didn't try to find a new belt. Being in a big city with so many shops and shopping malls, I figured this would be an easy half hour's work, at worst. However embarrassing it may be to say, height is not the only dimension in which a German-American is likely to be larger than a Vietnamese person. Along the way, I lost track of how many young female sales clerks had giggled at my efforts to make a Vietnamese belt go all the way around me. I promise I visited a good half-dozen shops despite the negative peer pressure, but the simple fact is that virtually nobody in Vietnam is as tall or as wide as me, so I would be leaving the country with, at best, the clothing and accessories I brought in. The belt would just have to hold up.

#

#justpassingthrough

Owing to the French colonial heritage, Catholics are Vietnam's second-largest religious group. As an adult convert to the Catholic Church, one of my great joys in traveling the world is walking into a building 9,000 miles from home where I know nobody and don't speak the language, and still feeling at home – no, being at home - in that building. The pilgrimage aspect of my travels has led me to grand European cathedrals, Latin Mass in Beijing, and even the odd roadside shrine in Brazil.

Though the Communist totalitarian government isn't exactly friendly to a religion that counts Christ as King of the Universe, the Church is too big to ignore or suppress completely. There are nearly six million Catholics in Vietnam, and the faith is strong. I know this through two means of observation: first, attendance at weekday Mass and devotions in Ho Chi Minh City, and second, the presence of first- and second-generation Vietnamese-Americans among the parishes I serve in Northern Virginia. In fact, several Catholic musicians with whom I've worked closely at home are Vietnamese-Americans.

Each day, I make it a point to attend Mass in whatever place I happen to find myself. I might not know the language, but I can make up for that, in part, by reading the lectionary texts online before I head to the church. Most of the other ritual texts are the same at every Mass, so I understand what's being said even if I can't exactly translate the words and sentences I'm hearing. Of course, this is where it would really come in handy if the Church would simply celebrate the Latin Rite in Latin, a language that belongs to nobody but can be familiar (or at least familiar enough) to all. But that's a discussion for another forum.

Though having a French-inspired colonial form, the Cathedral Basilica of Our Lady of the Immaculate Conception (which was initially named Notre-Dame de Saigon) is a building suited for the jungle climate in which it was built in the 1870's. It's made of orange-pink bricks imported from Toulouse. There's little else to say about the place, except to remember the way the rosary was chanted. It was pentatonic, mesmerizing, and led with the aid of giant projection screens on either side of the nave.

#

My solo adventures overseas inevitably focus more on cities and less on rural areas, and there are several good, logical reasons for this. First, the intercontinental flights land at big airports, which are usually near cities. Second, cities usually have the most to do and to see in a small area: museums, historic monuments, restaurants, great churches. Third, public transportation is usually cheap ($0.30 US per Metro ride in Mexico City is pretty good bang for the buck, I'd say), almost always reliable, and avoids the hassle and expense of renting, driving, and parking a car. Fourth, you might be surprised to learn that outside a few notoriously expensive cities (London, Tokyo, New York, Sydney, San Francisco), there are often some great deals to be found on city hotels, especially if you go at times that aren't peak season for tourism or business. Fifth, sunshine and fresh air and exercise are great for beating jet lag, which is even more important when you make such short trips as I do, and walking around a city naturally accomplishes this while also functioning as transportation. In most respects, I could be a world traveler who visits only cities and be quite happy with my life.

But there's more to the world than cities, so whenever it's at all practical, I get out of the city where the airline happens to have deposited me, and I see the countryside. To an American, the most obvious way to achieve rural mobility is in a car. I've driven cars on all six inhabited continents (my first rental was out of Munich Airport, and I drove it in five countries) and have always loved the freedom of having my own wheels and a set of keys. Sometimes a city's public transit network extends well outside of town, and some parts of the world (Europe and Japan come to mind) have excellent intercity high-speed rail systems. There's also such thing as a long-distance bus: I hear those are a great way to cover long distances in Argentina, for example, though I've never tried it myself.

One further option for getting out of town is the package day trip. Here, you pay a fixed fee to a tour operator for a package that includes transportation (usually by coach), sightseeing, a tour guide, relevant meals, and the company of other travelers. As a certified introvert, I shy away from these in most cases; if I can get there by car or by train, read a book or even just the museum captions, choose my own meals, and avoid the risks of human company, I usually do. Sometimes, though, a package tour makes sense, and can offer significant advantages. Such was the case when I decided to visit Cu Chi, a site associated with the American War, located deep in the jungle up the Saigon River from Ho Chi Minh City.

Having learned of Cu Chi through my pre-trip research, I knew I wanted to work in a visit if I could. The internet is an amazing thing and I read stories from several other travelers who'd been there. Again, my first preference is to get someplace independently, with a minimum of fuss. Reading some accounts of visits by other Americans, I learned that I'd have to walk to a bus station in Ho Chi Minh City, take a particular bus in a particular direction to a particular place, transfer to another bus, get off at an intersection in the jungle, then walk over a mile to the entrance of Cu Chi. Since I don't speak the language and am considerably larger than most Vietnamese folks, this all sounded less than ideal. That's when I discovered a particular tour company operating out of Ho Chi Minh City that offered a package daytrip to Cu Chi by boat.

After a short van ride from my hotel, which saved me the trouble of walking across any motorbike-filled streets en route to the dock, I boarded a boat at the edge of the river with eleven other tourists and a Vietnamese crew consisting of a captain, a mechanic, a hostess, and a tour guide. The plan was that we'd ride upriver for about an hour and a half, tour Cu Chi, eat lunch and make the trip back down the river and be returned to our respective hotels by mid-afternoon.

Riding upstream, we passed under some serious bridges carrying vehicular and rail traffic, through some suburbs, and up into the jungle, refreshed by the warm breeze. Rural Vietnam was as green as anyplace I'd ever been, and it sure was nice to be rid of the motorbikes and their exhaust fumes for a few hours! Now, here was something straight out of National Geographic: Vietnamese fishermen with those conical hats, riding in boats whose gunwales rise only a few inches out of the water. We waved, they waved back. East met West.

Along the river there are various towns and hamlets, each with its own marina of some description. Having skipped the public bus system in favor of the boat ride, I don't know how good the Vietnamese road network actually is outside the city. But I can't imagine there's a better way to get from place to place than by taking a boat on the Saigon River, certainly not a more pleasant way, though maybe in a downpour that equation might change. We were served a snack of colorful, tasty fresh fruit. (Have you ever peeled a passion fruit before? There are multiple YouTube videos with instructions if you're interested in learning how it's done.) At Cu Chi, the marina wasn't marked by the sort of signage Pedro uses to lure folks into South Of The Border, but compared to the green of the jungle environment, it stood out like a sore thumb.

Some places are genuinely significant by nature or by history, and some places are horribly cheesy tourist traps. Cu Chi manages to be both of these at once, rather like Niagara Falls. During the American War, the Viet Cong had as their objective the disruption of American and South Vietnamese operations, guerrilla-style. Remember how I said Vietnamese people are smaller than Americans generally? Well, here the Viet Cong used that biological reality to their advantage. At Cu Chi, they built a complex of tunnels and caves just big enough for themselves to crawl through. That in itself is pretty cool from an engineering/ingenuity standpoint, but the reason it worked from a tactical standpoint is that the complex was built almost directly under a major American logistics base. If you can imagine thinking you were safely out of a live-fire zone, propping up your feet, resting, having the enemy pop out of a hole in the ground to shoot your fellow soldier, then having him disappear into a tunnel too small for you to chase him, you've grasped the diabolical genius of Cu Chi.

The American soldiers in Vietnam knew where the trouble was coming from: since they couldn't chase the Viet Cong into the tunnels, they dropped bombs on the whole place. Today, many of the bomb craters are small ponds in the jungle, standing out for their unusually perfect shapes. The rest of the park is a sort of outdoor museum of the war, with various exhibits illustrating the kinds of booby traps and other security measures with which that war was so viciously fought. We're talking about holes in the ground covered with leaves disguising a set of metal teeth that would cut off the leg of someone unfortunate enough to step there. It's a surreal experience, and more than a little sobering, to go as an American and be shown where tiny people came out of the ground to defeat your country, which is supposedly the most powerful on earth.

Near the climax of the tour, we were given the opportunity to crawl through one of the tunnels. We were assured this particular tunnel, about the length of a football field, had been enlarged so that foreign visitors could fit inside. To get there, first I had to climb down a hole into the former Communist Party office, which struck me as being more equal that some of the other holes in the ground, inasmuch as it included an electric light and a place to sit and have tea with guests. Unfortunately, the steps down into that cave did something funny to my knee and ankle, which were still feeling a little less than useful after my recent Dreamliner ride from Japan. As soon as I got down there and snapped a photo with the tunnel entrance, I elected to hobble back out and walk the remaining distance at ground level.

Reading this, you might get the impression that Cu Chi is a glossed-over-for-the-tourists version of its old self. You'd be right, but I haven't yet mentioned that Cu Chi is also one of the few places in Vietnam where a member of the general public can legally discharge a firearm. That's right: behind one of the gift shops there's a firing range where you can rent a gun and buy ammunition. Never having fired a gun before, this didn't seem like the place for me to start, but that didn't really matter. All through the tour about what this place was like during the war, visitors can hear the nearly constant sound of gunfire. Can it get more realistic than that?

#

So after those insightful days in Ho Chi Minh City, there I was standing in my hotel room, ready to pack and catch a cab to the airport and head home. But the second of my four planned flights, the long one from Hong Kong to Los Angeles, was cancelled. Looking at the airline's app, I could see that I hadn't been auto-rebooked, an indication that there was no suitable seat available at a time that made sense to the airline's computers.

Not being the village idiot, I didn't wait for the airline to make up its mind. After all, a parish church was counting on me to be on its organ bench Sunday morning, and failing to be there was not an option for me. I checked another subscription website that keeps track of availability on airlines worldwide, and I could see why the airline's computers didn't immediately help… their only other Hong Kong flight, going to Dallas, was completely full. There was availability through Tokyo, but I didn't have enough time to get to the airport to make the connecting flight, a judgment that I promise has nothing to do with the seating on the Dreamliner that had put my right foot in such a lousy condition three days earlier.

An airline cancelling a flight, even for weather, has the duty to refund the unused portion of the ticket, but the couple hundred dollars that might have yielded me would not buy a transpacific ticket on the day of travel. The airline also has the duty, generally speaking, to sign the passenger over to a competing airline with available space, absorbing the cost of buying that seat on the new airline. The hitch was that while I was ticketed in Business Class having used an upgrade, the underlying fare basis was deep-discount economy. If they signed me over to, say, Korean Air Lines and sent me through Seoul, I would be stuck in economy and then probably have to fight to get the upgrade certificate back for future use, if the computers even cooperated in the first place. To avoid those escalating indignities, I'd have to stay within a particular alliance of airlines, which wasn't showing any viable transpacific options. It was time to get creative.

I briefly explored itineraries connecting through mainland China, and I think there was availability through Shanghai on some combination of airlines. The hitch there is that Americans must have a visa to enter China; an exception allows in-transit travelers to pass through without a visa, but in practice it would be up to a gate agent working for a Chinese airline in Vietnam to know that detail about U.S. passports, or else up to me to persuade him or her of that reality without speaking either of the relevant languages. This sounded like a recipe for trouble, compounded by the reality that Chinese airspace sometimes gets closed for hours at a time without warning so that the PLA Air Force can practice their technique, plus the fact that itineraries with multiple carriers have an elevated risk of not going smoothly as computer systems struggle to communicate properly. I pictured myself stuck in a Chinese airport with a damaged ticket, no visa, no local language skills, and no internet connectivity. No, thank you.

Drumming my fingers on the desk in my hotel room, I stared at the defunct belt buckle while trying to think of another way home. And then I remembered another cardinal rule of recovering from flight cancellations: the normal routing rules don't apply. What does that mean? Well, say you're buying a ticket from Miami to San Francisco. If an airline happens to operate that route nonstop, you can buy a nonstop ticket. You can also buy itineraries connecting through just about any U.S. hub, so you could fly Miami-Atlanta-San Francisco, Miami-Phoenix- San Francisco, Miami-Chicago- San Francisco, or something like that. The fare rules might specify that you can't be ticketed to fly Miami-New York-

San Francisco, likely because the airline wants to keep its New York-San Francisco seats available for higher-paying local traffic on that route, or else for connections with the international flights on either end of. But, if you're ticketed Miami-Chicago-San Francisco and on travel day O'Hare is shut down because of a blizzard, they can (and must, if there's a reason to insist) rebook you onto Miami-New York-San Francisco if seats happen to be open, even though that's against the fare rules.

Now, extrapolate that principle to my situation. The ticket from Washington to Ho Chi Minh City required that I travel across the northern Pacific. In fact, my route was already against the rules because my originally-ticketed flights had been retimed; through several rounds of rebooking I'd ended up with a plan that allowed me to get rest, see friends in New York, and earn more frequent-flyer miles. But now that HKG-LAX was cancelled, I could reasonably ask for literally any route in the world that had available seats, as long that route led me back home to Washington. Since I wanted to preserve my business class upgrade, I needed to stay within the alliance.

Having already exhausted alliance airlines from the U.S., Hong Kong, and Japan, I tried the other airline that flies from North America across the Pacific, which is based in Australia. Unfortunately, that airline didn't have a schedule that would get me home in time. At that point early on Friday, I did some quick mental reckoning about time zones and realized that if I could get to Europe or the Middle East by Saturday morning, I could get to Washington by Saturday evening. I checked a middle eastern airline, but their flight from Hong Kong that night was already full. Next I tried a favourite European airline: yes, both of their Friday night flights from Hong Kong to London's Heathrow had a few seats in Business Class. Neither of their Heathrow-to-Dulles flights on Saturday had availability, but Heathrow to Philadelphia did, and my own airline could get me from Philadelphia to Washington with time to spare. Bingo.

Next, I called my airline, which had issued the ticket. Even after the operator looked up my itinerary, she couldn't figure out what to do. (This

#justpassingthrough

is part of the technique... you can't just call and say "I want", you have to let them try the most obvious solutions and when those don't work, you can suggest an alternative for which you might be willing to settle.) So I suggested she try routing me the long way around. Either her mind or her computer couldn't process that idea, and by strange coincidence the call got dropped when it went on hold.

I tried again and got a zippier agent who seemed to understand the problem and, in due course, my proposed solution. He told me he could get me to London in business class, but then I'd have to fly coach across the Atlantic. I asked him to check the later LHR-PHL flight. To his astonishment, it had availability in business. He dourly informed me I would be stuck at Heathrow for about seven hours, and I told him I'd be able to deal with that.

You might think that was the end of it, but you'd be one of those annoying optimists. Now that I had reservations for SGN-HKG-LHR-PHL-DCA, the software for three different airlines had to cooperate, issue me a new ticket, and accept me for travel. Mercifully, my US passport would be sufficient to let me into Hong Kong and the United Kingdom without visas, so I would only have to worry about airline problems and not diplomatic ones. If all went something close to the new plan, I'd be home in time for Saturday dinner, sleep, and Sunday morning. I even remembered to e-mail my two friends in New York with my regrets.

Oh, and since I was now beltless, I'd have to keep pulling up my pants.

#

The Rex Hotel was a good choice because the staff seemed both eager and able to please. I didn't ask for a lot of extras; in the era of the smartphone, a concierge is almost obsolete. But I did appreciate their help getting a cab to the airport at 4:30 a.m. The driver was talkative, and

I was quite sincere in telling him that I'd thoroughly enjoyed my first visit to Vietnam, though I might have exercised editorial discretion by leaving out any mention of the motorbikes. Oh, the motorbikes. Please save me from the motorbikes.

#

The name "Hong Kong" sounds to me like a video game, and my subconscious assumptions about the place were of a faceless, soulless, ultramodern international trading port where western imperialist-originating capitalists tried to hold Chinese Communism at bay through advanced mathematical computations and a spot of tea. A British colony until June 30, 1997, Hong Kong has long been a place where East and West meet, engage in trade, and occasionally clash. Since I now had most of the day here (my layover went from 9:55 a.m. until 11:45 p.m.), I hoped to gain at least a little bit of perspective to challenge or confirm my assumptions about the place.

Hong Kong is a "Special Administrative Region" of the People's Republic of China. So while the Chinese flag flies here, there, and everywhere, Hong Kong does maintain bits of its own identity. Its currency is the Hong Kong Dollar. It keeps English as an official language, and the contest between the Cantonese (local) and Mandarin (national) Chinese languages is one of those rivalries with social, political, and economic ramifications, to say nothing of purely linguistic ones, I don't begin to understand. Traffic in Hong Kong moves on the left side of the road, instead of the right side like mainland Chinese traffic. Mainland visa rules don't apply here, so Americans can get in for business and tourism just by having a valid passport. And the economy is a quite a bit more laissez-faire, as befits Hong Kong's status as one of the world's busiest shipping ports.

It was a bit of a trek through the terminal to the immigration control area, made longer because I kept having to park my luggage to pull up my pants. My revised plan for the day, now that I had a few more hours than I originally scheduled, involved taking the Mass Transit Railway (MTR) into central Hong Kong, finding the cathedral for Mass, going up to Victoria Peak on the tram, eating a couple meals, and maybe finding a museum or two.

Hong Kong's public transportation infrastructure is legendary – given the small territory's mountainous topography and busy waterways, it would have to be excellent to be at all useful – and I couldn't wait for my inner five-year-old to experience it. So, naturally, after I put my bags in storage, I found that the MTR train was not operating from the airport due to damaged cables. I pulled out my phone, eager to figure out which bus I'd have to take to get into the city. I kept finding websites that told me to take the MTR train, which was not at all helpful advice just now. Earlier that morning, I'd successfully negotiated with an airline to send me home the wrong way around the globe; now, I couldn't figure out how to travel 20 miles downtown from the airport without resorting to an expensive cab ride…until I saw the person holding the sign announcing free shuttle van rides into town while the MTR was closed.

The overgrown van had big windows, so I could observe the freeways, the planes coming and going, the sunny sky, the beautiful blue water full of ships, the vacant train tracks, and the tens of thousands of shipping containers stacked like so many Legos in Hong Kong's port. I was expecting big-time port-ness, but this was bigger. My jaw must have been agape at the volume of stuff I saw being shipped before my very eyes.

The van dumped about ten of us outside of Hong Kong Central Station. I hadn't expected Hong Kong Island to be so vertical, a complete contrast to Ho Chi Minh City, which (it had just now occurred to me) was pancake-flat. Given the time, I wanted to find lunch and then head to the Hong Kong Museum of History. The MTR seemed to be operating downtown, but I opted to take the Star Ferry across Hong Kong Harbour. In order to get to the ferry, I had to cross a few streets. In order to get across the streets, I had to use the elevated walkway. In order to get to the elevated walkway, I had to navigate through a shopping center. In order to get to the shopping center, I had to find my way out of the train station. The view from the ferry was worth it, though, and being seated gave me a respite from the continual ritual of pulling up my beltless pants.

And even after so much rigamarole, I was not at the museum, but only on the correct side of the water, on the Kowloon Peninsula. I've heard so much about the food in Hong Kong, and wanted very much to try some honest-to-goodness Cantonese food, or Sichuan, or whatever kind of Chinese food I could find. So, naturally, I grabbed a cheeseburger in the first Irish pub I passed.

From there, my journey to the Hong Kong Museum of History stayed just as complicated as it had been before lunch. I needed to find the MTR station, several blocks away, and getting there required me to descend a staircase under a major intersection, navigate a blocks-long maze of underground passageways, and pull up my pants repeatedly. I could go on, but by now you have the impression that my journey home was many tedious steps interspersed with a few glimpses of really cool stuff underscored by the constant fear of becoming de-pantsed.

I was beginning to despair of ever finding the Hong Kong Museum of History, or of finding it at all enjoyable, or of ever traveling again. I'd been up since 3:30 a.m. and dealt with several rounds of incompetence. And then, in fairly short order, there were two day-brightening developments.

First, as I walked up Chatham Road in Tsim Sha Tsui (or maybe it was Salisbury Road?) I passed some sort of advertising display, likely for a travel and tourism-related business, that took up the middle of a pedestrian plaza. The centerpiece was a Phileas Fogg-style balloon proclaiming "Around the World With a Smile". And that's when it hit me: my broken belt somehow symbolized my cancelled transpacific flight, and I was now on a trip around the world.

There's a scant portion of the world's population that can afford to travel around the world, and a small fraction of those with enough curiosity and tenacity and grit to carry it off. And here I was: a single guy in my early 30's, a self-employed liturgical musician, wandering around Hong Kong in the midst of a round-the-world trip. It's something I'd always wanted to do, that I'd planned to do several times before, for which I'd twice held tickets I then had to cancel because life happened, and here I was finally circumnavigating the globe just because it was the only way to get home in time for work. It's rare to have a moment so life-changing, especially when it isn't tied to a wedding or a funeral or a birth or a graduation, but there I was, having one in the plaza in front of a travel agency. Fortunately, I remembered to pull up my pants.

Having enjoyed that feel-good moment, I kept walking toward the Hong Kong Museum of History. Presently, I found myself wandering through an area with all kinds of clothing stores. Hong Kong is a center for the fashion industry in Asia, and since I enjoy clothes shopping about as much as I enjoy traffic jams, I had put that fact in the "useless information" section of my brain. Pulling up my pants yet again, I walked past souvenir peddlers selling t-shirts, tailors offering fine suits, shoe stores, and a leather goods shop.

Whoa, horse. Leather goods? I backed up. I went in. They had a belt my size. I bought it for a very reasonable price. I put it on. I stopped worrying about my pants falling down. I'd wasted a couple hours in Vietnam looking for something not sold in my size in their entire country, but now I'd been in Hong Kong a couple hours and found it by accident. Brilliant.

This was turning out to be a good day, after all. And that's the thing about days: any day you live through is a good day, and I have a hunch the one you don't live through can also turn out to be pretty nice, too, if you've had your priorities straight. Today, I could continue going Around the World With a Smile without needing to pull up my pants every few steps.

#

Around the World By Accident

The Hong Kong Museum of History is superb. It does a comprehensive job of telling the story of the place and its people from the beginning of recorded history (and, through the wonders of science, long before that) through the handover from the United Kingdom to mainland China in 1997. I could have spent weeks wading through a written historical narrative, but this gave me what I needed to know, and a good bit more. It's the sort of place that has something for everyone: brightly-lit displays, interactive exhibits, informative captions, and quite a bit of space. The whole family could visit and nobody would be disappointed. If you're ever flying around the world (with or without a smile) and you have a couple spare hours and you're within a couple thousand miles of Hong Kong, go to the Hong Kong Museum of History. Seriously, just do it.

Earlier, I described Hong Kong as an East-meets-West kind of place. There are other places matching that description: Istanbul is one, I'm told (it had been a planned stop on one of my cancelled around-the-world trips), and Berlin was one, at least when I was in pre-school. But to wander through Hong Kong really is to cross London with old Shanghai, adding traces of Paris, San Francisco, and Tokyo. Heading from the museum to an MTR station felt like an around-the-world journey in itself, such were the contrasts from block to block on Kowloon Peninsula.

At length, I found the requisite MTR station and headed for my next objective, Hong Kong's Cathedral of the Immaculate Conception. On the map, it looks to be just a few blocks' walk from where I would disembark, but that's where two dimensional paper maps fail, to say nothing of electronic ones. In order to reach the cathedral on the Mid-Levels of Hong Kong Island (we're back south of the Harbour, if you're keeping track), you have to get up the hill. To get up the hill, you could take a bus or a taxi. But why would you do that if the world's longest pedestrian escalator system will do the job for free? The thing climbs 443 feet over a horizontal half mile. It takes between 10 and 20 minutes to climb, depending on how much you walk. It's a one-way system, moving downhill for four hours in the morning and then uphill until midnight, favoring rush-hour pedestrian traffic.

The tropical white cathedral is on the quietest street I found all day in Hong Kong. The organ case is (sadly) empty, but the evening sun shines through it in a beautiful way. After Mass, it was about 6:00, so I decided to head to Victoria Peak before returning to the airport. I meandered my way down the hill toward the Peak Tram station, heading past an imposing, standoffishly secure United States Consulate along the way. Unfortunately, I hadn't figured on a 90-minute wait for the tram, and mental calculations told me that going up, and then potentially having another significant wait to come back down, would jeopardize my travel home in the way that setting off a cannon endangers a fragile cease-fire agreement.

And that turned out to be a wise calculation, if I do say so myself. In my favor, the MTR was once again operating to the airport, a thoroughly first-world train experience complete with wi-fi. I reunited with my luggage and proceeded to the (European) Airline B counter to check in. Reaching an agent at the business class desk, I handed over my passport expecting to receive a couple of boarding passes in short order. But the agent told me he couldn't check me in since Airline A's computers hadn't finished reticketing my reservation, and he sent me to the Airline A check-in desk to get it sorted.

So I wheeled my luggage a significant distance across Hong Kong International Airport's vast check-in hall, now limping from whatever the Japanese Dreamliner and the Viet Cong had done to my right foot, aggravated by a week of walking with pants falling down as well as the five or six miles I'd already walked that day. When I got to the Airline A desk, I found it closed. This was natural enough, since their last flight of the day, on which I had until this morning held a confirmed reservation, had long since been cancelled. I hobbled back to Airline B, and the guy I'd seen before avoided making eye contact, so I found a new agent. I explained that I held an Airline A ticket, had already flown a segment on Airline C that morning, and needed to check in for the Airline B flights to

London and then Philadelphia. She looked at me as though I had three heads, and pityingly explained that I needed to go see an Airline A agent. She told me where those agents hide when the Airline A desk is closed, so off I went once again. I found the contractors at the place where the Airline B agent had sent me. They told me they couldn't help me, and I should go see Airline B because you check in with the operating carrier. I gave them the look. One of them couldn't avoid eye contact, and reluctantly she asked how she could help me. I explained that I needed to get my reservation re-issued because of the flight change. When she pulled up my record, her eyes got really big. Yes, I explained, that really was the correct itinerary, and no, I did not want to change flights again.

After the better part of an hour hobbling back and forth across the landside terminal, my pants behaving perfectly, I finally got to one of the famous Hong Kong business class lounges, ordered an Old Fashioned, and finished uploading the day's pictures to Facebook. There was also a second message from the woman I'd told I was over the northern Pacific. Her reply implied that she didn't believe me, and also that I travel too much for her taste. These were two seemingly contradictory notions, which my married friends tell me is a red flag. Sigh.

As you might imagine, beating jet lag is a pet project of mine. On this trip, my body had just caught up on the sheer amount of sleep I needed to recover from the outbound journey, and was still settling into southeast Asian time when I headed for home. The flight from Hong Kong to London left just before midnight, and was scheduled to arrive in the United Kingdom well before sunrise. The twelve-hour flight offered plenty of time to eat dinner, sleep for a full night in the Airline B flat bed seat, and eat breakfast before landing. The only challenge was staying awake until nearly 2:00 a.m. on a day when I'd awoken at 3:30 a.m. and thoroughly exhausted myself hobbling around Hong Kong and all over its airport.

The Chinese government was being cooperative tonight, and with no military-related airspace restrictions, I slept from someplace over Inner

#justpassingthrough

Mongolia to the Baltic Sea in the airline A-branded pajamas I'd saved from my trip to Australia earlier in the year.

#

London is what's known in the airline industry as a "premium" market. In fact, it's the textbook example of one. Lots of business and government travelers fly to and from London, and airlines make a great deal of money on flights there, with the UK's substantial tourist traffic (again, outbound and inbound) putting considerable gravy on top. That means the airlines serving Heathrow, London's favored intercontinental airport, trip over one another to offer the finest amenities on the ground. One of my personal favorites is the arrivals lounge: the idea is that after you land, clear immigration, and retrieve any checked luggage, you can go to a quietly atmospheric club to eat a complimentary breakfast, use Wi-Fi, and (here's the key for me) take a shower in one of the dozens of shower suites they've installed in the back. There's even a clothes-pressing service that will return your clothes, freshly ironed, to a compartment inside the door of your shower suite while you're bathing. Combined with the flatbed seats offered in business and first class, the overall goal is to allow business travelers to go straight to work in London just as if they'd slept in a hotel the night before. Time is money, you know.

I wasn't quite a business traveler on this trip, but with seven hours until my next flight, I wanted to be clean and refreshed before I headed into central London for the morning (Saturday, in case you've lost track). So it was that I got in the shower suite, unpacked the clothes I had planned to wear into New York, turned on the water, and lathered up. And then the water stopped.

After a minute or two, there was still no water. Was it the whole lounge that had lost water, or just my shower suite? Would it be out for just a couple minutes, or all day? I decided that since I'd arrived on one of the first flights of the day and hadn't needed to wait for luggage to come out, there likely weren't many people in the lounge using the showers. So I used the towel to un-sudsify myself, got dressed, re-packed my bag in the hope of being assigned to a different suite, and went to find the attendant.

Now, I figure some pretty self-important people use that lounge on any given day, and every last one of them has just come off a long-haul flight. Thus, it makes sense to me that the lounge attendants would be very sensitive to any kind of customer dissatisfaction, plus they're British and British people are super-duper polite, so I tried to be as non-demanding as possible when I reported that the water had stopped working in my shower suite.

I said, "I'm sorry, but the water in suite number forty-six is not working," The reply was simply, "I am sorry, sir," accompanied by no motion or further action or attempt to explain. It took me a minute to realize what had happened: having coming three-quarters of the way around the world in five days, and having dealt with customer service professionals in Japan, Vietnam, and China, and now being in England at the premier lounge for the highest-paying customers of an English airline, I had encountered a first for this trip: a customer-facing employee who couldn't communicate in basic English. The man had apparently been trained to apologize when someone seemed unhappy, and didn't seem to have any training or empowerment to improve the experience. Here I was in a place whose primary purpose is for people to take showers, just before the morning rush, and nobody cared that the water wasn't working. Was this normal?

Having gotten no reaction, I saw that a couple other travelers were also reporting the water outage. After a few minutes, word came that the water was back on, so I returned to my suite, got undressed, turned on the water, and lathered up.

And then it quit again. Missing the reliability of the shower in Vietnam (or even just the torrential rainstorms), I resolved to get out of here and find a public restroom to brush my teeth and shave. I used the towel to de-lather again, got dressed in my clean clothes, and just as I opened the door to leave for the last time, the water came back on.

#

If I were a grumpy person spoiled by all this luxury, the erratic shower might have turned into the straw that broke the camel's back. You might even expect the following paragraphs to be all about the incompetence of London, owing to its being overrun by American tourists who think they're accomplished world travelers because they endured that unbearably long flight across the ocean and got a passport stamp not involving a maple leaf. But I never have thoughts like that.

Actually, this was my eleventh lifetime visit to the United Kingdom, so I had the advantage of arriving with no unrealistic expectations. My first visit was when I was eleven years old, when my mother let me be the 50th person on a group tour featuring the college handbell choir she directed. My second visit had been with my sister when she was 14 and I was 21; for four of the longest minutes of my life, we'd been separated by a closing door while we were both minding the gap on the Central Line. My third, fourth, fifth, and sixth visits had involved left-sided driving all over England and Wales. The tenth visit had put me in an international conference on the Catholic liturgy when a certain Cardinal famously got himself in trouble with Pope Francis by promoting a particular traditional liturgical practice. I'd seen this island in all four seasons, and had few illusions. Today was simply a matter of going for a nice walk in a familiar and enjoyable place to pass the time between flights.

Descending into the bowels of Terminal 5, I found my way to the Heathrow Express train, much like the one I'd taken the previous evening in Hong Kong. It offers comfortable seating for the 22-minute journey to Paddington Station, plus electrical outlets and wi-fi. Once again, I'd left my bags in storage at the airport and brought only my phone with me. During the ride, I visited one of my favorite websites, which features a listing of daily Mass times, to figure out which Mass I'd attend. The familiar (and therefore safe and reliable) option was the 8:00 a.m. Mass at Westminster Cathedral, but I opted to aim for the 9:30 a.m. Mass at St. Etheldreda parish.

At Paddington, I transferred to the Circle Line and surfaced at Westminster station, where the Houses of Parliament and Westminster Abbey are reflected in the waters of the River Thames. It was sunny and about 52 degrees, and the quietness of Saturday morning in the British capital contrasted vividly with the hustle and bustle of Hong Kong and Ho Chi Minh City. Walking downriver on Westminster Embankment, I crossed to Southwark at Waterloo Bridge. There were a few boats on the river, some active Londoners walking their dogs, and no motorbikes.

I headed back to the left (north) bank of the river, and into the City of London proper, known as the Square Mile because it's really that small a place, via the Millennium Bridge, which affords pedestrians a grand view of St. Paul's Cathedral. I strolled up to Sir Christopher Wren's magnificent baroque structure, whose dome famously survived the Blitz and became a symbol for Britain's defiance of Adolf Hitler's attempts to demoralize the British via air raids.

And I kept going right on past London's Anglican cathedral to find my way to St. Etheldreda's, located above a tavern in an apartment block off an alley off a side street; the alley in question is known as Ely Place. Built in 1290, St. Etheldreda's was originally the chapel used by the Bishops of Ely when they visited London. The story goes that King Henry VIII and Catherine of Aragon dined at this tavern in 1531, in separate rooms, which some sage observers took as a sign that their marriage might have been in trouble.

Having timed my walk up the Thames fairly precisely, I walked past the tavern door, through the office hallway, up the back steps, and into the Gothic splendor of St. Etheldreda's about ten minutes before the 9:30 a.m. Mass, only to find I was nearly alone. Standing there in the dark church, with nobody but Jesus himself to keep me company, was one of those rare moments of forced quiet in my impromptu around-the-world journey. The rear window of the church is a brightly-colored stained-glass depiction of the English martyrs who'd given their lives for their Catholic faith under the oppressive Protestant regimes of Henry VIII and some of his successors. That's the thing about a beautiful old church: you've got good company even when it looks like you're alone.

I also wondered why nobody was coming to Mass, so I went back down to the office hallway where I found a custodian. Helpfully, the custodian didn't know anything about the Mass schedule, so he pushed the intercom button to call to the priest's residence, then walked away. Soon, Fr. Dayoff answered (no, that's not his real name). No, Father informed me, there is no Saturday morning Mass at St. Etheldreda's, and where would I get such a preposterous idea? It's hard to tell with the well-mannered British, but I think he might even have been annoyed with me for daring to allow his custodian to push the intercom button. But since he plainly wasn't going to come down and celebrate a Mass just because I'd showed up, I asked him whether another nearby parish might have a Mass that morning.

Perhaps Father was surprised by the earnest persistence of his American interlocutor, but I detected a change in his tone. I might try St. Peter's, he said, a short walk to the north. Father mentioned the church was Italian, so I looked forward to the possibility of interesting art and architecture.

Leaving St. Etheldreda's, I made a mental note to cross-check the Mass times listing next time I used it in a foreign country (it's usually quite reliable domestically) and then I headed north. Not wanting to splurge on cell data connectivity, I found a pub with wi-fi and leaned against the outside wall while checking the exact location of St. Peter's. It was next door, which is to say that if I hadn't been so focused on my phone and looking for a pub with wi-fi, I would have been in the church by now. It was a splendid, brightly-colored little place, not quite as well hidden as St.

Etheldreda's and, also by contrast, populated by a few other Saturday morning Mass-goers.

Let's pause here for just a moment and review: I was supposed to be in New York this morning, on my way home from Vietnam and Hong Kong. Instead, I was in London, disoriented from my rerouting and two flips of the body clock that week, only partly showered, having been proud of myself for finding the hidden church and deflated when my reason for being there turned out not to exist. Just when it couldn't have gotten any weirder, Father appeared and said, "Nel nome del Padre e del Filgio e dello Spirito Santo". Now, I'm used to Mass being in English, but I also have experience in several other languages, and my overtaxed brain took a moment to rule out Latin, French, Spanish, German, and Portuguese before settling on "Italian". Then, I remembered what Fr. Dayoff had said: St. Peter's was the Italian church. So I'd come to England and, for the second time in four hours, discovered that English was not the spoken language. I'd also discovered that there's a small but devout Italian-speaking community in Clerkenwell, information whose usefulness to me is limited, but it might make an interesting side story if I ever decide to write a book.

Mass was over about 10:30 a.m., and I now had exactly 135 minutes until my flight to PHL was slated to depart. Will it ruin the mood if I tell you I was a little nervous about making that flight? I had to walk a quarter mile to Farringdon Tube station, ride the Circle/Metropolitan train six stops to Paddington, take the Heathrow Express 23 minutes to Terminal Five, retrieve my stored luggage, clear security, ride the train to an outer concourse, walk up to a quarter mile to my gate, and board the flight. Logic told me I could do it just fine, especially since I'd been through check-in the previous evening at HKG (and had I ever been through check-in!), but it was Saturday, and we Washingtonians get nervous about public transit on Saturdays.

Well, logic was right yet again. I got to the gate (it was, in fact, the farthest gate from the terminal entrance) in time to walk through one of the world's longest jetways onto yet another Boeing 777 and be stopped by security amidst the stream of Economy passengers. They insisted that my carry-on bag was too big. Remembering against all odds what country I was in, I ruled out a direct refutation of that incompetent idea even though I'd have won, and I got clever. As I bent over to pick up my bag, refreshingly unworried about my pants falling down thanks to the new belt, I flashed my Business Class boarding pass and mentioned the seat number out loud, and magically my bag was now of the proper size once again. Perhaps I even received an apology for the dreadful inconvenience.

I'd like to tell you that my unexpected crossing of the Atlantic on a trans-Pacific trip was life-changing. But what I really remember is that a flight attendant named Pippa brought me Kir Royale and a slightly-burnt chicken curry for lunch, followed a few hours later by tea and sandwiches, and that the plane didn't crash. Transiting PHL was mind-numbingly uneventful, and the short hop back to DCA even more so.

And after a warm greeting from two of my favorite toddlers, the people who call me "Uncle Matt" who I'd also gone to see after buying this plane ticket, I rode the Metro home. The kitchen trash was right where I'd left it, and my framed photo of St. Paul's Cathedral in the Blitz was still on the wall over the bookshelf.

When I return home from an adventure, I dump my suitcase onto my bed. By this method, I make sure the suitcase actually gets emptied and its contents are placed in their proper places no later than when I go to bed that night. With two flips of the body clock under my new belt, I had incentive to get that done quickly. Despite the disorientation that comes from over 48 hours of nearly nonstop travel, I was lucid enough to reflect on what I'd just done: As planned, I had explored a little bit of Vietnam. I'd managed not to get flattened by the motorcycles. As I hadn't planned, I'd had a nice walk through London despite the lack of a proper shower, where improbably I'd attended Mass in Italian. I'd broken my belt and returned with a new one from Hong Kong. I'd circumnavigated planet earth in Business Class, with only my carry-on luggage, by myself, for all of $412.26…by accident.

The East Coast's Main Street

Statistics are dangerous things: they can be used to illustrate truth, to mislead, to deflect from the larger truth of a matter, to shock, to entertain. They can also be used to get to know how and why a person, a place, a situation got that way. So here's a statistic about me:

Before my twenty-first birthday, I had witnessed three high-speed crashes on I-95.

The first time, I was a junior in high school. At 17, I'd had my license for less than a year, and we lived in Rochester, New York. My mother, a professional pianist, was the accompanist for the Odyssey Select Choir, my high school's elite ensemble, which was performing that May in a competition in Williamsburg, Virginia. I'd gotten special permission to skip the long bus rides to and from Williamsburg in order to accompany her, and to share the hours of driving required, so that she could be present for the competition.

We'd stopped for lunch in Annapolis, Maryland, where I'd had to drive the family minivan over a curb and onto the sidewalk to let an ambulance pass us. That made an impression on my teenage mind! I drove us west along US 50 and the southern arc of the Capital Beltway, which carries both I-95 and I-495, crossing the Potomac River via the Woodrow Wilson Bridge.

The Woodrow Wilson Bridge opened as a six-lane span in 1961, part of the I-495 Capital Beltway, during the early years of the Dwight D. Eisenhower National System of Interstate and Defense Highways. There's a story that as Allied Supreme Commander during the 1944-5 conclusion of World War II, Ike encountered Hitler's network of Autobahnen, designed to carry troops and materiel quickly from one part of the Reich to another, and decided America needed these highways, too. It's only partly true, though President Eisenhower did sign into law the federal legislation creating the network, which is still not quite complete.

#justpassingthrough

As originally envisioned, I-95 was to go north from the Beltway through Arlington, cross the Potomac near the Pentagon, pass under Capitol Hill, and then make its way through Northeast DC's Edgewood and Brookland neighborhoods and College Park, Maryland before crossing the Beltway again and heading to Baltimore. However, planners couldn't find a way around a few landmarks such as Howard University and the newly-completed National Shrine of the Immaculate Conception (the national place of pilgrimage where in 1963 Jackie Kennedy famously refused to allow her husband's funeral to be held), so the freeway was truncated at New York Avenue and redesignated I-395 inside the Beltway. I-95 was routed across the Woodrow Wilson Bridge and around the southern and eastern segments of the I-495 Capital Beltway in Virginia and Maryland.

The knock-on effects of rerouting I-95 were considerable: now, traffic moving between Florida and the northeastern megalopolis (Walt Disney World opened in 1971, but Florida's beaches are considerably older) would have to use the Woodrow Wilson Bridge to cross the Potomac. While most of the Beltway grew to eight lanes or more to carry the increased traffic, the Woodrow Wilson Bridge stubbornly remained only six lanes wide. The bottlenecking grew worse and worse over the years as the suburbs sprawled and more people drove more miles in more cars.

That's not all: the Potomac River itself is a transportation artery, carrying military, commercial and private boat traffic. Did I mention that the Woodrow Wilson Bridge was a bascule-style drawbridge? It had to open 260 times a year to allow big ships to travel between Washington and the Chesapeake Bay.

So you could say that by the time I first drove it in 2000, the Woodrow Wilson Bridge had become one of America's most notorious traffic bottlenecks. I don't recall the backup being too bad that Friday lunchtime, but maybe that's only because I shortly had to pass through the Springfield interchange, where I-95, I-395, and I-495, plus a plethora of local suburban arterial roads, cross paths in northern Virginia.

The East Coast's Main Street

It's difficult to describe in family-appropriate prose just how bad the Springfield interchange (known affectionately as the "Mixing Bowl") had gotten by 2000, but I'll try: Remember how I-95 was supposed to go directly into Washington and continue northeast? And how I-495 was supposed to be the suburban loop around Our Nation's Capital? Highway engineers built in Springfield an interchange designed to carry moderate suburban traffic loads. When it was designed, the thinking was that most traffic would pass through the interchange in a north-south, south-north, west-east, or east-west direction, with a fraction of traffic changing direction. However, with the cancellation of the I-95 freeway through Northeast DC, long-distance traffic between Baltimore/Philadelphia/New York/Boston and the southeastern United States now had to pass through the interchange northward-to-eastward and westbound-to-southbound. Add the explosive growth of northern Virginia's affluent suburbs and you had a recipe for daily weeping and gnashing of teeth.

In particular, the ramp carrying southbound I-95 traffic was comically inadequate: to stay on "the East Coast's Main Street", after squeezing through the Woodrow Wilson Bridge's legendary bottleneck, you had to exit the Capital Beltway onto a two-lane ramp with a 35-m.p.h. curve. And then, while merging onto the main southbound highway the two lanes merged down to one. That's right... a highway that had three or four through lanes per direction in the rest of the metro area was reduced to just one lane while merging onto itself. It was actually that bad.

Having passed through that exercise in hazing for new drivers, I figured it now would be smooth sailing from here south to Williamsburg on the open highways of the rural South. But since I'm writing about it nearly two decades later, you already know that's not quite how things went down.

Being, then as now, a driver heavily invested in the concept of lane discipline, I settled into the right lane of southbound I-95, a decision that turned out to be very fortunate, indeed. I lived these high school years in suburban Rochester, New York, where the driving culture is a product of New York State's relatively rigorous training requirements for new drivers, general Midwestern-type levelheadedness, and a healthy respect for what our long, nasty winters could do to road surfaces and braking action. The level of aggression shown by so many drivers on I-95 in Northern Virginia, to say nothing of raw speed, scandalized me: didn't people know that getting caught doing 73 while tailgating in a 55 zone could get you a traffic ticket…or worse? Yikes!

Just then, perhaps about three miles south of the Mixing Bowl, the first crash happened before my eyes. I retained mental still shots: a tanker truck bursting into flames across the left two lanes of the road, a small passenger car being smashed to pieces, people leaping over the concrete barrier along the left shoulder separating us from the reversible HOV lanes. For my part, I swerved as far right as I could in a successful bid to avoid getting the family minivan involved in the conflagration. Briefly, I wondered whether I should stop and make sure 911 was called. But I didn't yet possess a personal cellphone, my mother was somehow still asleep with her phone hidden in her purse, and as I quickly realized, thousands of drivers would be trapped in the ensuing traffic jam with every incentive to get police, ambulance, and fire services on the scene quickly. We continued southward.

#

Two and a half years later, on a cold February day in 2003, I was driving north on I-95 from southeastern Virginia to my college home in Princeton, New Jersey, concerned about beating the approaching snow and ice storm back to Westminster Choir College. Passing through the Mixing Bowl northbound-to-eastbound, I managed to get across the Woodrow Wilson Bridge once again without too much trouble. It was midday, and (I can say, knowing the metropolitan area as I do now) the weather forecast had probably scared lots of people into staying home.

The East Coast's Main Street

A few miles into Maryland, perhaps someplace around Suitland Parkway, I noticed that the rain had morphed into something a little more solid. As an upstate New York driver, I was a little concerned with the precipitation, moderately concerned about the road surface, and a lot concerned about the Southern drivers around me. Switching to the second-from-right lane to pass a slow-moving vehicle, I saw another car was in the third lane getting ready to pass me. But then, as I checked my side-view mirrors to get a sense of when it would be safe to move back to the right, the car I had just passed suddenly spun out, hitting the vehicle approaching from the left. My good training kicked in, and I kept my foot steady on the accelerator, aware of the twin dangers of the out-of-control collided vehicles spinning just behind me and the icy pavement underneath me. Once again, I was able to continue without a scratch – without even a delay! – because I'd been observing lane discipline and keeping my distance.

#

If one is really brave, one can stay on I-95 after crossing the George Washington Bridge into New York City. It becomes the Cross-Bronx Expressway, one of the most-potholed and worst-congested pieces of freeway real estate I've ever experienced. And I experienced it a lot: during my junior year of college, still living in Princeton, I had the good sense (read: ludicrous idea) to accept a part-time position as a church music director on the North Shore of Lawnguy Land (usually spelled "Long Island"). So, every Thursday I'd leave Princeton in the afternoon to fight my way to New Brunswick and the New Jersey Turnpike, past Newark-Liberty International Airport (where I'd try not to be distracted by the heavy metal using the two runways parallel to the Turnpike), across the George Washington Bridge, and on through the Bronx. A few miles into the City and State of New York, I'd cross the Throgs Neck and proceed via Northern Boulevard to Manhasset.

#justpassingthrough

When rehearsal was done, I'd do the reverse trip in as little as half as much time, rejoicing that my late-evening arrival meant there would usually be ample parking in Westminster Choir College's parking lot. I'd get into my room and my roommate, who hailed from Connecticut and thus knew the hazards I had just braved, would usually not bother asking how the drive had been. I'd gotten back in one piece, and on most days that was enough of an answer.

One Sunday in Lent, I didn't return to Seabrook Hall until well after dinner. I handed my Connecticut-born roommate, with whom I'd had endless discussions about the correct pronunciation and accenting of most of the names of cities and towns in his home state, a copy of the Sunday New Haven Register. He was confused, and wondered how I'd gotten one of those. I told him I'd been to Connecticut, and he didn't have much of a reaction. Was I that predictable?

The same roommate once saw me stash my Rand McNally Road Atlas in the gap between my dorm bed and the wall, and dubbed the atlas "the other woman". So, by our junior year, nobody was very surprised to hear that I'd gone for a Sunday afternoon drive to Connecticut on I-95. In fact, I don't think anybody even missed me for the five or six extra hours I was gone. Their lack of curiosity almost deprived them of the best part of the story: I had also been to Rhode Island, the only northeastern state I had never visited before. I'd gone up there out of curiosity, crossed some pretty bridges into Newport, and then pointed myself back to Princeton. This was in 2004; I wouldn't return to the Ocean State until 2016, when I arrived in the morning by air and left in the evening by train…but that's for another chapter.

#

Not all of I-95 is in the northeast corridor, with its congestion and frequently foul weather. South of Petersburg, Virginia, the route is almost entirely rural all the way to Florida. And even in Florida, apart from the

Jacksonville metropolitan area, the road maintains a low-friction rural character. That makes this the fun part of I-95 to drive. How much of a power trip must it be, too, to wear a Virginia police uniform and wait in the median for Norbert Nutmeg (the dad of three from New Haven taking his family to visit the Mouse), or Gordon Garden (the snowbird from Metuchen), to go dashing past at 11 mph over the limit and issue a summons for reckless driving. In Virginia, this means going 16 over the limit, or any speed above 80, and it carries a maximum penalty of one year in jail!

That's all second-hand, of course, as I've never been issued a traffic citation in this country. But ask me later about Morocco.

You can't be associated with Westminster Choir College, or at least with the Westminster Choir, for too long without going to Charleston, South Carolina for the Spoleto Festival USA. Each spring, the members of the Westminster Choir are contracted by the Festival to perform as their premiere chamber choir, as the backbone of a symphony chorus, and as an opera chorus. All this unfolds in an intense four-week period centered around Memorial Day, beginning in mid-May.

When you need to get from Princeton to Charleston, you either fly or drive. Many prefer to fly, as the 551-mile flight from Philadelphia International Airport to Charleston International Airport is much quicker than the 723-mile drive down I-95. I always drove to Charleston; there's something very good for the soul about catapulting past Philadelphia, Baltimore, and Washington, squeezing across the Woodrow Wilson Bridge and through the Springfield Mixing Bowl, and then having little but open, flat road ahead for hundreds of sunny miles.

But not even those miles are always sunny. The odd devastating hurricane aside, the southeastern United States is prone to experiencing intense thunderstorms, especially in the spring and fall. I became acquainted with this ugly side of Southern weather in an up-close-and-personal way during my first Spoleto Festival, in 2003, but the worst story of all dates from the drive home. We'd just performed our final Saturday afternoon concert at the then-Episcopalian Cathedral of St. Luke and St. Paul, doubtless including some of Joseph Flummerfelt's signature Brahms partsongs. We all had to be in the Princeton University Chapel on Monday morning to record Charles Ives's "Psalm 90" and Samuel Barber's "Agnus Dei", along with some Stravinsky in Slavonic and maybe another similarly light piece or two. (The album is known as "Heaven to Earth" – take a listen!) I had to make a stop in southeastern Virginia along the way, so once again this was a job for I-95.

With such gloriously beautiful music in my head, and my white tie and tails mercifully exchanged for shorts and a t-shirt, I maneuvered my car up I-26 and onto I-95, stopping almost immediately for dinner at Santee, where South Carolina Route 6 is the center of a typical explosion of traveler-oriented commerce. Dinner having been inhaled, I drove away from the fast-food restaurant and turned onto the I-95 north ramp.

As soon as I'd committed to the onramp, the deluge began with a suddenness worthy of Vietnam: I could barely see, and was far more nervous about the merge I'd shortly have to perform that I had been about the concert two hours before. Would traffic on I-95 be able to see me? Would those vehicles be going slowly enough to take action to avoid me (the onramp not being long enough for my little car to accelerate to 70 mph in the rain before merging), given the sudden start of the downpour? It was dusk, so would everybody have headlights on? Once I merged into northbound traffic, what would conditions be like on the causeway bridge across Lake Marion? Would I be able to maintain control in the event of crosswinds? There was no place to stop and wait, so the only thing left to do was press on toward the goal, hoping for the best. I reached the end of the ramp and, with visibility quite limited, kept my foot on the accelerator as I nudged my car into the right travel lane, seeing no cars behind me. I was moving about 55 or 60 by now, wishing there was some other visible traffic whose speed I could match. Nothing was in sight, so I had to rely on my own instincts.

The East Coast's Main Street

Just then, out of nowhere, a vehicle appeared in my rearview mirror. I saw it moving across the dashed line into the left lane in order to pass my car with a significant speed differential, its headlights dark. Once I saw the pickup truck was in the other lane, I eased off the accelerator to minimize the amount of time my car would be in close proximity to that truck, which I judged was moving in excess of 80 m.p.h. This wasn't Virginia, but in these conditions, that had to qualify as reckless driving.

My calculation proved adequate for the safety of my vehicle and its occupants. I watched, though, as the pickup truck got past me and then began to move – without signaling, so maybe the driver was a Marylander – back into the right lane ahead of me. And I watched in helpless horror as it continued to slide across the right lane and the right shoulder, briefly becoming airborne before taking out a Big Green Sign for the next exit and landing upside-down in the drainage ditch to the right of the roadway.

Realizing that other drivers might not see the overturned vehicle, and that the occupants might be seriously injured, I gingerly braked and pulled into an impeccably-located rest area less than a half mile from where I'd entered I-95. I whipped out my cell phone, reached Orangeburg County 911, and told the operator about the vehicle in the ditch. The weather being what it was, I elected to wait at the rest area for the worst of the storm to pass. After a couple minutes, I saw a South Carolina state trooper go rushing past the rest area looking for the crashed pickup truck, having missed the scene entirely. As with the other incidents, I don't know how this one turned out.

#

The following semester, the fall of 2003, was one of the worst times of my life, so bad that I will protect the innocent and the guilty by leaving out the details. When I finally made it out the other side of the semester from you-know-where, I wanted some warmth, some sunlight. I was still about a month too young to rent a car, so I had to drive myself wherever

#justpassingthrough

I was going, in turn ruling out the possibility of air travel. At Christmas, I would be free from December 25 at noon after Mass in Highland Park, New Jersey until December 31 at dinner time in Oakfield, New York, where I was due for the big New Year's Eve Party with my grandparents – an annual tradition. I considered my options for someplace warm that I could visit by road in that timeframe (consulting the "other woman", which I brought out from behind my dorm room bed a bit more often than usual that semester), and quickly narrowed it down: I'd be in Key West for a little while on the 27th, meet relatives at Universal Orlando on the 28th, and even slip in a visit to my mother in western Pennsylvania the evening of the 30th.

The next step was to reserve hotel rooms along the way. In this era before smart phones, I wasn't brave enough, as my maternal grandparents were in their traveling heyday, to set out in the morning not knowing where I'd be sleeping that night, especially not with the long days of driving I'd planned, especially not in Florida during Christmas week.

And, in case there was any doubt, "the way" was I-95. So on Christmas Day, after singing two Masses at which my roommate played the organ, I drove onto the New Jersey Turnpike, crossed the Delaware Memorial Bridge to join I-95, got through Baltimore, around the Capital Beltway, and over the Woodrow Wilson Bridge, and then crawled through the Springfield Mixing Bowl (now partway through an eight-year reconstruction) before setting my sights southward in earnest, easily reaching my planned overnight in Benson, North Carolina on Christmas night, exhausted from my professional exertions that morning and the previous night and also from writing this long sentence.

And then on December 26th, 2003, I set a personal record that would stand for just over a decade. After driving from Benson, North Carolina south along I-95 through South Carolina, past Savannah and Jacksonville, beyond the I-4 split for Orlando, past the space coast, down through metropolitan South Florida, right out the other side of Miami where I-95 dumps its traffic onto US 1 south for the last time, I reached my hotel in

Florida City. The distance was 799 miles, the farthest I had ever traveled by car in a single day, almost all of it on the sun-kissed asphalt of I-95.

The 27th, too, was a notable day when I crossed an item off my bucket list. Continuing south from Florida City along US 1, I left the mainland and drove all the way to Key West, where US 1 ends 90 miles from Cuba. The Overseas Highway's route was originally the Overseas Railroad, part of the Florida East Coast Railway, connecting the mainland with Key West via the long line of islands known as the Florida Keys. But the 1935 Labor Day Hurricane (which happened before such storms were given ironically cute names) washed out some of the bridges, so the State of Florida bought what was left over and set to work making it into a road for motor cars.

When I parked in Key West, the temperature was 76 degrees, according to the local bank. I had no particular agenda and wouldn't be staying long, so I just started walking. Oh, was it glorious to be out of the northeastern chill (even in Georgia at lunchtime the previous day, it had been under 40 degrees) and enjoying a subtropical breeze!

Back to Key West: my aunt called (whose family I planned to meet in Orlando the next day), and in order to help her with directions, I had to consult the other woman, who…which was resting comfortably in my parked car. I returned there forthwith and gave directions more or less immediately. By this point, a glance at the clock revealed that I really ought to head back north in order to make it to Orlando by bedtime. And that was the extent of my second visit to Key West.

Was it worth driving 1400 miles from New Jersey to breathe warm fresh air for half an hour? Yes.

#

That 799-mile record, as I said, was carefully calculated to be the farthest I ever hoped to drive in a single day, the nearly clear route of I-95 in the Southeast being conducive to fast and efficient travel, at least when it wasn't raining. I would have been happy to let that personal record stand until the day I die. But...

#

As a kid, I was into rockets and space travel. Forget traveling around the world in five and a half days: astronauts could do it in ninety minutes! Sure, the philosophy and history of space travel interested me, but I was a very normal boy in the sense that I was awed by the big machines involved and wanted to know how they worked. To that end, I watched on CNN Live every time a space shuttle launched or landed, even in the middle of the night. (Once I saw a liftoff in person. I was just seven, and we'd sat up waiting for Atlantis to blast off on mission STS-40 in a midnight-3:00 a.m. window for several nights in a row.) I studied the countdown procedures meticulously, knew which systems activated at which points in the count, when the failures typically occurred, and what radio calls would indicate whether the solution could be found in time to meet the launch window.

I never really outgrew the fascination. Oh, sure, I went into music professionally, but organ music, among other types, which features a large, loud, complicated machine. See the pattern? Anyway, I was sad when the Space Shuttle program came to an end in 2011, though any machine that killed fourteen people in my lifetime due to icing in Florida was certainly suspect, even before anybody considers the financial overruns and futility of flying circles around the earth hundreds of times.

But as a serious traveler, I had enormous respect, bordering reverence, for people who would allow themselves to be strapped onto a giant bomb and ride it into the sky essentially just for the experience and the views and the science and a government paycheck. As I've grown older, I've gained equal admiration for the thousands of people on the ground who made it all happen successfully as often as it did. And I'd always wanted to visit the special places where earthlings departed for the heavens.

The East Coast's Main Street

Thus, when in early 2014, I caught wind that NASA was giving special behind-the-scenes tours of the Kennedy Space Center's Launch Complex 39, I paid top dollar for a scarce spot on a tour. For this trip, having rather more money than time, in stark contrast to the situation in my college years, I drove Sylvia the Silver Sentra from Little Rome to Dulles International Airport one Wednesday morning in February. As a bonus, I was getting out of DC in advance of some weather system that was going to obliterate the mid-Atlantic region with a few inches of flaky precipitation.

Landing at Orlando International was set for 10:39 a.m. and my tour would be at 1:00 p.m. That would be just enough time to deplane, get my rental car, head to KSC, eat lunch, and line up for the tour. So, naturally, I got in line behind a few families picking up cars for their Mouse-hunting expeditions. The group immediately in front of me was a real treat: Dad was grousing about the line he'd been in for ten minutes, calling people at home to complain about it when Mom decided to love the kids instead of rewarding the complaints. I got the distinct feeling their visit to a land of Magic would contain many similar moments in lines of various lengths, and I felt sorry for the kids and the mom.

Anyway, I made it down the Beeline Expressway to the Space Coast, waving at I-95 when I crossed it. How odd that I wouldn't be on The East Coast's Main Street at all during this trip.

The tour group I joined was worthy of the title "elite". By virtue of the $90 ticket cost, most families with half-interested members were cut out. The people on the bus were lifelong space enthusiasts, and included some retired space program workers who hadn't been on Launch Complex 39 since they worked on the Apollo moon launches.

Talking about "Launch Complex 39" might not sound as exciting as talking about a moon landing or even a launch into low earth orbit, simply because Launch Complex 39 has never moved. That's not entirely true: its two launch pads are linked to the Vehicle Assembly Building by several miles of purpose-built "crawlerway". The Crawler Transporters themselves, of which two were built in the 1960's and have been moving rockets at 1 mph ever since (slow enough to avoid even a Virginia reckless driving citation) are on the National Register of Historic Places. These giant tractors were designed to carry an entire assembled rocket, pointing straight into the sky it was built to penetrate, from the Vehicle Assembly Building to Pad 39A or 39B.

The Vehicle Assembly Building (VAB) itself was the first in-earnest stop on my three-hour tour this February afternoon. According to statistics I found on the internet (Al Gore's creation being especially informative about all things Florida), the VAB is 526 feet tall, less than half the height of the Empire State Building, but it is the world's tallest single-story building (in the sense that you can walk in the door at ground level and look all the way up to the roof, when the view isn't blocked by the clouds that form inside) and the tallest building in the United States outside a major urban area.

Because the VAB is wider than it is tall, and there are no buildings around it more than a few yards high, it's impossible to gain an appreciation for the sheer size of it until you see a rocket come inching out the side, or unless you walk inside yourself. And walk inside is what we did: these tours marked the first time the public had been allowed inside since 1976. I was in total awe of that place: at 129,428,000 cubic feet, it's the largest room I'll ever enter. And given some of the churches I've visited, that's saying something.

Yet that was just the warm-up round. Back on the bus, we rode alongside the crawlerway, tracing the route astronauts had been taking to Pad 39A ever since Frank Borman, Jim Lovell, and Bill Anders boarded Apollo 8 in December of 1968.

The tour bus stopped southeast of Pad 39A while the guide talked about the pad's technical features. Perhaps we heard about the 290-foot tower designed to hold the 300,000 gallons of water that would be poured onto the launch pad at liftoff in order to prevent a space shuttle from being torn apart by its own sound waves. Or maybe we were made to notice the twin tanks that held cryogenic liquid hydrogen and liquid oxygen located at opposite sides of the pad in order to prevent unauthorized fraternization until ignition was commanded.

What I really mean to tell you is that I don't remember precisely what the guide was saying because I was so enamored with what I saw. Pad 39A had been left essentially untouched since the launch of Space Shuttle Discovery on STS-135 two and half years prior. Of course, they'd removed the Orbiter Access Arm, a jetway-like swinging bridge that extended from the Fixed Service Structure 147 feet above the pad to allow astronauts and technicians to enter the orbiter's crew cabin. The fixed service structure itself is a relic of the Apollo program, built from segments of the same launch gantry that stood beside a Saturn V rocket. You can't say they didn't try to be thrifty with the tax dollars!

Where we went next was sobering in the extreme: our guide led us into the flame trench beneath and behind the pad. Here was concrete and brick that had been scorched by rocket exhaust over and over again since 1968. When Neil Armstrong, Buzz Aldrin, and Mike Collins left the ground for the first lunar landing that following July, the exhaust of five F-1 rocket engines burning kerosene and liquid oxygen for a total of nearly eight million pounds of thrust – each engine individually the most powerful liquid-fuel rocket engine ever made – poured through here, causing the sound-suppression water to billow into great clouds of steam as the 363-foot rocket lumbered into the sky.

Standing in that flame trench, I contemplated the twelve Saturn V rockets that had left earth here... the eighty-two space shuttle flights that had launched here... the men and women who rode into orbit from here, not entirely sure whether their vehicle was going to hold together, or whether a small leak would develop into a big problem, or whether ice from the cryogenic fuels would fall off and knock a hole in the wrong place. The Apollo 1 fire had happened down the road at Pad 34, and Challenger's ill-fated 51-L launch in 1986 was from neighboring Pad 39B. But STS-107, the science mission that would claim Columbia and the lives of seven crew members on re-entry during my sophomore year of college, had left from Pad 39A a decade earlier. And Apollo 13, whose crew launched for the moon but barely made it safely back to earth, had blasted from this place in 1970. I'd studied their plight a lot in my younger years.

I stood for a few minutes contemplating the violence, the majesty, the danger, the beauty of it all, even the age of some of this equipment: most of us wouldn't be caught dead driving a thirty-year-old car, yet the space program made it into 2011 relying on vehicles designed in the 1970's. Yes, maybe it was high time for America to move away from the "space race" model of government-run space travel. But darned if I wasn't sad to see those vehicles retired to museums!

Reflecting on this tour years later, I'm struck by the fundamental similarity among journeys of all kinds: we make a plan, we get the necessary equipment, we pack, we tell friends and family where we're going and when we plan to return. But did the people with whom I'd shared I-95 expect to be in those crashes? Do we ever really know where the journey is going to lead or how it will end?

#

Having come and seen what I came to see, it was time to head home. I had planned to spend Wednesday night at Cocoa Beach and then fly out of Orlando International at 8:10 a.m. Thursday. Mid-tour on Wednesday, the airline sent word that my flight would now be departing at 1:00 p.m. Thursday, but I should still be at the gate in time for the scheduled 8:10 a.m. departure. Right.

Since it seemed like the snow at points north was fouling things up, I called before bed and got myself rebooked on a Thursday afternoon flight from Orlando so that I didn't have to sit at the airport all day amongst those who didn't understand why they weren't still at Walt Disney World. This gave me Thursday morning to walk on the beach and then drive to the airport, which sounded like a good plan at bedtime Wednesday.

Unfortunately, it wasn't such a good plan when I woke up Thursday. My flight would now be leaving late in the evening, so I would be stranded in Florida for an extra day due to the northeastern snow business. Darnitall.

On recommendations from friends who knew the area, I got on I-95 and headed to Jacksonville – so, yes, indeed I would be on that road after all – and visited the museum where someone from a choir I directed had interned one summer of college. I saw the very old pot she'd glued together for display, and dutifully photographed it to prove I'd been there. It wasn't as exciting as Pad 39A, but it sure beat trying to drive in a Carolina snowstorm. Plus, in the unlikely event I decided to drive home, Jacksonville was in the correct direction.

Around lunchtime Thursday, I got notification that all flights from Orlando to Dulles were cancelled for the day, so this time I rebooked on a flight from Tampa Friday morning. That seemed safe; the pressing concern was that I needed to play for two Masses Saturday morning. Thursday afternoon, I slid back down I-95 and stopped at St. Augustine, the oldest settlement in the United States continuously inhabited by Europeans. I learned that the place received its name because a Spanish admiral had first sighted it on St. Augustine's feast day, August 28, 1565. After paying a visit to the Cathedral-Basilica of St. Augustine (built in the late eighteenth century, it's Florida's oldest church) I furthered my cultural education by touring the St. Augustine Pirate and Treasure Museum.

With Jacksonville and St. Augustine in my history books, I set sail for I-4, passing through Orlando and eventually landed in a cheap hotel a couple miles from Tampa International Airport. And after a short night's rest, I rose early enough to drive to the airport, return my rental car, clear security, and arrive at the gate just in time to learn that my third attempted flight home would now be leaving at least seven hours late.

I'd had enough. Eating an overpriced, understuffed breakfast burrito in the terminal, I took matters into my own hands. The airline, mostly through no fault of its own, couldn't be relied upon to get me home on any particular schedule, so I would have to drive. The car rental agent couldn't mentally process what the computer could: that I was renting a car Friday morning at 8:30 a.m. in Tampa, to be returned to Dulles Airport in Virginia within 24 hours. He tried to tell me I was making a mistake, not of the moral or prudential type, but just of the technical type. I assured him that, yes, my plan was to drive to Dulles Airport as soon as he pushed his buttons and handed me some keys. He slowly accepted that I was not crazy, but just eager to get home.

And so, having slept only about four hours, I got behind the wheel of a rental car to continue the longest driving day of my life. I wasted no time scooting onto I-275 and heading north to I-75.

Here's a compare-and-contrast: I-95 is the East Coast's Main Street, an express route from the northeastern megalopolis through flat coastal Southeastern regions to the sunny East Coast of Florida. I-75, on the other hand, links some of the major cities of the interior east – Detroit, Cincinnati, Atlanta – with Florida's Gulf Coast. And that's the key: Midwesterners vacation on the laid-back Gulf Coast, traveling via I-75 through Appalachia. Northeasterners barrel down I-95 towards the cosmopolitan Atlantic metropolis of Miami. They mix only in the Orlando area.

Today, I stayed on I-75 only as far north as Ocala, where I picked up US 301 to roll through the Southern part of Florida, which is also the northern part (notice the caps). That's a thing about Florida, too: the geographically northern parts are culturally of a piece with the South, like neighboring Georgia and Alabama (I ate fried chicken for lunch because the other choice was fried catfish), while the southern reaches of the Sunshine State are full of immigrants and refugees from Havana, Port-au-Prince, Sao Paulo, and Brooklyn. Florida is upside-down.

Mercifully, US 301 eventually intersected with I-10, which I used to go east to I-295 near Jacksonville before joining I-95 for the long trip north. Usually when I spend a whole day on the road, I schedule a break every two hours or so, alternating between a food stop and a fuel stop; today, not wanting to waste a single minute, I stopped only when I really needed to stop. So, after lunch somewhere in Southern northern Florida, my next stop was in Hardeeville, South Carolina, where I later figured out one of the planes that flew over me as I refueled was the Tampa-Dulles flight I had abandoned. Oops... I'd made a bad call in retrospect, but it was water under the bridge now.

After that, I covered another 200+ miles, recognizing the site where that pickup truck had hydroplaned near Santee eleven years prior, and rocketing right past Pedro at South of the Border, before stopping at a Subway restaurant in Lumberton, North Carolina. Here, I waited in line fifteen minutes behind one other customer ordering one sandwich, watching the sun drop below the horizon as the clock ticked. Fifteen hours remained until I had to be at work in Little Rome.

The rental car was performing well. The next fuel stop was at a gas station north of Rocky Mount, but since the restroom was not working, I also stopped at the Welcome to Virginia stop just over the next state line. This next part was, psychologically, the most dangerous part of the drive: Virginia was practically my home territory, and it was already dark outside, but I still had to drive nearly four hours before I'd see a bed. Oh, and now I was in an area where the roads could be icy.

I persevered through Petersburg and Richmond and past Fredericksburg. Now the road surfaces were wet and people were driving like they'd just survived nuclear Armageddon. Yes, this was starting to feel like home. At the Mixing Bowl, I "turned left" toward Tysons Corner. Coming around a bend, I got to test the rental car's brakes when a snowplow backed into the through lanes of the Capital Beltway. Oh, yes, this is definitely my target region! I edged onto the Dulles Access Road and remembered to stop and fill the gas tank in order to avoid paying $9 per gallon, or whatever the rental company charges when you don't fill the gas tank.

#

#justpassingthrough

Dulles Airport is many things: Its capacious runway layout means that weather rarely causes delays unless conditions are bad enough to halt air traffic altogether. There is ample parking for planes and cars. And the retro moon buggies remind me, at least from afar, of something you'd find at the Kennedy Space Center. But as the clock ticked past midnight, I learned that Dulles was not designed to facilitate pedestrian transfers from rental car return to short-term parking. In fact, from the rental lot I couldn't even see the terminal or parking decks. I hopped on a shuttle bus to the terminal, but when it passed near the parking garage and I asked the driver to let me off, the mumbling contained the phrase "bus not stop here". There was a stop sign, so I walked toward the door and again asked for leave to disembark. The driver protested that he wasn't supposed to do this, but I promised not to tell anybody (I guess I'm breaking that now…sorry!), so he opened the door and left me and my luggage in the adjacent pile of snow.

My name is Matt, and as you've figured out, I do what it takes to get home; when I finally pulled Sylvia the Silver Sentra into her icy Little Roman parking space, it was nearly 1:00 a.m. Saturday. I'd driven about 960 miles in a waking day, and that, my dear readers, is a record I truly hope will stand as long as I live.

The Sandbox

Dear Matt,
Don't die. And have an awesome time!!

P.S. Don't die.

This was the sticky note I found affixed to the *Lonely Planet* guidebook for the Arabian peninsula, which I'd left sitting on a shared desk.

Of course, the Middle East has its share of conflicts. On the surface, they tend to look like old-fashioned land grabs, but this region's conflicts force their way into our headlines with two hooks, religion and oil, that most conflicts elsewhere on the globe simply cannot offer.

On one hand, there's a plot of land smaller than my Little Roman ZIP code claimed as "holy" by Jews, who have built their Temple there two and a half times; by Christians, who revere the place where God Incarnate, Jesus, died and rose and ascended; and most recently by Muslims, who celebrate the Prophet Mohammed's night journey from Mecca to the Far ("Aqsa") Mosque in Jerusalem. People get, well, territorial about land where they think holy things happened.

On the other hand, there's a lot of oil in the Middle East and North Africa. Oil is known as "black gold" for a reason – he who pumps it prints money – and the drawing of lines in the sand can leave a sheikh destitute while the neighboring emir rolls in dough. Add that any disruption to oil supply and/or shipping, as is caused when there's a regional war, can lead to world economic turmoil, and suddenly major powers from every continent have material interests in the region's geopolitics. This leads to conflict, and people don't like to take unnecessary trips into what is – or what they fear might become – a war zone.

#justpassingthrough

I've made three separate trips to "The Sandbox" and lived to tell the tale. The first time I was apprehensive, but the experience of Arab hospitality, the glory of nearly-guaranteed sunshine, the stark beauty of deserts, the absence of droves of American tourists, and the close proximity of so much that's of historical and cultural interest, to say nothing of the cheap gasoline prices, have made the Middle East, North Africa, and the Persian Gulf region one of my favorite parts of the world to explore.

And this is part of why we travel. As Mark Twain put it:

Travel is fatal to prejudice, bigotry, and narrow-mindedness, and many of our people need it sorely on these accounts. Broad, wholesome, charitable views of men and things cannot be acquired by vegetating in one little corner of the earth all one's lifetime.

#

My second Sandbox visit was one of my trips whose genesis lay in the concept of mileage running. You see, in order to obtain and maintain a high status in an airline's frequent flyer program, it's necessary to fly a certain number of miles in a year. For lower status levels, it might be as few as 20,000 miles, while at least one U.S. carrier has a top tier for those who fly over 125,000 miles per year (which would be about halfway from Pad 39A to the moon). Once you have status, you begin to get attached to the perks: complimentary upgrades, priority access to boarding and ticket counters and security checkpoints, free flight changes, extra baggage allowances, access to lounges with showers that sometimes work, and so forth. It follows that if you hold, say, a mid-level status that requires 50,000 miles a year, and your work/family travel adds up to just 46,000 miles this year, you might be tempted to look for a cheap trip, usually without regard for the destination, since you'll just get right back on the plane and come home, that will allow you to earn those last 4000 miles (easily accomplished by, say, a North American transcontinental round trip in 12-15 hours) toward next year's status. That trip is known as a

The Sandbox

mileage run, and yes, there are parts of the internet where people share mileage run-friendly fares, experiences, and tips on how to explain the practice to friends and family who already suspect you're a hump short of a full camel.

Most of my mileage runs over the years have been exactly that sort of trip, though I usually try to build in at least a few hours in the destination city. And then in the summer of 2013, my favorite mileage running web forum began to go crazy over a fare in the $600-700 range for round-trip travel from various North American cities to Bahrain. In turn, there were question-and-answer sessions on how to obtain a Bahrain visa, whether the setup of the Bahrain airport would allow a flight connection without having to pass through immigration and/or security (in order to enter and exit Bahrain without leaving the airport), and what the transit experience would entail at Kuwait City. The airline in question flew regularly from Dulles Airport to Kuwait City and on to Bahrain. The main profit center was government and military travel and cargo, so the back of the huge plane often went out empty, hence why the airline was so heavily discounting the economy fares.

I was intrigued, to say the least, and began playing with various travel sales websites trying to get the fare to work on an itinerary that originated at Dulles. You'd think that would be the cheapest of all (since the flight to the Sandbox was nonstop from Dulles), but no, it was much more expensive to leave directly from Dulles than to connect from some other city; Los Angeles and Chicago seemed to be favorites. So, what I ended up buying was a Chicago-to-Bahrain fare with a multi-day stopover in Kuwait City on the return, all bookended by a Dulles-to-Chicago round-trip. In other words, I would fly:

Day One: IAD-ORD-IAD-KWI-BAH (arriving Day Two)
Day Four: BAH-KWI
Day Seven: KWI-IAD-ORD-IAD (arriving Day Eight)

#justpassingthrough

No, you can't skip the first two legs without having the rest of your itinerary cancelled, and you can't skip the last two legs if you want to see your checked baggage sometime this decade.

I booked this trip for late February and early March, mainly to coincide with a gap in my work schedule, but also to take advantage of mild winter weather in the Persian Gulf region.

#

So it was that I turned up at Dulles Airport on a Monday in late February 2014, soon after my record-setting adventure on I-95. I parked Sylvia the Silver Sentra in the same garage where she'd waited for me to come home from Florida a couple weeks earlier, and rather optimistically left my winter coat in the car. I didn't want to drag it all over the Middle East, and the forecast was for mild weather on my return.

On an unrelated note, weather forecasts aren't very reliable more than about three days out, but that fact probably isn't important to this story.

I'll spare you some of the details of the out-and-back to Chicago, but I will mention that at my first flight's scheduled departure time, I looked out the aircraft window and saw the captain standing inside the engine. Things cascaded from there, but due to quick thinking and some kind of providence, I found myself back at Dulles that evening, sweaty and winded, settling into my rear-facing Business Class seat for the long trek to Kuwait City, just in time. Yes, I'd gone wimpy and used miles to upgrade to a flying bed.

Records indicate that I watched "Parkland", about what had happened at that Dallas hospital on a November day just over fifty years earlier, while dining on beef tenderloin in asiago broth with gnocchi and asparagus. Side observation: asparagus is commonly served with dinner in premium cabins (maybe because it's cheap in bulk?), and the whole plane gives olfactory evidence of this fact a few hours into flight, especially in the lavatories. After a couple rounds of dessert and the corresponding

The Sandbox

beverages, I changed into my pajamas, put my seat in bed mode, and slept from Newfoundland to Romania. I changed back into my street clothes in time to eat breakfast over northern Iraq. Though it was somewhat cloudy, I caught a glimpse of Baghdad (recognizable from cruise altitude because it sits on a distinctive bend in the Tigris River) as I partook of a cheddar omelette.

Soon, the Triple-Seven landed in Kuwait. The terminal smelled horribly of cigarette smoke, but I was able to spend most of my transit time in a smoke-free lounge area. Unintentionally, I'd timed my pass-through to coincide with Kuwait Liberation Day, celebrating that glorious occasion in 1991 when a coalition of nations drove Saddam Hussein's armies from the tiny but oil-rich emirate, so there were special decorations throughout the airport.

In a little over an hour, I got out of the smoke-filled airport, re-boarding the plane for the hop to Manama, Bahrain, located on an island in the Persian Gulf just 261 miles away.

I figured it would be an uneventful and quiet flight, but I ended up next to a talkative Kuwaiti matriarch. Her monologue started shortly after takeoff, when the moving map showed the Islamic Republic of Iran a few dozen miles off the port side. Without naming the country, the woman pronounced it "a monster". I was not overly inclined to argue with her, and she proceeded to inform me that Iran's problem is that it's full of Shi'ites, who are not really Muslim. (Replace "Shi'ite" with "Catholic" and "Muslim" with "Christian", and the scene would be not unlike some get-togethers this Catholic convert has attended.)

The educational lecture wasn't over. Obama was "no good". Oh, and since JFK preferred blondes, Jackie Kennedy must have been "no good". Notwithstanding these facts, Americans are the best people in the world, in contrast to Saudis (whose airspace we were using) who are too rich because they all have private jets. Next, I was encouraged to agree that all choirs should be made of black people, because the late Whitney Houston was the best singer ever.

#justpassingthrough

Then came the kicker. The woman pulled out her photo array and showed me her twenty-five-year-old daughter, who was single and practically the attorney general of Kuwait, yet was somehow flying coach on this flight while her mother rode up front. Was I interested? I briefly considered the mother-in-law stories I'd be able to tell, but then I politely declined. You have to be careful of this sort of thing in the Sandbox; one distinctive Arabic custom is that when a guest expresses admiration for something, the host must give the thing to the guest. It's all well and good if the thing is a salt shaker or a picture frame, but one must be careful when talking of someone's beautiful single daughter... or of someone's wife.

I managed to deplane in Bahrain with my bachelorhood intact, and found (as if this wasn't already my lucky day) that my prepaid e-visa came through when the border officer scanned my passport. I was in Bahrain. The sun had gone down on Tuesday, so all I needed was to rent a car, drive twelve minutes to the Holiday Inn Express everyone in the mileage running forum had recommended, and fall into bed so that tomorrow could be a great day.

#

Bahrain is an archipelago in the Persian Gulf. Its nearest neighbors are Saudi Arabia to the west and Qatar to the southeast. The Iranian coast is about 150 miles to the northeast. It's not a big country at all, less than a quarter the size of Rhode Island. The urban concentration of Manama is at the north end, while the south end is more rural but also hosts the energy industry and some military bases. I had given myself two days here, which ended up being just about right for seeing the highlights.

Wednesday morning, I drove straight to the Beit al-Quran, a museum containing old Korans and some stunning examples of Islamic calligraphy. All Korans are in Arabic; Muslim tradition is that the Koran was given to Mohammed in completed Arabic form, so this is the only version that's authoritative. Now, here's a thing about Islamic art: Islam's brand of monotheism holds that Allah is a strictly heavenly being and can't be seen here on earth. This is in stark contrast to the Christian dogma of the Incarnation, which holds that God came to earth and became one of us, and that we humans are the very image of God. For reasons others could articulate better, traditional Islamic art never depicts Allah or his creatures, but is only abstract. Nonetheless, one exhibit that caught my eye put a Koranic verse in Arabic calligraphy, arranged in such a way as to form the outline of a fish. I guess that's kosher.

Next, I made my way to the Al-Fateh Grand Mosque. Most mosques (whether they're the friendly neighborhood kind or a showpiece in the center of a big city) only allow Muslims inside. But here the signage loudly proclaims that the mosque "welcomes people of all faiths and tourists". I seemed to qualify, so I parked and went in, and they warmly invited me to take a seat and told me what time I could expect a tour in German. Since I didn't want to wait that long, I conceded that an English tour would suffice. They asked me to remove my shoes, which wasn't a problem since I'd remembered to wear socks without holes in them that day.

The tour was highly instructive. The lady tour guide, covered in a single black garment with just a slit for her eyes, showed us the main prayer room, which could comfortably hold several thousand people. There are five times of prayer daily, which are calculated according to the movement of the sun and announced by the muezzin for the whole neighborhood to hear; this chant adds a distinctive sonic component to the atmosphere of any Muslim city. In the front of the prayer room the imam has a chair whence he proclaims the lesson from Allah, and also a cubicle where he leads the gestures of prayer for the assembled faithful. The art, for reasons already mentioned, consists entirely of geometric patterns in textiles, mosaic, stained glass, and light bulbs. It is quite beautiful, actually.

#justpassingthrough

As informative as the tour was, and as glad as I am that I took the time to visit, parts of the experience made me angry. As a Christian, I believe that God is Three Persons, a belief that the tour guide and the printed literature preemptively derided as polytheistic. One of those Persons is Jesus, who is fully human even as he remains fully divine, and who rose from the dead in victory over sin and hell. It took quite some self-restraint not to argue with the tour guide when she described Jesus as a dead prophet ("peace be upon him"), and in that kept-to-myself moment, I experienced in a new and personal way how it is that wars break out so readily in the Sandbox. But my God Incarnate says that he who lives by the sword dies by the sword, so I held my tongue, wandered off to a corner by myself, and silently prayed "Glory be to the Father, and to the Son, and to the Holy Spirit..." in reparation.

#

Heading to a nearby restaurant, I found lunch in the form of a lamb skewer. It was served not on a plate but as chunks of spiced meat intermixed with peppers, all suspended above a plate of perfectly-salted French fries. The taste was amazing, and the experience of forking the meat off the hanging skewer is something I've yet to encounter in America.

After a morning of intentionally intense exposure to Islamic art and practice, I took advantage of the warm, sunny afternoon and drove into what passes for countryside in Bahrain. My next stop was the Al-Areen Wildlife Park, where my twin goals were to observe the non-human animals and to observe the human animals.

The uncrowdedness of the park allowed visitors to have close encounters with flamingoes, camels, goats, ostriches, ducks, and other creatures native to that part of the world but inaccessible to Bahraini city-dwellers most of the time. A highlight, which I unintentionally caught on video, was when I happened upon a pair of African spurred tortoises were

The Sandbox

publicly engaged in becoming a larger family of African spurred tortoises. At one point, a third African spurred tortoise, from its size probably another female, waddled into the picture. Big daddy African spurred tortoise made his non-amusement clear, and the interloper ran away while the mommy African spurred tortoise just kept her head inside her shell.

The people-watching was rich here, too. Owing to my near-total unfamiliarity with the Arabic language, I observed human interactions more or less the same way I observed that of the camels and ostriches and tortoises. No, the behavior wasn't the same, but I did enjoy watching a young couple (he dressed in slacks and a shirt like me, she covered head-to-toe in black) as they chased their child around and through a pond full of oblivious ducks.

Heading further south by car, I managed to find the Tree of Life, which is a tourist attraction because there are no other trees in the area. There is some mystery surrounding the tree: even though it stands two miles from the nearest known water source, it has survived for more than four hundred years and grown to a height of over thirty feet, with many sprawling branches. Some people, most of them employed as Bahraini tourism officials, seem to think this was the site of the Garden of Eden; most other scholars seem to think the Garden of Eden was probably in southern Iraq. Mystery aside, it's a grand tree surrounded by desert sand.

#

My second day in Bahrain was further devoted to learning about the history and culture of the place by way of vehicle-based exploration. That is to say, I drove around the island some more.

The Bahrain National Museum is the nation's largest, and dates from 1988. It tells the story of Bahrain through a wide variety of multimedia and 3D exhibits, beginning with its Dilmun civilization roots over three thousand years ago. A center for trading pearls, the archipelago was ruled in turn by the Persians, the Greeks, and maybe the Seleucids, before being conquered for Islam in 629 A.D. From then until the fifteenth century, Bahrain was ruled by a series of local sheikhs, having trade relationships with Baghdad to the northwest and Persia to the east. Then, for a few hundred more years, Bahrain was ruled by Europeans, first the Portuguese and then the British, who left their mark in the form of English as a widely-used second language while continuing to prop up various puppet sheikhs. The big change came in 1932, with the discovery of oil, which made Bahrain suddenly get more important in the hierarchy of the British Empire.

Bahrain didn't become independent until 1971, after a long series of United Nations talks involving the Trucial States (the seven emirates that now comprise the United Arab Emirates), Qatar, Iran, and the United Kingdom. When the British vacated Bahrain's naval bases, the United States Navy immediately moved in. Unlike some other states in the region (like Saudi Arabia, where, as you'll recall, they're all too rich and own private planes) Bahrain came out of the politically turbulent 1970's with a fairly prosperous middle class owing to the relative diversity of its economy; in addition to the energy industry, tiny Bahrain is a center for trade and banking. In turn, prosperity has made Bahrain a magnet for immigrants from all over south Asia. As I drove around and saw the various cultures intermixing, I mused that Bahrain is part Tampa, part Las Vegas, and part Coruscant.

There are some impressive exhibits in the Bahrain National Museum: a diorama showing pearl divers dodging sharks in the Gulf to obtain pearls; replicas of typical homes in various stages of Bahrain's history to illustrate family customs and economic trends; more Arabic calligraphy; the obligatory display of ancient pots and pans. But my favorite part was the map floor: an entire area of the museum has its floor covered with a satellite image of the island, and the walls feature satellite images showing how the very shape of the island has changed with time and development. If for some reason you ever find yourself with even a few hours in

Bahrain, catch a cab from the airport and see this museum; if you have a little more time, add the aforementioned mosque.

But I still had a half day left before my flight to Kuwait, and I planned to do more exploring.

#

When I said Bahrain is part Las Vegas, I meant that it's a weekend playground for those who want to escape the strictness of Saudi Arabia, whose laws don't allow the possession of alcohol or the viewing of female skin. Bahrain is an island nation with no land borders, but there is a bridge to the Saudi mainland. In 1967, Bahrain changed from driving on the left to driving on the right in order to match the rest of the region, which is an event I'm very sorry I didn't get to witness but in which I'm much less sorry I didn't get to participate. The Bahraini and Saudi authorities talked for a long time – perhaps over drinks, but not in Saudi Arabia – and in 1986 the King Fahd Causeway was opened, linking Manama with Dammam and Dhahran and Khobar in northeastern Saudi Arabia. (Those old enough to remember the 1991 Gulf War will remember CNN reporter Charles Jaco doing live standups from the U.S. military base in Dhahran with air raid sirens blaring and Iraqi SCUD missiles incoming. You may have read the urban legend that Jaco's broadcasts were an early form of CNN making fake news, but my research into the visual evidence has satisfied me that Jaco was really there and the SCUDs were really incoming.) Nearest the Saudi end of the bridge is Khobar, a planned community full of ex-pats, including U.S. military personnel. The Khobar Towers, inhabited by U.S. airmen and their families, were bombed by Iranian-backed militants in 1996, and another terror attack took place in Khobar in 2004.

Since Saudi Arabia doesn't grant tourist visas to Americans, and since my rental car was not insured outside of Bahrain, there was no possibility of entering Saudi Arabia today. My mission was simply to drive to the midpoint of the King Fahd Causeway, where an artificial island houses the border control facilities for both countries as well as some restaurants, gas stations, and a mosque. I was going to eat lunch in the Tower Restaurant, which promised views of the Saudi side of the border, and then return to Bahrain's main island. Unfortunately, there was construction going on at the time to expand the border processing facility, and the Tower Restaurant was closed. The only other lunch option was (wait for it) McDonald's, which shares a parking lot with the island's mosque. Yes, I ate there, and it was just as good as at home. Refreshingly, there were individuals, families, and small groups occupying the dining area just as they would in America. So maybe the Middle East wasn't so exotic as Coruscant, after all.

There was little (but not no) traffic on the King Fahd Causeway that Thursday midday. I'm told that's not the case at the end of a weekend or during the Eid holiday after Ramadan. In fact, I read at least one explicit warning not to drive the bridge when a bunch of drunk Saudi men use it as a racetrack to get home to their totally-covered, not-allowed-to-drive women after a weekend of binge drinking and other forms of debauchery in Bahrain. I guess Bahrain International doesn't have enough parking spaces for them all to fly there in their private jets.

Returning to Bahrain's main island, I made my next stop at the Center for Traditional Handicrafts. There, I bought a small replica of a traditional Bahraini gate, made of painted gypsum, which now hangs on a wall in my home. In the process, I encountered a pair of Italians who wanted to converse with the Arabic-speaking craftsman. Fortuitously, I was able to facilitate international peace and harmony, to say nothing of trade and commerce, by translating between their Engtalian and his Arablish.

With just a few hours until my flight back to Kuwait, I parked in a downtown garage and explored the Bahrain souq. Some cities (in my experience: Jerusalem, Marrakech) have a traditional-looking marketplace where people buy and sell everything from fresh vegetables to spices to recently-slaughtered goats to flowers to brightly-colored scarves to

The Sandbox

electronics. This marketplace didn't quite fit the "traditional-looking" bill, but it was a labyrinthine place with just about everything for sale, all prices being negotiable.

The only thing I bought, and then only because the establishment selling it had free wi-fi for customers, was a dish of rahash-flavored ice cream. A search of the internet in 2018 doesn't turn up much agreement on a definition of rahash, but it might be a dessert consisting of ground sesame seeds mixed with hot sugar syrup, possessing the approximate texture of jelly. To be clear, I didn't have rahash, but rather rahash-flavored ice cream. Just the same, it was delicious.

While I ate the rahash-flavored ice cream, I marveled at the change I'd received from the cashier: One Bahraini half dinar note, depicting the Bahrain International Circuit. (Motorists can sign up for a time to drive on the race course, an opportunity I had declined in favor of the copulating tortoises and Tree of Life.) I also received, apparently in error, a Saudi fifty-riyal note, depicting the Al-Aqsa Mosque in Jerusalem. There's lots I might say about this, but instead I'll ask you a question: How would it be if Mexico printed money showing the St. Louis arch?

#

Driving into Bahrain International Airport, I looked for the sign pointing me toward rental car return. Since the staff had delivered the car to me curbside on arrival, I had no idea where to go. I did encounter a vehicular security checkpoint staffed by drowsy men with very large weapons, but I must not have made much of an impression on them because when I came back for another attempt to locate rental car return a few minutes later, they waved me through once again. That was a relief, but I still didn't know where in the world to park my rental car. I did, though, remember where the office was in the terminal; having more time than local language skills, I parked the car in short-term parking and went inside. As it would turn out, there is no special rental car return lot in

71

Bahrain. You just go to the counter and hand them the key and tell them where the car is parked and assure them the gas tank is full and they trust you because they have your credit card information. Then you fly away.

The triple-seven flew back up the eastern Arabian coastline, shadowing Saudi Arabia's Highway 95. Unlike our I-95, this is mostly a two-lane road notorious for being overrun with speeding oil tanker trucks. Had I been able to drive rather than fly, the journey from Bahrain International Airport would have taken me five hours, crossing the King Fahd Causeway and heading up Saudi Highway 95 to the Saudi-Kuwaiti border at Khafji, and thence up to the Kuwait International Airport. But the flight was well under one hour, and since it was after bedtime when the wheels touched down, and since there were no offers of betrothal to consider, I was eager to pick up my Kuwaiti rental car and get some sleep.

#

A few months after I had watched (at age seven) the space shuttle punch through a cloud deck in the middle of a Florida night in 1990, Saddam Hussein sent his armies to punch into Kuwait. Calling Kuwait Iraq's "Nineteenth Province", the August 2, 1990 invasion gained him control of Kuwait's oil production and threatened (implicitly and then explicitly) neighboring Saudi Arabia. The ensuing occupation and subsequent U.S.-led, U.N.-backed Operation Desert Storm gripped my seven-year-old mind. I watched on CNN in January 1991 as John Holliman, Bernard Shaw, and Peter Arnett bravely reported live from Baghdad's Al-Rashid Hotel while American and Allied planes dropped bombs all over the city. Subconsciously, this became my first real experience of geopolitical history, just as the Vietnam War had been for many in my parents' generation decades earlier, and as the Second World War was for my grandparents' generation before that.

My own arrival into Kuwait City wasn't like Saddam's, exactly, but it was memorable nonetheless. Deplaning, I followed the signs to immigration and customs. Being a non-incompetent traveler and having done my homework, I know that an American tourist could simply land at KWI and be admitted to the country without obtaining a visa in advance. You can thus imagine my alarm and annoyance when I arrived at the immigration counter and the non-smiling officer demanded to see my visa in addition to my passport. Since "But I'm an American" doesn't tend to play too well in this type of situation, I apologized and explained that I didn't think I needed one.

She sternly directed me to go back up to the boarding gate area, a fcat I eventually accomplished by dragging my bags up a semi-hidden flight of stairs, and visit the visa-on-arrival desk. After being photographed and fingerprinted, and forking over some sum of money I had obtained from a nearby ATM, a tourist visa for Kuwait was placed in my passport and I returned to the passport control queue. I got a different agent just as friendly as the first, and was stamped into the country.

Thinking that I'd collected my war story for the evening, I claimed my bag, which fortunately was still on the carousel despite my delay in getting there to fetch it, and stood in line for security screening. This seemed a bit odd considering I was not planning to board another plane, but I played along. Looking into things later, it turned out that this baggage inspection is how the Kuwaiti government keeps its people safe from the evils of alcohol, whose sale, possession, and consumption are completely banned in Kuwait, just as in Saudi Arabia. Word is that when the border police find alcoholic beverages they charge the offenders an arm and a leg (hopefully not literally) in fines, and then take the contraband to an off-airport location for, um, disposal.

Next, I found the counter for the car rental agency where I held a reservation. The representative didn't like my DC driver's license for some reason, and declined to rent me a car. I tried a second rental agency, but they found something not to like about my credit card, as did a third. I began to wonder how this was going to end up; a fourth rental company had no cars available. Finally, on the fifth try, I found an agency with cars available that would accept my DC driver's license and my weird "VISA"-branded credit card. Since we were standing in the middle of the terminal, I asked where I could find the car, expecting, as at Bahrain two days prior, that someone would drive it to the curb and wish me a pleasant stay, Meester Mooller! But the reply was simply a gesture toward the garage. So I rolled my luggage into the one big parking garage at Kuwait International Airport, armed with just a remote opener and an ignition key and a description of the car and license plate number, and somehow found the vehicle.

With my hotel red-dotted on an offline Google map, supplemented by narrative directions and a neighborhood map I'd printed, I gingerly pulled out of the parking garage and set sail for Kuwait City. It was now well past midnight. There's a thoroughly modern suburban freeway linking KWI with central Kuwait City; I was glad not to have to find my way while dodging rush hour traffic. Going by a merge point, I noticed that a vehicle was approaching very quickly from behind and passed me on the right. Then, out of nowhere, two police cars appeared with lights ablaze, one passing me on each side… I half-expected my car to spin in their wake. Mind you, I was doing precisely the 120 kph limit, and these cars were blurs. I'd been off the airport less than two minutes, and already I'd been through a high-speed police chase.

Coming into the central city from the suburbs, I eased off the motorway and found my way onto the First Ring Road, following the printed directions that I had memorized. But then, at the place where I needed to turn right to reach the hotel, I found a barricade. How I eventually found my way there I'm not sure, but it involved good geographical instincts, the lack of anyplace else to go, and the pronounced desire to be in bed. And even when I found the hotel, all the parking spaces were full, so I surveyed the surroundings and noticed that a few cars were parked on the sidewalk. Jumping the curb into what I hoped wasn't a small cliff, I parked and checked-in, keenly lamenting the fact that Kuwait is a completely "dry" country.

The Sandbox

\#

As on any international excursion, I arrived in Kuwait City with a list of places to visit and bits of history to understand. But first I had a somewhat unusual agenda item to cross off. A friend of mine from school had signed up to wear a uniform and protect her fellow Americans and was currently deployed near Kuwait City. Since I was due to serve musically at her wedding in Annapolis later that year, I sent word that we would have to have a bridal music consultation while I was in town. Awaking on Friday morning, I got confirmation that my friend and her entourage had gotten permission to leave their base and come into the city for lunch. So, with the vague sense that the episode could have been taken from a spy novel, I drove to the Kuwait Towers at an appointed rendezvous time. A few minutes later, two SUVs pulled up, and out piled not only the bride-to-be but six fellow male Americans.

After introductions and greetings, we headed to a nearby building for lunch. Called the Green Apple restaurant, the place I'd found turned out to be a multi-story establishment with a different type of cuisine on each level. We opted for the Iranian floor and were not disappointed: lunch consisted of mountains of grilled meat, voluminous piles of rice, leafy salad (a rarity in the Sandbox), warm bread, tea, and tasty mocktails.

It was a humbling visit for me. Here were young men (and one woman) fundamentally no different from me, and they'd opted to give years of their lives in service to our country, while I stayed home and reaped the reward of security and comfort and reasonable gasoline prices their service and their potential sacrifices helped to buy.

Returning to my hotel to rest (it had been a short night of sleep after the annoyances at the airport) I plotted my next move. I wanted to attend daily Mass, but since this was Friday, Masses were actually of the following Sunday. That's because in the Islamic world Sunday is a workday, and Holy Mother Church desires that all the faithful should be able to fulfill their Sunday obligation without undue hardship. Unlike Bahrain (with just one parish holding Masses in the different languages of different expat groups, plus English and Arabic), Kuwait had a number of parishes spread over its populated areas.

While it's still a small country, Kuwait dwarfs Bahrain and has a land area similar to that of New Jersey; when I drove from Kuwait City to the expat community at Ahmadi, I was driving a distance similar to the entire length of Bahrain, but only about a sixth the width of Kuwait. It was so straight and flat that I even used cruise control.

In a desert country awash in oil wealth, having water is considered a luxury and a sign of prosperity; Ahmadi has lots of green plants and even some large trees. The town was covered with lights and festive decorations left over from Kuwait Liberation Day. The national colors are red (for the blood of the martyrs), white (for pearls), green (for Islam), and black (for oil); since black light doesn't show up too well, blue was substituted in many displays. Our Lady of Arabia Catholic Church was outlined with Christmas lights and covered with bright stars. A poster advertised an upcoming benefit performance of Handel's Messiah, the charitable cause being the construction of a new cathedral in Bahrain. Oddly, I'd seen and heard nothing about that project when I visited Bahrain's only parish church earlier in the week. Maybe the new cathedral was going to be a surprise gift.

The central blocks of Ahmadi were well-lit by multi-colored strings of bulbs and various other kinds of embellishments, the only obvious requirement being that it all look as cheesy as possible. On this Friday night, people were out in great numbers to celebrate Kuwait's liberation from the Iraqi occupation. The kids all seemed to have squirt guns (this being the Middle East, many of them were SuperSoaker-grade weapons) and they weren't shy about squirting passing cars, including mine. Here in the desert, the very fact they were using water recreationally speaks to the greatness of the occasion. The town's water storage tank admonishes, in English:

The Sandbox

SAVE WATER
IT WILL SAVE YOU LATER

\#

Saturday morning, I set out to find what I could about the legacy of that Iraqi aggression and the international effort to reverse it. My first destination was the "Kuwait House For National Works", otherwise known as the "Not To Forget Museum", or maybe the "Kuwait House of National Memorial Museum", whose sign specifies that the contents center around "Saddam Hussain Regime Crimes". Unfortunately for me, Google maps placed the museum incorrectly, and I drove all over the Shuwaikh part of town looking for it. I also drove quite a bit looking for an ATM, striking out at grocery stores, hardware stores, and shopping malls before I finally located a bank. In case you're wondering, no, they won't do cash-back when you buy groceries.

Anyway, I'd given up on finding much of anything, since the museum wasn't where Google left it and I didn't know how to ask directions, never mind how to follow them, in Arabic. It's not that I didn't try: my guidebook listed a phone number for the museum, but when I called it I couldn't even verify I had reached the right place, such was the language barrier. That's when I gave up on finding the museum, pulled onto a back street to turn around, and promptly discovered I was at the museum with its three or more names.

This museum should have been called the "Not To Gloss Over Anything Museum". In a prosperous country that rebuilt its buildings quickly after the Iraqis were defeated, the museum's job seemed to be keeping the painful memory alive for future generations. Inside were detailed descriptions of the Iraqi Baathists' war crimes: memos instructing troops to sneak up behind innocent civilians and shoot them, wall-to-wall dioramas with visual and sound effects to create a "you-are-there" feeling at the major battle scenes, allusions to the rape of Kuwaiti women by Iraqi troops. There is a generous amount of space detailing the contributions of each nation of the Allied coalition, accompanied by expressions of gratitude for liberating Kuwait, and maps showing how the ground phase of Operation Desert Storm was carried out. There's also the head from that big Saddam statue toppled in Baghdad after the 2003 invasion.

#

Needing to clear my head and desiring some sunshine, I aimed for the north side of Kuwait Bay in the hope of getting a good view of the Kuwait City skyline in the late afternoon sun. My sources told me that I should head toward Basra, Iraq, but that I would encounter a Kuwaiti military checkpoint a few miles outside Kuwait City, long before I could reach the Iraqi border, designed to keep bad guys away from Kuwait City and good guys away from Iraq. I should turn right at that location and be rewarded with the desired vantage point a few miles down the side road.

Not in any particular hurry, I drove through Al-Jahra and continued north on Highway 80, following the signs for the Abdaly border crossing and Basra. I was enjoying the sunshine and the freedom from city traffic, but it seemed like I should have reached that checkpoint and turnoff by now. Looking at the time and my speed, I realized I'd traveled much farther than I'd planned and would need to turn around soon. With hostilities apparently coming to an end in Iraq (this was shortly before ISIS became known as the menace of the decade), the Kuwaiti government had removed its checkpoint and was allowing every Tom, Dick, and Mohammed to access the Iraqi border.

In 1991, Highway 80 earned the dark moniker "Highway of Death". Facing defeat at the end of the occupation of Kuwait, Saddam Hussein's troops got in their tanks and drove north. Due to some unknown factor (perhaps vehicle breakdowns, perhaps the low visibility caused by the oil well fires they had set) many Iraqi soldiers abandoned their vehicles, including tanks, on the road and fled on foot into the surrounding countryside. In turn, Allied leadership dispatched airborne forces to destroy the equipment to make sure it wouldn't be used again. This so-called "turkey shoot" became the stuff of hush-toned CNN documentaries and international human rights protests. History isn't entirely clear on what happened, and I wasn't around in 1991 to examine things myself, but it seems that very few Iraqis were killed in this Allied operation, that the trail of burning abandoned vehicles shown on television gave the appearance of a far deadlier attack than what actually took place, and that the Baathist propaganda machine had spun the story.

At any rate, all that mess was long gone, and Highway 80 was a four-to-six-lane divided highway carrying a fraction of its designed traffic capacity between Kuwait City and Basra. The main hazards I encountered were not air-to-ground ordnance, but herds of camels and goats wandering into the road willy-nilly. I was careful not to hit the livestock, and reached the vicinity of the Kuwait-Iraq border crossing before I turned around. As at the Saudi border two days before, there was no possibility of entering Iraq spontaneously as a solo tourist, never mind driving my hard-won rental car across the border. And Basra isn't supposed to be an exciting place to visit, anyway.

Before returning to my hotel and imagining what it would be like to sip a glass of wine at the end of a draining day, I stopped at the Maritime Museum to explore Kuwait's more distant past. This establishment doesn't hold a candle to the museum I'd seen in Bahrain, but it did have some worthwhile exhibits. Notably, those include several traditional ships (right there in the middle of the parking lot!) used in the pearling industry as well as a collection of traditional musical instruments from the region, including plucked strings, wind, and percussion.

#

#justpassingthrough

For the first time in a long time, I woke up on Sunday morning and did the unthinkable: I drove to someplace other than a church. My destination was in the Al-Qurain neighborhood, a comfortable suburb made of cul-de-sacs and dead-end streets, much like, say, the Northern Virginia suburbs of Washington. I had my destination marked on an electronic map, and was using my phone once again like a radio direction finder, winding my way off the freeway (that goes to Khafji and becomes Saudi Arabia's Route 95) southeast of Kuwait International Airport into the target neighborhood. It looked quiet, happy, calm, prosperous. And well it should have looked prosperous, since Kuwait has a GDP per capita that outranks every country on this planet except Qatar, Luxembourg, Singapore, and Brunei. That means the people of Kuwait are wealthier on average than Americans, Canadians, Australians, virtually all Europeans, most other Gulf citizens, and even the Saudis with their private airplanes.

Wealth can make us targets of the jealous incompetents of the world, as can professional success, good looks, power, and a host of other factors. That, aside from sheer lunatic megalomania, is probably what drove Saddam Hussein to send his army to rape and pillage Kuwait in 1990. The occupiers continued to show their true brutal colors until the very end: in late February of 1991, as retreating Iraqi troops were flooding onto Highway 80 trying to make it to Basra, and as American and Allied troops poured over the border from Saudi Arabia, the Iraqis were still shooting up Kuwaiti civilians here in Al-Qurain.

And just so that nobody forgets about it, while the rest of the neighborhood rebuilt after the war, one house in the Al-Qurain subdivision stands as the Iraqis left it, except for some judicious structural reinforcement to keep it from collapsing. From my parking space, a half dozen blast holes remained visible in the exterior walls, leaving both floors exposed to the elements. Exhibits inside include a narrative about the 19 Kuwaiti men who holed up here, determined to fight the barbaric invaders to the bitter end. There's a pair of trousers on display with multiple bullet holes. There's a framed memo, under the heading of "In the

Name of God, Most Gracious, Most Merciful", instructing Iraqi troops to "burn and destroy" the resistance, and to "annihilate any hostile demonstrations". To top it off, one of the Iraqi tanks still sits across the street, pointing its long-dead gun at the house museum.

The longer I spent in Kuwait, the more I wondered whether its prosperity, despite the very real benefits that come with good access to food, medicine, travel, and schooling, might also be its weak link. Kuwaitis are less religious than the citizens of many other Muslim countries, and more obsessed with their own economic activity. In my subjective and anecdotal experience, they are less friendly and helpful toward strangers. It's a fairly universal concept that those who are caught up in the quest for material wealth have less time or inclination to ponder the things of the next world, never mind to be concerned for the well-being of neighbors in this one. In other words, while the invasion's physical scars were quickly repaired, it's possible that far deeper wounds remained.

Speaking of buildings, I'll mention here that Kuwait's National Assembly Building was finished in 1982 and underwent significant damage during, and reconstruction after, the Iraqi occupation. It's a striking enough building in its own right, but the noteworthy thing is that it's the second-best-known work of Danish architect Jørn Utzon, much better known for having designed the Sydney Opera House. That Kuwait has a nationally important building in the same league as the Sydney Opera House is another way of saying, "Hey, look, we have black gold shooting out of the ground and we're rolling in dough".

Having seen most of what passed for historically important in Kuwait, I planned to spend Sunday afternoon enjoying myself at the Kuwait Scientific Center and along the Corniche, also known as Arabian Gulf Road. Note the term "Arabian Gulf" here; it's the name Arab countries generally use for the Sinus Persicus (the Latin name I saw on a map at the Bahrain National Museum), or Persian Gulf. The reason for this is geopolitical: these Arab countries are rivals of Persia historically, and the current Iranian regime is as much a threat to Kuwait and Bahrain and the

81

UAE and Saudi Arabia as it is to Israel or any western power, if not more so. The pan-Arab sentiment is high, as is the desire for solidarity against Iranian influence. There's also the Sunni-Shi'ite divide at work here.

The Corniche is utterly gorgeous. The Persian, er, Arabian Gulf was a slightly deeper blue than the sky, and that day a few puffy white clouds rolled overhead. In the distance, around a curve in the coastline, I could see the shiny modern skyscrapers of Kuwait City. In the foreground were palm trees, high-end restaurants like Applebee's (without cocktails), walking paths, those sorts of gazebos and pavilions that in America would have a three-year waitlist for engagement photo shoots, and pebbly beaches. The Scientific Center itself is housed in a beautifully modern building; if it had been built in Baltimore or Cleveland or Kansas City it would be a major draw, but this Sunday it was almost completely empty. I went into the IMAX theatre and saw the 3-D movie about sharks. The narrative was in Arabic with English subtitles, but the beauty of a shark documentary is that you can get the idea without understanding the words. And the Sinus Persicus is chock-full of sharks.

My flight was set to depart just after midnight, so before I headed back to the airport I dropped in to the Holy Name Cathedral for Sunday evening Mass. Now, technically I'd already fulfilled my Sunday obligation with Mass in Ahmadi Friday night. But I couldn't not go, and since I'd checked out of my hotel and the sun had set, going to Mass and receiving Jesus seemed loads better than going to the airport and breathing stale cigarette smoke all evening. The cathedral is the seat of the Apostolic Vicariate of Northern Arabia, a missionary diocese-like structure whose territory also includes Bahrain, Qatar, and Saudi Arabia. Mind you, there are officially no churches in Saudi Arabia, no priests, and certainly no sacramental wine, but that doesn't mean the Church isn't there under cover.

Here in Kuwait City, there seemed to be some accommodation whereby the clergy could receive and store and use small quantities of wine for sacramental purposes, but of course the chalice never leaves the altar during Mass. Outside the cathedral, there's a plaque celebrating the warm relations between the Holy See and Kuwait, and thanking the Kuwaiti government for allowing Holy Mother Church to build a cathedral here.

What you don't see outside the cathedral is any form of a cross, and certainly not a crucifix with the likeness of Christ's body. This would offend Muslim sensibilities by depicting any human form, but especially the form of the Incarnate, humble, vulnerable, once-dead Second Person of the Trinity. Inside, there is a simple but elegant altar under a baldachin, stained glass, holy water fonts depicting demons fleeing in sorrowful fear, and rows of uncomfortable pews with clunky kneelers.

I was curious what the music would be, both in terms of repertoire and the instruments for leadership. Imagine my chagrin when the opening song, led with guitars, turned out to be "Be Not Afraid". At least here the bit about crossing the barren desert and not dying of thirst was cast in a new, closer-to-home light. Sunday evening Mass was packed; I stood in the side aisle leaning against a confessional, barely able to see the projection screens with the song lyrics.

#

Barren deserts having been crossed, and fear having been cast out, it was time for me to begin the long journey home. Plans called for me to drive to Kuwait International Airport, return the rental car, check my bag, clear security and passport control, fly overnight to Dulles, clear USCBP passport control, collect and recheck my bag, battle the Blueshirts, fly to Chicago, collect my bag (because a bag tag can't have the same airport on it twice, because who flies such an itinerary?), recheck my bag, deal with the Blueshirts again, take a shower in the O'Hare business class lounge, fly back to Dulles, collect my bag at the domestic bag claim, get back to Sylvia the Silver Sentra, and drive home in time to get to a Monday evening choir rehearsal.

#justpassingthrough

Nothing on that list seemed like it ought to be difficult, except maybe the TSA part. And it all started well enough. I parked the rental car in whatever general parking space I could find, returned the key to that one rental agency where they liked my credit card and my DC driver's license, and got in the check-in line.

About the check-in line: it was out the door and around the block. I noticed that many, if not most, of the folks in line appeared to be of South Asian extraction. The Gulf states play host to a great many people from places like India, Bangladesh, Indonesia, and the Philippines, who come to work on whatever construction project the local sheikh is paying for, earn lots of money, buy stuff, and take it home to their families. This explained why nearly everyone in line had a big-screen TV atop a massive pile of luggage to check. After I'd waited perhaps half an hour in that line, a security officer approached me to ask on what airline I was flying. He escorted me in the door and to the back of a shorter, but still substantial, line.

By the time I reached the check-in counter, I had learned via e-mail that my flight was delayed for several hours. On further investigation I discovered that Dulles Airport was closed due to a snowstorm. The airline was doing a smart thing by delaying the flight's departure from Kuwait City so that it would approach Dulles just after the airport was projected to reopen. Otherwise, we might have needed to fly in circles for a few hours and then divert to Newark or Albany or Montreal or whatever happened to be the closest airport when the crew ran out of duty time or the plane's fuel ran low. And I knew I didn't need to be stuck in Canada with only my dirty clothes from the Middle East, eh.

Of course, this put my connection to Chicago in jeopardy, and thus also my final flight back to Dulles. Chicago was another place I didn't particularly want to be stuck in early March without my winter coat (which, you remember, was in my car at Dulles). So I made a brilliant move: I asked the ticket agent to remove me from the Dulles-Chicago-Dulles segments since I would miss my connection. Unfortunately, this ticket agent was merely a contractor. He didn't understand the airline rules I was invoking generally, nor specifically how I knew I would miss my connection, nor in particular why I was so confident the snowy weather would continue all day tomorrow. I cut him a break since it doesn't snow much in Kuwait, and I asked him merely to short-check my bag to Dulles rather than to O'Hare. Now he wondered why I was planning not to fly the last leg of my trip to Chicago; this was technically a violation of the routing rules for which I should be charged a substantial fare difference and change fee. I reminded him of the delay and the certainty of missing the connection, but he just didn't get it, so my bag got tagged to Chicago even though I wouldn't be going there. No matter, I decided. I didn't need a suitcase full of dirty short-sleeve shirts in order to attend the evening's choir rehearsal in a snowstorm, and my address was on the outside of the bag. I'd deal with the fallout once I got home.

Midnight came and went. So did the announced new departure time of 2:30 a.m., or whenever it was supposed to be. Finally, around 4:00 a.m., my flight took off from Kuwait City and I ate dinner. It must have been good, because when I woke up the Triple Seven was over Quebec, and it was time for breakfast. Sure enough, the flight landed on Runway 1-Right just after it had been plowed, and just behind an also-delayed flight inbound from Brazil. No domestic flights were yet operating, so I was now officially, in addition to really, not going to Chicago. The good news, in theory, was that since my Chicago flight had been cancelled, my ticket record now reflected that I was ending my journey at Dulles, which should trigger the baggage system to have a handler pull my bag out of circulation and deliver it to me at the immigration checkpoint for non-connecting passengers.

You can guess how that turned out: after 45 minutes, the bags stopped coming onto the carousel, and mine wasn't among them. I found a baggage agent, who told me my bag had last been scanned leaving the terminal in Kuwait City. Recalling that the plane had been parked away from the KWI terminal and boarding had been done by bus, I asked if that meant the bag had fallen off a truck between the terminal and the plane. I looked out at the still-falling Northern Virginia snow, and wondered whether my bag had made a conscious decision to stay where it was warm. More seriously, I wondered whether I'd ever see it again.

Somehow, I made it out through the bitter cold to Sylvia the Silver Sentra and my winter coat (so much for the week-old forecast of mild weather today!), and fought my way home via the Dulles Access Road. At least I think that's how I got home; I couldn't really see the road at all. After a brief nap, I made it to choir rehearsal as planned. Arriving back home for the night, I took my time getting ready for bed, marveling once again that I had experienced for myself so many of the places I'd seen on television as a young boy.

Just then, after 11:00 p.m., my phone rang. I had a delivery. My bag hadn't fallen off the wagon in Kuwait, but had merely gotten stuck someplace in the bowels of the Dulles baggage system. The baggage delivery man was missing a couple front teeth; I guess he's in a rough profession.

Sensing that I'm a fairly nice guy, the delivery man tried to engage me in conversation, but it was time for bed. After all, I'd gone to the Sandbox. I'd found the Tree of Life. I'd narrowly escaped an arranged marriage. I'd driven to the gates of two different Middle Eastern forbidden lands. I'd had a great time. I'd crossed the barren desert and I hadn't died, of thirst or otherwise.

Visa Waiver

As I was reminded during my eventful arrival into Kuwait City, getting a visa can be a real pain in the rump. Of the thirty-three countries I've visited as of January 2018, only two (China and Vietnam) required me to get a paper visa for a short stay. All of western and central Europe can be visited visa-free by American passport holders, as can many countries around the Pacific Rim and in Latin America.

I generally avoid visiting countries that require a visa in advance of travel. That's not a matter of principle, nor even just one of cost. Getting a visa the old-fashioned way often requires two separate visits to the consulate or embassy, or, if you don't live in a city with an "embassy row", a check to a third-party handler. It can require being without your passport for days or weeks at a time, which is a logistical headache when you're a frequent international traveler. You might just say that on my mental world map, countries that don't allow visa-free entry are darkened as though mythical or downright forbidden.

And that's why, in 2016, I was so excited when Brazil announced a temporary visa waiver for Americans covering the time just before and during the Olympics in Rio de Janeiro… and that my then-favorite airline was dumping excess pre-Olympic capacity in the form of deep-discount fares with no Saturday night stay requirement.

The psychological floodgates opened. After years of convincing myself that Brazil was a mosquito-infested, overheated wasteland in which crime rates were so high that I would likely be shot on arrival, suddenly I had about two weeks of touring I wanted to accomplish in what couldn't be longer than a five-day visit. I wanted to spend three days or so in Rio, plus that long in Sao Paulo, maybe with side trips to Brasilia and Iguazu Falls and various other points. That would be like visiting New York and Chicago, plus side trips to Niagara Falls and the Grand Canyon, during a week-long first visit to the U.S. when you don't know any English.

#justpassingthrough

Try as I might, I just couldn't get all that touring shoehorned into a five-day itinerary. I pared it down: I'd spend some time in Rio and then hop out to Iguazu Falls with a brief foray into neighboring Paraguay just to say I'd been there. But the flight schedules didn't line up (Rio and Sao Paulo each have two commercial airports... what a logistical nightmare it would have been to depart from one and return to the other!), and Paraguay requires a visa after all, so its proverbial doors immediately darkened.

I played with the possibilities for a while. And by that, I mean I'm sure I put in at least the equivalent of a forty-hour work week deciding how much time I really wanted to spend in each place, what I wanted to see, and (importantly in a continental-scale country where you don't speak the language) how I'd get around. Eventually, I settled on a more modest plan for my first visit to Brazil:

Arriving in Rio de Janeiro on Monday, I would spend until Thursday morning in that city, getting around by Metro, on foot, and in taxi cabs. Then I would pick up a rental car and drive down the Atlantic coast to Paraty, a Portuguese colonial-era town. Friday morning, I'd head to the pilgrimage town of Aparecida before returning my rental car at the international airport outside of Sao Paulo and flying home. It was a good plan, and had the built-in advantage of allowing me to arrive late in Rio (in the event of, say, a flight delay) and not mess up the rest of the itinerary, which was more "delicate" in the sense that it involved long hours of driving without much extra daylight. Daylight was a commodity; I'd be visiting in mid-June, the depth of southern hemisphere winter, though it was unlikely to be very cold outside.

#

After playing a couple of Masses at one of my favorite parishes in Washington, I returned to Little Rome, packed my bags, and took the Metro to National Airport. I would be flying from DCA to Dallas, then

Visa Waiver

overnight from DFW to Sao-Paulo Guarulhos, and after a stop long enough for a shower and a stroll, finally over to Rio de Janeiro. It all went very well until boarding time for the first flight, which is to say it never really started going very well at all.

Somehow, my upgrade from DCA to DFW was still waitlisted, even though the long-haul one had cleared. So I was stuffed in an economy window seat, my elbow trying to bend the laws of physics and occupy the same space on the same armrest as the elbow of the poor guy in the middle seat. Departure time came and went, but the plane remained at the gate with the door open. My connection at DFW was set for two and a half hours, so I wasn't worried. The pilot activated the P.A. and mumbled something about a brief delay. Whatever.

A short while later, we got the real story. The catering department had messed up and put our flight's dinner service carts on another plane that had since departed on a flight not long enough to require meal service. Lucky those people, poor us having to wait until DFW to get dinner. Except the powers-that-be weren't going to allow that: the absence of beverages on a summer flight to Texas was probably a no-go in the eyes of the legal department, so we'd have to wait until the caterer scared up some carts with food.

After an hour of waiting in that cramped window seat and going nowhere in particular nor anywhere in general, I used my phone to look for alternate routes to Rio de Janeiro. I could leave in an hour and a half and connect through JFK and skip the Sao Paulo stop. I could stick with the flight to DFW and (if indeed I missed the planned Sao Paulo flight) catch the midnight flight to Lima, connect, and arrive at Rio de Janeiro within a couple hours of on-time. Believe it or not, I could also get a cab to Dulles Airport, fly overnight to Heathrow, and then get to Brazil by Monday evening.

I'm not saying my decision was at all influenced my ongoing captivity in the sardine can-style economy cabin of a full 737, but I decided right then not to chance the DFW connection any longer, not even for a good story about the leftovers the caterer could stuff onto the carts for dinner. It was one hundred percent about getting to Brazil without missing a day.

I excused myself, telling the guy in the middle seat it was his lucky day. I took my carry-on bags (I usually don't check bags, not that doing so has ever led to a problem), flashed a smile at the flight attendants, and rolled back up the jetway, pausing long enough to let the gate agent unload me electronically from the flight from which I was already quite unloaded physically and even more unloaded psychologically.

As my lungs gradually expanded back to normal size in the relative spaciousness of the terminal, I made my way to the airline's frequent flyer/business class lounge for rebooking. Lounges are great: not only do many of them have showers and buffets and bars and free wi-fi, but they have dedicated agents who can handle rebookings and flight changes in the event of a problem. The agent first told me that the flight I had just disembarked, scheduled to leave over an hour earlier, was still "on time" in the airline's computer system. I mentioned the catering problem, and the response was a knowing, sympathetic roll of the eyes.

Getting down to business, I asked in an unintentionally pointed tone how the airline was going to get me to Rio de Janeiro that evening. The agent tried to put me on the JFK route, but the hop to JFK was suddenly delayed a couple of hours and that was no-go. The solution I chose had all the beauty of the British Airways route via Heathrow, and none of the drawbacks (Heathrow, Heathrow, and the possibility of getting stuck at Heathrow): I would fly this evening to Miami, be put up in a hotel Sunday night at the airline's expense, and take a daylight flight with a Brazilian carrier, to arrive in Rio de Janeiro on Monday evening. This plan lasted as long as it took the agent to make a few keystrokes, but the computer told her she couldn't put me on the other airline's flight due to, well, the fact it didn't want her to do that. I proposed the Heathrow option – heretofore a joke in my mind, but now utterly in earnest – and she stifled a "hasn't this guy ever looked at a map" chuckle.

Visa Waiver

At great length, several same-night connecting options having evaporated in the twenty minutes or so the agent was trying to help me, the computer spit out a receipt. I would fly to Miami tonight, be lodged at airline expense, and fly Monday evening to Sao Paulo and then Tuesday on to Rio de Janeiro. I was not happy about the 24-hour delay, but now I was able to call my sister's family – my mother was visiting, too – and they all came to the airport for an evening of fun with Uncle Matt, watching the big machines come and go. The original flight to Dallas eventually left about two and a half hours late, with who-knows-what catering carts on board. I would have missed my connection and been stuck in Texas overnight, so the decision to get off the plane turned out to have been a wise one.

The Miami flight departed right on schedule, about 9:00 p.m. My instructions were to sit back, enjoy the ride, and see a customer service agent in Miami to claim my no-cost room at the airport hotel. But when I got to Miami, I couldn't find a customer service agent. I called the reservations line, explaining that I was due a free room, but was told that only airport agents can handle that kind of request. When I did find someone working for the airline, it was a janitor who pointed me toward the lost baggage office, which is always a fun place to visit in the wee hours. The baggage agent told me in the most what-kind-of-idiot-are-you tone that I should come back to the airport in the morning, when customer service was open, to discuss a free hotel room for the night.

It was now the morning, about 12:45 a.m. to be exact, and I decided to break down and pay for a hotel room myself. Google showed me that the airport hotel I'd heard so much about was actually built into the terminal, so I rolled my bags up to the reception desk and explained the situation. Here, the lady's response was much more helpful: the hotel had plenty of unclaimed rooms, but they were being held by the airline for potential displaced customers, and I should speak with the airline's customer service to claim one of them. Otherwise, they were fully booked. My bleary eyes stared into hers, looking for a hint of comprehension that she'd just said something completely ridiculous, or maybe for the glint that precedes a burst of raucous "got ya!" laughter. There was nothing of the sort.

Having attempted to make a soul-to-soul connection and struck out, I turned back to the almighty Google, and found a room at the local Deluxe Inn (not its real name) available for about $65.00, with free airport shuttle service. I scooped it up faster than you can say "catering fail" - which, you remember, was the root cause of all this - and rode to the hotel.

Other than having no windows with which to say "Welcome to the Sunshine State", the room at Deluxe Inn was perfectly adequate. I slept until nearly 9:00 a.m., and made sure to pack the receipt gingerly as I mentally rehearsed various not-suitable-for-kids versions of the letter I was going to write to the airline claiming reimbursement.

Now I had an unexpected gift of most of a day to explore Miami. I didn't have a car, so I'd mostly be restricted to places I could reach via the city's somewhat limited Metro rail network. That meant, in turn, that I needed to do something with my bags for the day. Storage would be free in the airline lounge, but first I needed to go through security to access that lounge. And, in turn, I would need a boarding pass to get through security. So I got in line at the ticket counter and, after waiting fifteen minutes or so, reached an agent who told me I would be denied boarding to Brazil because I lacked the proper visa. I explained the temporary visa waiver to the agent, who gave me that special "what-are-you-drinking-I-want-some" look and promptly walked off in some unexplained direction with my passport in her hand. Perplexed, I followed at a distance and eventually caught up to a gaggle of agents, each looking alternately at a computer screen and at my passport.

After several minutes of intense scowling and staring, the head-honcho agent solemnly informed me that Brazil has a temporary visa waiver in place due to the Olympics, and that by exception I would be allowed to travel after all. I thanked them profusely for their kindness in allowing me to proceed with my entirely lawful journey, and I tried really hard not to think judgmental thoughts about Miami International Airport and the people who work there. But I quickly cheered up when I remembered the next step would be my third inspection by the TSA Blueshirts on a trip that so far had involved leaving the ground exactly once.

My luggage having been tucked in a back corner of the lounge, I walked with some jollity off the airport grounds and onto Miami's Metro system. First stop would be the Gesu, a downtown parish run by Jesuits with Masses and Confessions several times a day. After lunch, I again boarded the Metro, making my way south to the Vizcaya stop, where I had three destinations in mind.

The first of these was the pedestrian bridge from the station into the exclusive-looking surrounding neighborhood and its subtropical rainforest environment. This bridge is special because it crosses I-95 at the very southern end of that ribbon of asphalt and concrete that, apart from a gap in central New Jersey where Princetonians nixed the highway's construction due to greenspace concerns, could carry traffic from here to the Canadian border at Houlton, Maine. In fact, this (very) pedestrian bridge affords a view of the first "I-95 North" sign as the East Coast's Main Street separates from US 1, the East Coast's Back Alley. I had driven under this bridge on December 26, 2003, my second-longest driving day ever.

Next, I walked to the shore of Biscayne Bay (not to be confused with the Bay of Biscay, across the Atlantic, whose waves crash onto the shores of Spain and France) and the Vizcaya Museum and Gardens. Built from 1914 to 1922, this house resembles a Venetian style villa, complete with boat access for visitors, and had been the winter home of James Deering, a Chicago farming equipment magnate who suffered from "pernicious anemia". Like other such house museums as the Biltmore Estate in North Carolina, Hearst Castle in California, Vizcaya affords a glimpse into the lifestyles of the rich and almost-famous in bygone times. There are lots of modern-for-the-time design features, some precious imported art works, and a pair of neon signs reminding guests to TAKE THE GIFTS

#justpassingthrough

OF THIS HOUR and PUT SERIOUS THINGS ASIDE. If you're ever in Miami looking for something to do, and if it's not Tuesday (when Vizcaya is closed), go to Vizcaya.

While you're at it, head to the almost-adjacent Our Lady of Charity National Shrine. It may resemble the sort of thing that gets launched into space a couple hundred miles up I-95, but it's a nice little Catholic oasis dedicated to the national patroness of Cuba. At any rate, that's where I went next.

As the sun got closer and closer to the Everglades, I rode the Metro back to Miami International Airport. I used my same boarding pass from the morning to get past the Blueshirts, who didn't seem to notice or care that I was traveling on an overseas flight apparently with no luggage. Having retrieved said luggage from the lounge, at long last I was off to Brazil.

#

Tuesday dawned for me over the vast urban expanse of Sao Paulo. It's South America's largest city, and the largest in the southern and western hemispheres, and as such it is named for one of Christendom's greatest saints. As St. Paul had come to the faith as one untimely born, so I had come to Brazil as one untimely landed.

The immigration agents here seemed to be familiar with the visa waiver, and soon I was free to move about Brazil, South America's largest and most populous country. Its system and structure of government very closely parallels that of the United States, inasmuch as it is a continental-scale federal republic with a president who serves for a four-year term (re-electable once) as head of state and government, checked and balanced against legislative and judicial branches. Brazil is comprised of twenty-six states, plus a federal district containing Brasilia, purpose-built on a swamp to be the national capital. In terms of natural environment, Brazil is dominated by the Amazon River (the world's second-longest, and the largest river by volume) and its surrounding rainforest, but it also boasts coastal flatlands, and some mountains. The principal language is Portuguese, and no, the people here don't like it when you use your high school Spanish as though it's pretty much the same language. It's not.

My first task was to wash that Miami right out of my hair and off the rest of me. No lounge with showers would be accessible to me as a departing domestic passenger, though a few posters in one of the frequent-flyer forums tried to convince the others that there's a way to sneak through such-and-such a checkpoint before immigration if you claim to be lacking such-and-such a document on the third Thursday of months that start with a waxing gibbous moon, or something like that. Call me unadventurous, but I was happy enough to pay $15 or so to use a commercial shower facility landside. Unlike the complimentary shower facilities at a certain British airport I'd almost transited en route to Brazil, the water was hot and continually available, but since the accidental round-the-world trip was still four months in the future, I didn't appreciate it fully.

Next, I headed up to the check-in counter to obtain a boarding pass for my flight to Rio de Janeiro in an hour or two; the way much of this chapter has gone so far, you won't be surprised when I tell you that the flight was cancelled. You also won't be surprised that when I asked the counter staff to rebook me they told me to call my airline because they're the ones who issued the ticket, nor that when I called my airline they told me I needed to approach the ticket counter staff for rebooking because that local airline had caused the cancellation. My airline was right: on a multi-airline ticket, the offending carrier has the responsibility to get you and your bags to the destination if they cancel a flight. Through a combination of sighs, eyerolls, and arm-crossing, soon I had in my hand a boarding pass to Rio de Janeiro's Santos Dumont Airport.

As the old ketchup commercials always said, good things come to those who wait. Arriving into SDU provides a memorable entrance to Rio de Janeiro: you get sweeping views of the city's artificial skyline as well as the mountains that line the coast, plus the blue waters of Guanabara Bay. Had SDU been a mileage run destination, and had I planned to reboard the same plane to fly right back out, it still would have been a trip memorable for the scenery. But landing at Santos Dumont is not for the faint of heart, nor for planes with questionable brake functionality, since its longest runway is a scant 4341 feet long, a half mile shorter than the main runway at DCA, which is itself an unusually short runway for use by 737s and A320s. But there was no splash that Tuesday afternoon, and soon I was in a taxi en route to my hotel. I had e-mailed from Miami to let them know I'd be checking in a little late. Cough.

Rio is famous for many things: its scenery, its nasty violent crime rate, its hedonistic party scene, and, not unrelated to these, its beaches. Naturally, my first activity was to inspect Copacabana. Perhaps it was because this was a workday, perhaps it was because of the Olympic-related construction projects ongoing, or perhaps it was the miserable weather (72 degrees and a few puffy clouds that made getting a tan too much work), but the beach was pretty empty that day. Which is exactly how I like my beaches.

Eating in Brazil is a manly affair. Dinner that first night consisted of "rooster filet" grilled with succulent simplicity, heaps of rice and fries, black beans, and a cassava-based mixture known as farofa, all washed down with a caipirinha. To top it all off, dessert was guava pudding doused in crème de cassis. After spending Sunday "night" in the Deluxe Inn and Monday night in the better-than-economy section of a Triple Seven and then eating this dinner, I slept exceptionally well Tuesday night.

#

There are a few world tourist attractions so iconic that you simply can't not visit them if you're in the neighborhood. Paris has the Eiffel Tower, Rome has the Colosseum, San Francisco has the Golden Gate Bridge, Miami has the south end of I-95. Rio de Janeiro has Cristo

Redentor, probably rivalling only the Statue of Liberty as the best-known outdoor statue in the western hemisphere. Getting there should be a cinch, right?

Well, no. While Rio does have a Metro system, and that system was enlarged in anticipation of the Olympics, the topography of the city makes it impractical to construct a traditional subway system in some parts of town. So to reach Cristo Redentor, I had to take a taxi to the lower station of Trem do Corcovado in the Cosme Velho neighborhood. And then I rode the Trem do Corcovado (Corcovado Rack Railway) itself, built in 1884 and consisting of exactly two trains of two cars each. Any more trains than this would be superfluous, as the steeply-inclined single track has only one siding where the two trains pass one another mid-journey as one ascends and the other descends. Since it's the only public way to get to such an important scenic site, the Trem do Corcovado has been ridden by such diverse personalities as Albert Einstein, Pope St. John Paul II, and Princess Diana. The ride up is not the stuff of luxury travel, but I assume it beats scaling the mountain's cliffs with climbing gear.

Cristo Redentor itself is a 98-foot statue atop a 26-foot pedestal. Construction took nine years, and the story goes that floodlights were to have been activated by Guglielmo Marconi from Italy, but bad weather meant that the switch had to be flipped in the more conventional way, on the same continent as the lights. Since 2006, there's been an official Catholic chapel on site, meaning that Catholic cariocas ("carioca" being the local slang term for a Rio local) can be baptized and married at Cristo Redentor. Though I was supposed to be away from the concerns of work, I couldn't help but imagine the sort of bridezilla who insists on such a wedding venue.

For being in such an exposed place, the mortar-and-soapstone statue has fared pretty well over the years. An exception occurred in 2008, when lightning damaged Our Lord's head, fingers, and eyebrows; repairs were made using stone from the same quarry where the original stone had been sourced.

The view from up there was simply incredible. You should go see it.

#

Having lost the first day of my visit to an airline catering error, for which I required lots of grace to forgive the airline, I moved quickly through Rio de Janeiro that sunny Wednesday. Next on the agenda was Mass at the cathedral, a structure designed in the 1960s that looks like a cross between Space Mountain and the Luxor casino from the outside, but nonetheless manages to impress with its daring stained glass inside.

After an al fresco lunch in the nearby square, I toured the Municipal Theater. It's not the only theater in the world to take its design from the Opera Garnier in Paris, but it still has an air of old-world elegance that stands in stark contrast to the cathedral and much of modern central Rio.

Continuing my cross-town campaign, I paid a visit to the Museum of the Republic, housed in Catete Palace, which served as Brazil's presidential palace until the government moved to Brasilia in 1960. It's probably an impressive museum, but at my whirlwind pace, and having just toured Vizcaya a couple days earlier, I wasn't that into it. I do recall seeing a retired presidential globe with most of the Northern Hemisphere blacked out. Perhaps those were the countries requiring visas for Brazilian citizens.

Last touring stop of the day was Brazil's Tomb of the Unknowns, actually a museum dedicated to Brazil's contributions to the twentieth century's great struggles. Did you know that 25,000 Brazilians helped to liberate Italy from Mussolini, and that 400 of them gave their lives? I was surprised to learn this, and the whole thing stands as a sobering reminder that defeating a great evil takes many partners working together. It's the same for Hitler, Hirohito, Mussolini, or Saddam Hussein, I suppose.

Visa Waiver

#

Thursday morning, even though I'd barely just arrived, it was time to begin phase two of my first visit to Brazil. I metroed to a stop near Santos Dumont airport (the airport with the great views on approach, plus the itsy-bitsy runways), pulled my bags through the tangle of roads that always grows next to an airport, and at length made it to the local office of an American rental car company. Thing was, this airport only handles domestic flights, so nobody in the rental office spoke anything but Portuguese. Since I didn't speak more than the few words of Portuguese I'd picked up around town, this could have made for a very interesting transaction in all the wrong ways, especially since they didn't have any cars in the category I'd reserved.

Fortunately, a big boss type just happened to be down from Boston visiting this particular branch office. He helpfully translated to facilitate the transaction, and then pulled me aside. Giving me his card, he strongly encouraged me to contact him if there were any issues, which made me wonder just what, other than the car itself, I was getting into. The whole interaction gave the impression that the office was, if not under suspicion, then at least on corporate radar in some undesirable way: poor sales performance, or perhaps a need for improvements to the staff-customer interaction. Before it was over, I spent nearly two hours at that rental office. Whatever the issue may have been, it's not that they don't try to get business. Since my visit to Rio, I've received at least one e-mail from the rental company in Portuguese per day, which is a nice contrast in my junk e-mail folder to the urgent messages I get from Nigerian princes and their lawyers with $32,000,00 million dollars to send me if I'd just get around to e-mailing them my bank account information and Social Security Number.

After picking up the car, my task was simply to drive to Paraty. Now, it's possible to make the journey in about four hours if you use the rodovia, Brazil's Autobahn-like network of modern, multilane, high-speed, grade-separated roadways. That seemed like the safe, conservative thing to do. So, even though most of my friends would describe me as being a safe, conservative guy, I decided against that plan. After all, Paraty was only a destination in the sense that I had a hotel reservation there; the real goal was to see rural coastal Brazil. In that light, I chose a route that stuck closer to the coast. I estimated it would take six hours to drive this way, so that when I added a few stops for food, gas, and sightseeing, I'd run out of daylight right about the same time as I ran out of road between me and Paraty. Since Paraty is a small place with little crime, I wasn't worried about arriving there in the dark and finding my hotel.

And so, leaving SDU on four wheels, I headed south past the Tomb of the Unknowns and turned right at Copacabana where the bay meets the ocean. Copacabana is famously crescent-shaped, and on reaching its end, I made another right turn to keep the ocean on my left. The next beach neighborhood was Ipanema. I wish I could tell you that I rolled down the window and crooned out "The Girl from Ipanema" while I waited for a light to turn green. I also wish I could tell you I made eye contact with a girl in Ipanema, but at least that day when she walked to the sea, she looked straight ahead and not at me. Obviously, with the traffic congestion, there's a reason she walks rather than drives.

Somehow, my mind was filled with the idea that Ipanema would be pretty much the end of urbanized Rio de Janeiro, but my mind was filled with the wrong idea yet again. While the swanky beachy parts of Rio were behind me, the city, or rather the suburban sprawl I detest so much closer to home, was not. In fact, Avenida das Americas was under pre-Olympic construction. The plan seemed to be for Olympic athletes, visitors, the press, and everybody else along the coast to use Avenida das Americas to get between Barra da Tijuca's myriad hotels and restaurants and the Metro-accessible venues at Copacabana, downtown, and farther north. That meant that dedicated bus and trolley lanes had to be constructed. All told, it was well past lunchtime before I saw anyplace rural. I reminded myself that the Olympics were the reason I'd saved three figures on a visa, but then I spent three light cycles at one intersection wondering whether the tradeoff had been worth the wear and tear on my right ankle, or whether it was always this bad and the Olympics were just a convenient excuse to tear stuff up.

In spite of the demoralizing effect of suburban congestion, I did manage to enjoy the beauty of coastal Brazil. I can't say that there was a whole lot of open-road rural driving; the frequency of towns, speed bumps, speed cameras ("Fiscalização Electrônica de Velocidade"), school bus stops, and slow-moving trucks made the driving a bit more tedious than I'd expected. But the scenery was indisputably beautiful as mountains met the sea under the sun.

#

Before the arrival of Europeans in South America, the area around the Bay of Paraty was inhabited by the Guaianás Indians. The natives called the whole area "Paraty", meaning "River of Fish" in their Tupi language, for the great swarms of Brazilian mullet fish that spawn in the area. Portuguese settlers were here as early as 1597, though what we now know as the village of Paraty wasn't officially established until 1667. Then, in 1696, gold was discovered in Minas Gerais, which had the predictable effect of making the region suddenly become important. Before long, a trail (the "Caminho do Ouro") was built from Paraty stretching 700 miles inland to the gold mining areas. The trail was used to move provisions and workers and slaves from Africa to the mines, and to bring gold back to Paraty for shipment to Rio de Janeiro and beyond.

You'd think that Paraty's importance would now be assured, but there's a reason why Paraty isn't up there with San Francisco as a post-Gold Rush port city: pirates. When the seaborne gold shipments fell prey to pirate attacks too often, a new land route was cultivated between the mines and Rio, and after a while there just wasn't as much accessible gold left to pull out of the ground. By the late eighteenth century, there was comparatively little economic activity, so nobody had money to tear down Paraty's old buildings and build new ones. Happily for us modern visitors, that means Paraty was preserved with its centuries-old buildings. Yes, there were briefer booms with the export of coffee and then cachaça, the latter being the key ingredient in Brazil's national cocktail, the caipirinha. It wasn't until the 1970s that the paved coastal road from Rio de Janeiro and Sao Paulo was built (on which I'd just arrived) and Paraty got a fresh coat of paint and a new industry: tourism.

Not being one for "tourist" destinations (Waikiki? Times Square? Shinjuku? No, thanks!), I primarily chose Paraty because I needed a place to stay along the coast. That is to say, I wasn't expecting much beyond a comfortable bed and some pretty buildings. But from the moment I drove into town, Paraty surprised me.

I mean that literally. At the very gate of town, I was greeted with a sign declaring "Jesus Christo é o Senhor do Paraty" ("Jesus Christ is the Lord of Paraty") and promptly got funneled into a network of one-way streets. I was looking for the Pousada do Sandi, a traditional inn ("pousada") with free parking, somewhere near the town center. Thanks to Google maps, I found the Pousada itself fairly easily, though there didn't seem to be an obvious place to park, free or otherwise. How inconsiderate of the seventeenth-century Portuguese not to build their streets wide enough for parallel parking! Since most of the streets were one-way, I eventually parked in a pay lot some distance from the Pousada and walked to check in and inquire about the free parking. As a side note, cobblestone streets aren't good for pulling roller bags.

The check-in clerk was friendly enough, but the language barrier was once again problematic. I did manage to learn that the free parking was about two blocks from the Pousada, near the post office. After putting my bags in my room, I returned to my rental car in the pay lot and set out in search of the free parking for Pousada do Sandi. Earlier, I mentioned that Paraty is full of one-way streets, but that's not entirely accurate;

Visa Waiver

actually, Paraty is more or less one big sinuous one-way street with a few side alleys and detours, the effect of which is that if you miss your stop you must drive out of town and make another approach through the whole street network. And that's exactly what I did.

"Jesus Christo é o Senhor do Paraty" even after dark. This time, I drove even more slowly looking for the post office. Have you ever driven through an unfamiliar town after dark where you don't speak or read the language, looking for a garage in an alley near a closed post office? I have, and it's just as difficult as it sounds. After leaving town a second time and being reminded yet again that "Jesus Christo é o Senhor do Paraty", I put my manly pride on the line, rolled down the window, and asked for help with directions.

In case you ever need to know, the Portuguese word for post office is "Correios", and attempting to identify one in the dark when it's closed is nigh unto impossible. But the kind couple I spoke with, apparently domestic tourists, pointed it out... about fifty yards behind me. I gave them a heartfelt "obrigado" ("thank you" is an indispensable phrase to know in the local language wherever you go) and once again drove out of town.

The fourth time was the charm. I entered Paraty knowing who is Lord and where the post office is and found the pitch-black alley across from it. Maneuvering my rental car at a snail's pace past multiple closed garage doors, I eventually found the one labeled "Estacionamento Pousada do Sandi Portão Automatico", pushed the call button, and drove in. They even have a cute little door-within-a-door so you can walk out of the parking courtyard once you've parked. At length, I reached my hotel room, mentally exhausted from the day's travels but relieved to have found my destination through sheer persistence.

It was about 6:30 p.m., so I had plenty of time to enjoy dinner at one of the local restaurants before turning in. The evening repast began with pumpkin-gorgonzola soup accompanied by a caipirinha, and reached its climax with pepper steak and fries alongside a Brazilian cabernet. There might also have been a sorbet dressed in chocolate sauce accompanied by Teacher's Whiskey. You could say that I quickly forgave Paraty and coastal Brazil for being so fiendishly difficult a place to drive and navigate.

At Pousada do Sandi, the colors are bright, and the maritime breeze is allowed to waft through the corridors and rooms. The floors are made of hard wood. In the morning, the view from my second-story room was worthy of a glossy travel magazine ad, filled with palm trees, colorfully-painted buildings, cobblestone streets, and hills silhouetted against a bright blue sky. The tropical breakfast buffet was also memorable. There, I helped myself to tapioca-starch crêpes with brown sugar and papaya and other delicious things. I had a couple hours to explore Paraty. From the attractions list I'd compiled, and given the compact smallness of the place, that would probably be enough. I set about to digest breakfast with a nice walk around town.

Paraty's climate is maritime, which is to say its seasons are moderated by the presence of the ocean nearby. At the same time, the town's waterfront is not on the ocean itself, nor even really on the larger Paraty Bay, but on the Baia Carioca, which means the water is calm enough for use by small sailing boats and for recreational fishing. Many locals have boats, and many more boats are available for hire by visitors, so that the docks and the canal are just as colorful as the streets on land. All in all, the blues of sea and sky, the dark green of the surrounding hills, and the various paints on houses and boats and foliage make Paraty one of the most colorfully beautiful places I've ever seen.

If all this sounds too heavenly to be true, walking on the non-golden pavements of Paraty, with or without baggage, is tough on the feet. The cobblestone pavement exists for a mundane reason: Paraty was a port where ships would be filled with gold for shipment to Rio de Janeiro, so the ships arrived full of ballast stones. In order for the gold to be loaded, the ballast had to be unloaded, and so the streets were paved with used ballast without too much concern for smoothness.

Visa Waiver

I stopped to see a church museum, which had various liturgical vestments, altar vessels, and paintings of long-departed clerics. There might also have been an art gallery or two. After an hour or so, I realized that while Paraty was a great place to relax and be away from it all, there wasn't a ton to do. And as a solo traveler, that meant it was time to pack up and move to the next destination. I still had an important pilgrimage stop to make, but I also had the hard-set requirement to make it to the Sao Paulo airport for my evening flight to Miami.

#

Driving out of Paraty in daylight for a change, I left coastal highway 101 and drove west into the mountains. The road was paved (with asphalt, not pre-owned ballast) and generally wide enough for two cars to pass. The switchbacks and sharp curves and steep hills were as severe as anything I've driven in West Virginia, the Alps, or the hills of Malibu. Reaching one peak, I stopped to take a picture at the state border dividing Rio de Janeiro state from Sao Paulo state.

Having crested that ridge and the state border, I descended into hilly farmland that reminded me of Appalachia, especially the western Pennsylvania hill country from which the Mueller family hails. As I pressed on toward my goal, there was a little church by the side of the road at which I felt compelled to stop. Please be assured that the mere presence of a church by the road is not the sum total of the compulsion; if it were, I wouldn't cover much ground in a country as Catholic as Brazil. Rather, what struck me was the way the church sat uphill from the road, and also the lines of multi-colored flags streaming from the tower to the road, in the elegant style one sees at a used car dealership back home. Fortunately, the church had a parking lot, so I increased the vehicle count to one. To enter the church, I had to ascend a flight of about twenty non-ADA-compliant steps.

#justpassingthrough

It was a pleasant little church inside, empty, and I wondered why it was out here in the country rather than in town where the people are. Lacking knowledge of the Portuguese language, I was left following other visual clues to figure out what it really was. One big clue was the statue of a Roman soldier carrying a small cross with "Haec dies", or "this is the day". These Latin words begin the Entrance Antiphon for Easter: "this is the day that the Lord has made," etc. What an odd thing for a Roman soldier to be holding. A nameplate proclaimed him to be St. Expedite, of whom I knew nothing before that day.

As it turns out, St. Expedite is venerated in various parts of the world. A festival in Sao Paulo is held each year, drawing hundreds of thousands on his feast day, April 19. Coincidentally, this is a date that most often falls during the Easter season with which "Haec dies" is associated. As with many of the early saints, his story is a bit murky in the historiographical sense. As best I can tell, he was a Roman soldier (hence the wardrobe) stationed in Armenia who, after converting to Christianity, was beheaded in the Diocletian persecution. Tempted by the devil in the form of a crow to delay his conversion for a day, he responded that today would be the day (hence the "Haec dies").

How St. Expedite came to be honored in such diverse parts of the world is also a bit of a mystery. According to one story, in 1781 a French convent received a shipment of relics in the mail marked "Expedite" (because otherwise the Correios will deliver at the pace of escargot), and somebody assumed that the relics inside belonged to St. Expedite. There's also a story that a package arrived at a New Orleans church containing statues of various saints, one of them unlabeled, so the "expedite" label was given to that statue.

Whatever the historical realities may have been, St. Expedite the Roman soldier is usually shown holding a cross with "Haec dies" or "Hodie" ("today") in his hand, and a crow underfoot. As any competent toddler can tell you, a crow says "caw, caw", but in Italian, it's usually rendered "cra, cra", and when that gets Latinized, it's "cras, cras", or "tomorrow".

St. Expedite is considered the patron saint for the swift winning of legal cases, and also for victory over procrastination (did you notice the "cras" in that word?).

This is one of the many joys of being Catholic. Not only can you go to the remote corners of the world and be one in faith with the locals, but you can make random stops and learn jagged little pieces of history, liturgy, hagiography, language, and geography. It's all too haphazard-looking to be made-up. That is to say, if somebody were going to contrive all this Catholic stuff like a crafty crow, he'd make the package much tidier, and he definitely wouldn't write "expedite" on the side of it and have the confusion of that word be part of the story.

All that is fascinating (I didn't figure it out until long after I got home) but today I needed to expedite my journey if I wanted to make it to my next destination on time. So I drove off before somebody could mistake the shrine for a used car dealership and buy my rental car.

#

There are shrines and then there are shrines. That little church in Nowheresville, Brazil is a little Shrine of St. Expedite. Some places are designated "National Shrines" by a country's bishops' conference in recognition of their importance in national Catholic life. Then there are "Basilicas", churches so designated by the Holy See because they have some elevated historical and/or ecclesiastical significance. This designation can be confusing, as the term "basilica" is also an architectural term applied to a building style commonly used in ancient churches. One could draw a Venn diagram with a bubble for "basilicas" partly overlapping a bubble for "Basilicas", with other interlocking bubbles for "shrines" and "National Shrines". To make matters even more confusing, there are two grades of capital-B Basilica: Major Basilicas, of which there are and ever shall be only four, all in Rome (St. Peter, St. Mary Major, St. John Lateran, and St. Paul-Outside-the-Walls), and minor Basilicas, of which there are hundreds throughout the world. Further confusing matters is that each diocese has a cathedral, one church, often a large one and often in the center of a major city, which is the seat of the local bishop; sometimes a cathedral is also designated as a Basilica and/or a shrine, but usually not.

So, in my own Little Rome ZIP code in Washington, there are three places formally designated as shrines by the Catholic Church. One is the Ukrainian Catholic National Shrine of the Holy Family, another is the St. John Paul II National Shrine, and a third is the Basilica of the National Shrine of the Immaculate Conception. Of these, all are places of pilgrimage and all are given the "national" designation by the United States Conference of Catholic Bishops. Only the latter one is a Basilica, so designated in 1990; before that, it was known simply as the "National Shrine of the Immaculate Conception". It is approximately in the architectural form of a basilica, but that is not the reason for the designation, which again is granted by Rome because the shrine, dedicated as it is to the national patroness of the United States, is of special importance in the life of the Church. None of the churches I just mentioned is a cathedral; that title belongs to St. Matthew's, elsewhere in Washington.

Are you thoroughly confused yet? That's okay. For the purpose of attending Mass on any given day, most of these are distinctions without meaningful differences.

My target this given day was the Basilica of the National Shrine of Our Lady of Aparecida. Let's take that title apart for a moment: It's a Basilica (with a capital B), meaning it is designated by the Holy See as a church of special significance, in this case, a popular place of pilgrimage in one of the world's largest Catholic countries. It's a shrine, a place of pilgrimage distinct from your ordinary neighborhood parish church. It's a National Shrine, designated by the bishops of Brazil as figuring prominently in their nation's Catholic life. And it's dedicated to Our Lady of Aparecida, the same Blessed Virgin Mary who gave birth to Jesus at Bethlehem, who is honored with titles like "Immaculate Conception" and

"Our Lady of Fatima" and "Our Lady of Lourdes" and "Our Lady of Guadalupe" and so forth.

As with the St. Expedite story, unraveling what is meant by "Our Lady of Aparecida" requires a knowledge of history, geography, language, and theology. One of the central tenets of Christianity is that God the almighty, omnipotent, infinitely vast Creator of the universe and judge of all, so loved us, his pitiable creatures, that he deigned to be born as one of us in a particular time and place, in ancient Palestine during the height of Roman influence. As the Son of God, Jesus was and is fully divine and is thus the epitome of humility for coming down here to be killed for our sake. But as the fully human Son of Man, he needed a mother from whom to be born. Mary is that mother. Catholic teaching holds that Jesus applied the same Easter grace to his mother as he does for the rest of us, cleansing her from sin, but that he did it decisively when she was conceived in his grandmother's womb; this is known as the Immaculate Conception. As a consequence of experiencing salvation at the earliest possible moment, she also experienced resurrection at the earliest possible moment; that is, when her earthly life was done, she was taken straight to heaven, body and soul (this is known as the Assumption) to reign as Queen Mother with her Son. That's the short version of the story, and I defer to others more knowledgeable to color your understanding if you're inclined to learn more.

But, of course, that's not the end of the story. The same God who came down here once to die for our sins and lead us to eternal life by his resurrection didn't just go up there and rest from his exertions until Judgement Day. He continues to intervene and lead us to heaven not only through the invisible work of the Holy Spirit in hearts and minds, but through the visible, tangible means of the sacraments: water, bread and wine, oil, the bodily union of man and wife, the ministry of the priest in reconciliation or confession. Occasionally, for reasons that aren't mine or yours to appreciate fully, the eternal, omnipotent King of the Universe sends those closest to him to deliver special messages to chosen people in specific places. Who better to send than the Queen Mother, the Blessed Virgin Mary herself?

As you recall from my overview of Paraty's place in Brazil's history, the seventeenth and eighteenth centuries saw a gold mining boom inland from the coast, approximately in what is now the state of Minas Gerais. One day in 1717, the state governor was passing through what is now Aparecida, and locals decided it might be a good idea to hold a feast in his honor; accordingly, three local fishermen went to the Paraíba River. They prayed through the intercession of Our Lady of the Immaculate Conception (as Catholics are wont to do; when you really need something, you ask the holiest people you know to join you in your prayers) for a good catch of fish. Their request was granted, but also in the net was the head of a statue of the Blessed Virgin Mary.

Near the head was eventually found the rest of the statue. You might expect, along the lines of the Guadalupe apparition in Mexico and its tilma, that I'm going to tell you the statue was of supernatural origin. In fact, it was attributed to a monk from Sao Paulo, who carved it from clay around 1650. It's only about three feet tall, and the loss of its coloring indicated that it had been in the water for quite a while before the fishermen found it. The word "Aparecida" (not previously associated with that place) is a loose cognate of "Apparition" or "appearance", but it also refers to "conception", which is in a sense how we all make our appearance. Thus the fishermen's official title for the statue, Nossa Senhora da Conceição Aparecida, translates approximately as "Our Lady of the Conception Appearance" or "Our Lady of the Conception Appeared", which makes for a tantalizingly frustrating inter-linguistic situation. (The word "Immaculate" was not officially added to this title until 1854 when the dogma behind it, which had been widely believed longer than anyone could remember, was made official.)

As has happened with the relics of miracles throughout Christian history, the found statue was venerated as a manifestation of the eternal and omnipotent God in this created world, a memento of an answer to the prayers of three humble men. By 1737 a small chapel had been built, and pilgrims began to visit in 1745. A larger church was erected beginning in 1834, while the present National Shrine of Our Lady of Aparecida was begun in 1955, receiving the Basilica title in 1980. At some point, Our Lady of Aparecida became the national patroness of Brazil, and in 1924 the hill around the shrine was designated as the city of Aparecida.

#

The Basilica of the National Shrine of Our Lady of Aparecida may be the second-largest church in the world, and is the largest with a Marian title. It is not the cathedral of the Archdiocese of Aparecida. That honor belongs to the Cathedral of St. Anthony in Guaratinguetá, a place nobody visits because they don't have the statue there; we can imagine that the Archdiocesan staff likes it that way.

Since the Basilica is a very large church and the main attraction within Aparecida, which is a very small city, I drove there on the assumption that it would be easy to find the Basilica and park in order to pay a visit. I was half right: the Basilica was easy to find, but the parking lot was not. Aparecida's network of one-way streets is larger than what I'd dealt with last night in Paraty, and lacks the convenience of being a simple conveyer belt that pulls you in one end of town and spits you out the other if you don't park first. Aparecida is a driver's nightmare, combining the density (it seemed) of midtown Manhattan with the driving habits of Rome, the narrow streets of Paraty, and the hilliness of Pittsburgh. It took me the better part of an hour first to understand the basic lay of the land, then to figure out which of the intersections had had their directional signs removed by souvenir hunters, then to find the obscure entrance to the largest church parking lot I've ever seen. I think I parked over a half mile from the Basilica itself.

Since it was now pushing 2:00 p.m. (the St. Expedite visit, ironically, had slowed me down somewhat), I was overdue for lunch. Not to worry, the Basilica has two giant mall-style food courts, with all the variety of cuisine you would expect; for some reason, I chose a cheap Brazilian burger joint. Digesting this, I was glad for the opportunity to walk the rest of the way to the Basilica. Imagine the King of Prussia Mall, or Tysons Corner, or the Mall of America; now imagine that every store there sells rosaries, Bibles, holy cards, miniature saint statues, full-size saint statues, posters of the Blessed Virgin Mary for your bedroom wall, and every other type of religious good known to man, all in an environment only slightly more spacious than a middle eastern souq, open to the Brazilian mountain breezes. That's what I had to walk through on my way from the food court into the Basilica.

But even when I emerged from that bit of holy purgatory, there was a still a plaza to cross. Like St. Peter's Square in Rome, the entrance to the Basilica is framed by a colonnade with statues of the apostles. Unlike St. Peter's in Rome, this Basilica offers a skyride. Paying a few reals, I rode to the top of a neighboring hill, passing over the valley of city streets through which I'd driven less than an hour ago. The view was utterly spectacular: not as high, certainly, as Corcovado where Cristo Redentor is built, nor as naturally scenic as the ocean-city-mountains tableau I'd seen from there, but rather, laid out in front of me, was the western hemisphere's largest church. Oh, and on top of the hill were more shops. Possessing limited cash resources and even more limited space in my baggage, I returned quickly to the Basilica's front porch.

#

To understand what happened next, one must understand the nature of pilgrimage and its central importance in the life of faith. My dictionary defines pilgrimage as "a journey, especially a long one, made to some sacred place as an act of religious devotion". To make a pilgrimage is to acknowledge that geography is important; otherwise, we could all just pray by ourselves at work or at home or at the Correios and call it a day.

Visa Waiver

Geography is important because the same God who created the earth and its fullness chose to be born into this world in a particular place, and not in any other place. In our neighborhoods, churches are important because they are the place where we gather with others to pray, and where we experience God's grace through the sacraments.

But pilgrimage predates the Christian Church. The ancient Hebrews made pilgrimages to Jerusalem, the Holy City with the Temple at its very center, especially for the major liturgical feasts of the year. They had special psalms they sang along the way, known as the Songs of Ascents:

Pilgrimage is rightly directed toward Jerusalem:

> *I rejoiced when they said to me,*
> *"Let us go to the house of the Lord."*
> *And now our feet are standing*
> *Within your gates, Jerusalem.*
> (Psalm 122:1-2)

Pilgrimage teaches us to look upward for protection along the journey:

> *I raise my eyes toward the mountains.*
> *From when shall come my help?*
> *My help comes from the Lord,*
> *The maker of heaven and earth.*
> *He will not allow your foot to slip;*
> *Or your guardian to sleep.*
> *Behold, the guardian of Israel*
> *Never slumbers nor sleeps.*
> (Psalm 121:1-4)

Pilgrimage changes our attitudes:

#justpassingthrough

> *Those who go forth weeping,*
> *Carrying sacks of seed,*
> *Will return with cries of joy,*
> *Carrying their bundled sheaves.*
> (Psalm 126:6)

Pilgrimage helps bring redemption from our sins:

> *Let Israel hope in the Lord,*
> *For with the Lord is mercy,*
> *With him is plenteous redemption.*
> (Psalm 130:7)

Pilgrimage, by placing us closely in contact with other pilgrims, helps us live more harmoniously with our neighbors:

> *How good and how pleasant it is,*
> *When brothers dwell together as one!*
> (Psalm 133:1)

Entrance into the place of pilgrimage puts us in the very Presence of God:

> *Let us enter his dwelling;*
> *Let us worship at his footstool.*
> *Arise, Lord, come to your resting place,*
> *You and your mighty ark.*
> (Psalm 132:7-8)

As a side note, Catholic typological tradition holds that the "mighty ark" here is a prefiguration of the Blessed Virgin herself. She who carried

Christ the priest, Christ the prophet, Christ the king in her womb is the fulfillment of the Ark of the Covenant, which contained the manna, the tablets of the law, and Aaron's scepter of power.

#

In 2016, Pope Francis acknowledged the long tradition of pilgrimage journeys as part of his worldwide decree of the Extraordinary Jubilee Year of Mercy. Each diocese around the globe was to designate one or more churches as a place of pilgrimage (the Aparecida Shrine being a natural choice) and in turn to designate one door as a holy door, an official entrance to the church where pilgrims could celebrate, in a tangible and concrete way, God's mercy on themselves and on the whole world. Attached to the pilgrimage journey was an indulgence: in addition to the journey itself, if one attended Holy Mass and received Communion, if one received the Sacrament of Penance (a.k.a. Confession), if one prayed for the intentions of the Holy Father, and if one did so while maintaining interior detachment from sin, one could apply a plenary indulgence to oneself or to a soul in purgatory.

Historically, pilgrimage has been a long and difficult journey. Imagine what a traveler must have encountered traveling from medieval France to the Holy Land, or even the long journey on foot many pilgrims still take to reach Santiago de Compostela in Spain. By comparison, my journey to Aparecida, though marked with some incompetence on the part of airlines and rental companies and road sign makers, was not an especially difficult one. Still, it had involved some effort, some time, and some money, and I hope that by the time I reached Aparecida and passed through the holy door (having been to Confession during my unplanned day in Miami), my interior disposition was significantly free from attachment to sin so that some soul is now in the presence of Christ for all eternity.

Whatever the effects may have been for another, the effects on me were profound. Ever after all the trouble getting to Brazil, even after the time I'd had finding the entrance to the Basilica's parking lot, even after passing through the food court and the dizzying array of gift shops, when I found the holy door, there on the door itself were two of my favorite psalms. I'd spent just enough time in Brazil struggling to read Portuguese that I recognized the texts: On the left side, Psalm 122, the Song of Ascents expressing joy at going up to Jerusalem; on the right, Psalm 100, about serving the Lord with gladness and coming before his presence with a song.

And then, walking through the doors, I found myself standing in the western hemisphere's largest church, tall, deep, wide, and brightly lit through massive windows. The statue that started this whole complex is in the far apsidal wall. At only three feet tall, it is dwarfed by the church built this big by necessity to accommodate all the pilgrims. In truth, I almost forgot to go look at the statue. In a side chapel, so many votive candles were lit that the air was nearly opaque with the sunlight coming through the window. The prayers were practically visible as they rose toward heaven.

If you're a non-Catholic, you may react to all this the way I did before I swam the Tiber: The story of fishing Mary out of the river is cool, the building is impressive, the food court is useful, the votive candles are beautiful, the gift shops are a little tacky, but… where's Jesus? The answer, of course, is that Jesus is present in the Mass. He's present in the proclaimed Word (a.k.a. the Bible), in the assembly of the faithful ("where two or three are gathered…"), and in the priest-celebrant. Most distinctively, Jesus is fully present, Body and Blood, Soul and Divinity, in the consecrated forms of bread and wine.

The doctrine of transubstantiation explains that when the priest-celebrant (by virtue of the sacrament of his ordination) pronounces the words of institution ("This is my Body…This is my Blood…") over the bread and wine, it is as though Christ himself were saying those words as he did at the Last Supper. While the elements still look, taste, smell, and otherwise behave like bread and wine, they have become, fully and irrevocably, the Body and Blood, Soul and Divinity of Christ, by the power of the Holy Spirit, offered to God the Father as a re-presentation of the one, perfect sacrifice of Christ on Calvary. No, it's not a new sacrifice, nor a temporary change, nor a simple memorial meal, nor a celebration of the community of persons at Mass.

And a church, whether it's your little neighborhood parish, your diocesan cathedral downtown, or the western hemisphere's largest pilgrimage church, is designed first and foremost as the place where the Mass is celebrated. All the stained glass, all the impressive doors, all the statuary (whether purpose-built or fished out of the river), all the organ pipes point to the altar, the place where the sacrifice of Christ on Calvary is re-presented.

So, without any great deal of consideration of other options, the overall timing of my visit to Aparecida was planned so that I could attend Mass. The Basilica has six Masses on weekdays, and the one at 4:00 p.m. suited my needs very well. Attending this Mass would allow me ample time to drive from Paraty and explore the complex before Mass, and enough time to drive to the airport and fly home afterward. My experience of weekday Mass is that it generally takes no more than a half hour, maybe slightly more if it's a major feast day or if an unusually large number of people are present to receive the Eucharist, so I figured I would be back in my car about 4:45 to head home.

I wish I could say that Mass at this Basilica was a pure delight. But it began with a verbal introduction of all the Extraordinary Ministers of Holy Communion, lectors, and altar servers by the priest who, I'm sorry to report, acted like a celebrity game show host at this juncture. There was a musician, a poor guy playing some kind of miscellaneous keyboard instrument with a microphone stuck in his face amplifying his voice far too loudly. The homily itself went on for a long time, which is never a transcendent experience when it's not in a language you understand, and often not even when it's in a language you do understand. Mass was celebrated in a side chapel off the crossing of the main Basilica, and it was so crowded that I half-expected somebody to cut a hole in the ceiling and lower people into the chapel that way.

But here's the thing: no matter how bad the homily, no matter how tacky the in-flight commentary, no matter how ugly the vestments, no matter how abysmal the music, the Mass is still good because Jesus is there, offering himself not only as God-made-human-flesh, but as human-flesh-made-food for us to eat. That's why it drives me nuts when somebody asks me "how was Mass?" Objectively, it's always good because it's Jesus, no matter how badly the other stuff gets screwed up. Unfortunately, some in positions of Church leadership seem to think that because Jesus is always there it doesn't matter about the rest. No, inappropriate music and a priestly personality cult don't negate the Presence of Christ; but they do distract and, I'd argue, set up the occasion for scandal and idolatry.

When Mass was finally finished just before 5:00 p.m., I hurried back to my rental car, glad to have received Jesus in the Eucharist, disgusted with much else about the celebration, and rededicated to living my own vocation as a liturgical musician in such a way as to reflect the beauty of goodness and the goodness of Truth. So, paradoxically, the pilgrimage changed me for the better in spite of itself.

#

It doesn't take long for a foreign country to become home. Now as the sun set on my fourth day in Brazil, my task was simply to drive to the airport, return the rental car, and get on the right plane. It was no different than flying home from London or Kuwait City or Hong Kong. The navigation in this case was utterly simple: just follow the Rodovia 116 west toward the airport, refill the gas tank someplace nearby, return the car, and be gone. The fact that I'd be driving in Friday evening rush hour traffic in the world's third-largest metropolitan area didn't really faze me after I'd spent my college years in the world's second-largest metropolitan area. I did manage to take a wrong turn from the gas station, delaying my arrival by a quarter-hour or so. All told, I didn't make it into the terminal until perhaps 90 minutes before departure. From there, the trip home was largely uneventful. I was in my door around lunchtime on Saturday after a Miami connection just long enough to take a shower in the lounge.

However, a day or two later, I couldn't quite seem to find my passport. I turned my apartment upside-down looking for it; I always carry the passport in my shirt pocket when I travel with it, and I couldn't for the life of me remember removing it from that pocket in either of the usual places. I called every business, every restaurant, every local church I'd visited, but the truth of the matter was that I had last seen my passport when I used it to pass through TSA Blueshirt security after clearing immigration in Miami. Losing my passport was a serious psychological blow. Arguably, it was my most prized possession; without it, I was trapped inside the borders of my own beautiful country. For a few hours, I wondered whether this was a sign from heaven that the formerly waterlogged statue at Aparecida would be the end of my foreign travel adventures. After a while, clearer thinking came as I planned to fly to London in a couple weeks for a conference on the sacred liturgy, and then to Australia a few weeks after that. Visa waivers or not, I needed a new passport, and fast.

Fortunately, St. Expedite was on the case.

Misericordes Sicut Pater

Aparecida wasn't my only holy door pilgrimage destination during the Extraordinary Jubilee Year of Mercy (2016, give or take). As best I can recall, it was at least my fifteenth. Earlier that year, something had possessed me to undertake a series of Lenten pilgrimages within the continental United States.

Well, to be exact, whatever possessed me took hold late in 2015.

On a few previous occasions, I had undertaken day trips by plane, leaving home in the morning, flying someplace, spending the day there, and returning home in the evening. This is a pretty cheap way to see a place, inasmuch as no hotels are required. If you can avoid a car rental by using public transport, so much the better. In turn, you don't need to take any baggage; if you've never done air travel with no bags, you should try it. Of course, this last advantage becomes a risk: What happens if your flight home gets cancelled and you're stuck in a strange city with no toothbrush? And as you might already have told yourself, taking a daytrip by plane can be tiring given the early wakeup calls, late-night returns, and hours on the pavement.

But all this is the stuff of pilgrimage travel, especially coupled with the indulgence gained by passing through a holy door, and the spiritual value of spending your time and money on such a journey.

My task was to identify cities I could visit, with the following conditions:

1. Flight schedule on my preferred airline allowing morning outbound travel and evening return home.

2. Public transportation in the destination city between the airport and the church with the holy door.

3. Mass schedule at the church with the holy door that complements the flight schedule to and from the city, allowing time to absorb minor flight delays without missing Mass.

#justpassingthrough

4. Availability along the way of restaurants and, ideally, museums and other points of interest to fill the rest of the day.

As I began to perform research, I also relaxed condition number one to include cities (primarily in the western USA) to which I could fly in the morning and return via overnight redeye flight.

Looking at all the cities and countries of North America, I narrowed my search to those cities with rail transit to and from the airport, then to those with holy doors accessible by transit, then to those with complementary flight times and Mass schedules. Looking at this list of nineteen cities, I eventually decided that, on Tuesday of each of the five full weeks of Lent, I would undertake a daytrip pilgrimage for the purpose of passing through a holy door at a North American cathedral. After a further process of elimination, I bought plane tickets from DCA to visit holy doors at five diocesan cathedrals:

- Diocese of Providence: Cathedral of St. Peter and St. Paul
- Diocese of Salt Lake City: Cathedral of the Madeleine
- Diocese of Brooklyn: Cathedral Basilica of St. James
- Archdiocese of Chicago: Cathedral of the Holy Name
- Archdiocese of Portland: Cathedral of St. Mary of the Immaculate Conception

This list was a marvelous study in variety, including a state capital in New England, the capital of Utah and of Mormonism, the cultural melting pot of New York City, the largest city in the Midwest, and the weirdness of Left Coast. Missing was anyplace likely to be particularly warm, but this was, after all, for Lent.

As I discussed at some length in the previous chapter, pilgrimage travel is an ancient spiritual discipline. In addition to whatever good works might be done along the way, and certainly in addition to whatever indulgences might be attached, pilgrimage is valuable in the spiritual life because it mirrors the lifelong journey toward heaven on which we all find ourselves.

#

Week One: Divine Providence

On Tuesday of the First Week of Lent (that's the sixth day after Ash Wednesday) I held a round-trip plane ticket for Providence, Rhode Island. This was mid-February, so travel carried the risk of winter weather disruptions. Indeed, Our Nation's Capital was recovering from a brush with snow and ice. Flights had been cancelled up and down the east coast. Frankly, I was amazed when I woke up and didn't find a text message saying my flight was cancelled.

Leaving home about 5:30 a.m., I brought little more than I would take for a day in Washington; only my phone charger and a piece of paper listing travel essentials and prayer intentions from friends weighed me down more than usual. But perhaps I could have used a bit more weight, because the four blocks between my home and the Metro station were one big sheet of ice. My first traveling prayer was probably for the sun to come and melt that ice before I had to skate home from the Metro station that evening.

My flight from DCA to Providence was delayed the better part of an hour because of very necessary de-icing. On deplaning, it was, er, providential that the first shop I passed in the terminal, a bookshop, had a giant poster of Pope Francis out front, with a quote so good that it can't have been uttered in one of his infamous cruising altitude press conferences:

"Mercy is the divine attitude that embraces, it is God's self-giving that welcomes, that leans down to forgive."

Providence's T.F. Green State Airport stretches my definition of "accessible by rail transit", as the rail service between the airport and downtown isn't a local subway system (Providence doesn't have one) but rather an MBTA (Massachusetts Bay Transit Authority) commuter rail line leading to Boston. Service is directional, with morning trains northbound from PVD to downtown and onward to Boston, and evening trains southbound from Boston to downtown Providence and PVD. And even then, the airport rail station is removed from the terminal, reached by a series of (mercifully) covered footbridges.

The downtown Providence rail station (shared by MBTA and Amtrak trains) is at the bottom of a hill. At the top of the hill is the Rhode Island State House. Not being encumbered by anything heavier than my winter coat, I skated up the hill, which was exactly as difficult as it sounds. Naturally, the main door was on the side of the State House that faces away from the train station. Stumbling inside, I was greeted by state troopers and metal detectors. Passing through without incident, I quickly joined a guided tour of the State House.

The State of Rhode Island and Providence Plantations has the longest official name of any state in the union. Rhode Island is also the smallest U.S. state by area; it is less than one-sixth the size of Kuwait, but about four times as large as Bahrain. It boycotted the Constitutional Convention, but became the thirteenth state to ratify the United States Constitution. It is the second most religiously homogenous state in the union (after Mormon Utah), with the highest percentage of Catholics (43%) in its population of just over one million. Rhode Island is a reliably liberal state in its politics: it abolished the death penalty early, was the third state to legalize marijuana for medical use, and didn't outlaw indoor prostitution until 2009 (it was always illegal outdoors, I guess). The Ocean State also ranks near the top of states for property taxes.

The State House tour was unexpectedly engaging. Take, for instance, the Gettysburg Gun: It was used by Union troops during the Civil War, at least until one day the cannonball somehow got stuck in the bore. One thing led to another and the cannon ended up on display in the State House entryway. About a hundred years later, somebody realized that there was still gunpowder inside the loaded cannon, that smoking was still

Misericordes Sicut Pater

allowed in the State House, and that this had the potential to escalate quickly into a real problem. At that point, historic preservationists delicately removed the cannon from public display, submerged it in water to render the powder inert, cut the bore open, emptied it of the now-soggy powder, stitched it back together, and returned it to public display for more generations to enjoy.

And the building itself is quite impressive. The dome, for example, is supposed to be the fourth-largest self-supporting dome in the world, after those of St. Peter's Basilica, the Minnesota State Capitol, and the Taj Mahal.

But the thing I really remember from that tour was when my phone suddenly started vibrating uncontrollably in my pocket. Sheepishly, I removed it to put it in airplane mode to avoid further disruption, but I read the text message anyway: my flight home was cancelled, and I was rebooked for tomorrow afternoon.

Emerging from the State House without having lit any literal gunpowder, I spent a few moments contemplating what to do next. And then I remembered that I'd just come from the train station, served as it is by multiple daily trains on the Northeast Corridor Line. With gravity on my side for a change, I skated back downhill to the providentially-located station and waddled, somewhat sore from all the skating, up to the Amtrak ticket desk. Having already consulted the online timetable, I asked about fares to Washington, DC for a couple of afternoon departures. I could take the ultra-fast, business-class Acela train at 3:45, arriving at Union Station at 9:55 p.m., or I could leave at 4:01 p.m. on the Northeast Regional train and get to Washington at 11:10 p.m. I looked at the considerable price difference, and decided that since the slow train would get me to Union Station in time to catch one of the last Metro trains home (the DC Metro shuts down around midnight on weeknights), the slow train would suffice.

I thanked the Amtrak ticket agent and skated out the door, then called my airline to request a refund of half the fare I'd paid because of the cancelled flight. All in all, the net cost increase was in the tens of dollars. I'd still get home tonight via a mode of transport virtually impervious to the less-than-ideal weather, so I figured this was a minor inconvenience and got on with my day.

Next stop, about a fifteen-minute walk from the State House and the train station, would be Providence's Cathedral of Saints Peter and Paul. The Diocese of Providence was carved out of the Diocese of Hartford (which is now the Archdiocese of Hartford) in 1872, and the Church of St. Peter and St. Paul was chosen as the cathedral. Soon, though, things fell apart. As the story goes, during Holy Thursday Mass in 1878, the ceiling began to fall on the congregation, making it obvious to just about everyone that a new cathedral would have to be built. By 1889, the present cathedral church was open for the salvation of souls, and remained largely unchanged, despite the best efforts of a few hurricanes, for nearly eighty years. But then, in the 1960s, the aftermath of the Second Vatican Council did what hurricanes could not, and the cathedral was renovated. Whatever you may think of the rearrangement of furniture, the cathedral remains an inspiringly grand structure with gorgeous rose windows, light-colored stone, imaginative side chapels, an imposing organ in the north transept, and arches pointing the way to heaven. A highlight is the Mother of Divine Providence Chapel, with a reredos painting of the Assumption.

The Cathedral has played a fairly significant role in the musical life of the Catholic Church in these United States. Liturgical musicians will have encountered the compositions of Alexander Peloquin, who served as cathedral music director from 1950 to 1991. In 1964, he composed the first English-language setting of the Mass for Catholic liturgical use. Peloquin composed a great long list of pieces of liturgical music; my personal favorite is his hauntingly stark, dissonant responsorial setting of Psalm 22, which is sung in the Palm Sunday liturgy as the first music after the giddy jubilation of the triumphal entry of Christ into Jerusalem.

Misericordes Sicut Pater

My own entry into the cathedral was not accompanied by swarms of children laying down palm branches, and I rode on no borrowed ass through the holy door. Festooned with flowers, the holy door here was (providentially, I hazard to say) an inner door, allowing one to pass through at one's leisure without exposure to the elements. Uniquely among the cathedrals I visited those Lenten Tuesdays, the Cathedral of St. Peter and St. Paul had a priest available for confessions just before the midday Mass; this being one of the requirements of the plenary indulgence attached to the holy door, I took full advantage. I'd love to tell you what I confessed, but I can't. That's not because I'm barred from telling (as the priest is), nor because I'm embarrassed to admit to you what I admitted to God through the ministry of that priest. Rather, I just can't remember what sins were absolved in there. And that's the thing about the Sacrament of Penance: you often don't remember your sins, just the fact that you're forgiven and God loves you and has had mercy on you. There's nothing else like it.

After Mass and a photography session and time for my phone to recharge, I found lunch. Providence seemed like a very nice city except for the rain, sleet, hail, snow, freezing rain, ice, mixed precipitation, fog, and so forth.

Soon, I arrived at the Rhode Island School of Design Museum. That place is heavy on modern art, with the predictable range of abstract paintings, nonsense sculptures, and the like. There was also the Lucy Truman Aldrich Collection of Porcelain Objects. One piece is simply a neon sign explaining that "HAPPINESS IS EXPENSIVE" (food for thought much?). Comically, right in the middle of the museum, there's a single large room filled with work of the European masters, some hung crookedly and all without the usual explanatory placards, as obviously an afterthought as anything I've ever seen.

Once my eyes had tired of modern art – it took about an hour, which was pretty good considering I'd been up since 4:30 a.m. or so – I walked back to the Amtrak station. Having originally psyched myself for another round of the quintessential airport experience, it was a little disarming to walk into the station, check the monitor to see which track my train would be on, and head down there with no shoe removal and no inquisition as to why I didn't have luggage like a normal traveler. I watched the Acela train pull away, the one I'd opted against for this journey, and shortly my Amtrak Northeast Regional train arrived, right on schedule. I boarded, took a seat, plugged in my phone, and got comfortable for the seven-hour journey back to Washington. My second lifetime visit to Rhode Island was now complete, the first since that Sunday afternoon in 2003 when I'd gotten curious about what was up I-95.

By the time this train got even as far as Mystic, Connecticut, the weather outside was simply horrid, and for some reason I developed a hankering for pizza. Amtrak's café car offers those little microwaved pizzas. They're not the best, but they did the job okay, except for the fact that the café car was out of plastic knives with which one would ordinarily cut one's pizza. I'll let you visualize how that went.

By the time I returned to my seat, just past the mouth of the Connecticut River, I noticed the train had slowed to a crawl. This wasn't my first Amtrak rodeo, so I didn't find the plot twist alarming. I was just glad not to be driving in this disgusting freezing rain, never mind trying to fly through it. After a while, though, people began to ask strangers why the train was moving so slowly along the Connecticut coast. Nobody knew why until the announcement came over the P.A. system: the train in front of ours had hit a rock and was restricted to a very slow speed.

How in the world does a train hit a rock? Did it take a wrong turn? Did the rock fall from the sky onto the track? I puzzled over this until we finally made the platform at New Haven. There, our half-empty train suddenly became jam-packed with people who'd just gotten off the wounded Acela train on which I was now even more glad not to have bought an expensive ticket.

Despite the delay, the rest of the journey was mostly uneventful: through New York and New Jersey and Philadelphia and Wilmington and

Baltimore much faster than I could have driven on I-95. The train got into Union Station right about midnight, and I caught the last Red Line train north to Little Rome, where the ice was long-gone from the sidewalks.

Prayer answered.

#

Week Two: Mormonville

A week later, on a morning that required no de-icing, I found myself boarding a larger plane than the one that had taken me to Providence. Departing from DCA at 7:00 a.m. on Tuesday of the Second Week of Lent, my ride took me first to Phoenix, which was experiencing a mild form of dry heat (mildly hot while still very dry, I mean). From there, the connecting flight headed north, affording a first-class view of the Grand Canyon. This brought back memories of the Aleatoric Road Trip four years earlier, in which I'd stayed in St. George, at the southwestern corner of Utah, after my first-ever visit to the Grand Canyon on the ground (North Rim). Flying north over the otherworldly landscapes of southern Utah, I hatched a plan to come on a hiking/driving trip here later that spring.

Arrival into Salt Lake City International Airport came a few minutes past noon. It was a gorgeous day along the Wasatch Front; the pale blue of the Great Salt Lake faded into the even paler blue of the winter sky, and the manmade skyline of Salt Lake City looked like toys compared to the snow-capped mountain peaks beyond. This compare-and-contrast between man's biggest works and God's medium-sized ones had to give the locals a head start in the humility department.

Heading quickly out of the uncrowded terminal, I boarded TRAX (short for "Transit Express"), the Utah Transit Authority's light rail system. Unlike the urban rail systems in large cities like New York or

Paris or Beijing, TRAX is an at-grade (i.e. ground-level) system operating down the middle of various city streets and suburban boulevards. As I rode the mostly-empty Green Line train into the city, I marveled at the interaction of the train with road traffic, pedestrians, and the odd bicycle. This was a metropolitan area that had grown around the automobile, with room to sprawl miles and miles in several directions.

Since this trip was planned at 28 hours door-to-door, I'd cheated a bit and brought a small just-in-case overnight bag, figuring that a costume change might even be a good idea at some point. Not needing to drag said bag around Salt Lake City all day, I dropped into a full-service hotel downtown, gave the luggage attendant a $20, and left my bag locked in a storage room. $20 isn't a huge sum in the grander scheme of things, but that and the extra stops (one for dropoff, one for pickup), were an occasion to ask myself in what other ways it costs a person to have more possessions than are strictly necessary.

If you've ever been to Salt Lake City – goodness, if you've ever spent eight seconds thinking about the place – you know that the main attraction is Temple Square, the world headquarters of the Church of Jesus Christ of Latter-Day Saints (LDS), a.k.a. Mormonism. The most famous buildings are the Temple (which, like Mormon Temples the world over, usually forbids entry to non-Mormons) and the 8000-seat Tabernacle (a non-liturgical gathering space, like an auditorium or lecture hall, open to all). There is also a twenty-seven-story office building and a multi-block conference center, along with other administrative and support buildings. They have a warm-and-cozy-but-still-corporate-looking visitor center with models of the other buildings. All in all, it's one of the best-maintained urban landscapes you'll ever see, neat and tidy in the same way as the pairs of young men in white shirts and black ties who knock on your door are neat and tidy.

Speaking of which, my brief visit to Temple Square answered a question that had been festering in my mind for some time: when all those clean-cut young men go biking around the world, what happens to the young women? Apparently a good many of them are here in Temple Square giving tours. About every twenty-five feet, there would be a modestly-dressed, highly attractive young lady, probably blonde, speaking proficient English in an exotic accent, her first name and home country listed on a nametag, giving information to groups of visitors, especially the middle-aged men. While I'm sure the actual process is more wholesome, I did briefly imagine those pairs of young men happening upon a beautiful young Mormon woman in a remote corner of, say, Norway, and having her shipped to Salt Lake City for tour guide duty.

The Tabernacle is a notable stop for any musician, especially those of us involved with organs and choral music, and the Tabernacle organ itself has quite a history. The original instrument came here in 1856, having been built by English Mormon Joseph Ridges in Australia and brought here by ship and then by covered wagon (Salt Lake City was not reachable by rail until 1869, when the Transcontinental Railroad was completed with that golden spike) to be installed in the original Tabernacle building. When the present building was planned, Ridges built a new, all-American instrument of about 1600 pipes with two manuals and pedal (an average-size instrument by today's standards) and it was completed in 1869. Further enlargements were undertaken, and by 1885 the instrument had 2648 pipes played by four manuals and pedal. The organ was rebuilt and enlarged by the Kimball Organ Company in 1901, and again by Austin in 1916, who added to it yet again in 1926 and 1940. A substantially new instrument, approaching the present size and scope and tonal design, was made by Aeolian-Skinner in the late 1940s, which retained a little of Bridges' original pipework and the organ case. A final rebuild was undertaken in the 1980s by Schoenstein & Co., a San Francisco firm known for its work in developing innovative consoles that allow organists seamless control over the tonal resources of large instruments such as this behemoth of over 200 ranks.

The organ is complemented by the 360-voice Mormon Tabernacle Choir. The choir has been a part of Salt Lake City's cultural fabric since its first performance in 1847, only weeks after the first Mormon pioneers arrived in Utah. It now takes part in regular radio, television, and internet programming, through which the LDS Church reaches many who are loathe to speak with those door-to-door missionaries. It is one of the few choirs in America that might outshine the Westminster Choir (of which I am an alumnus) for name-brand recognition.

But during my five-minute visit to the Tabernacle, I could only imagine what the organ and choir sounded like. Here, too, those pretty guides were giving tours to small groups of (mostly male) visitors.

The atmosphere in Temple Square is a bit intoxicating. In addition to the tour guides of outrageous attractiveness, I noticed that everybody smiled. A lot. Too much. So, while I still possessed some part of my willpower, I left on my own two feet and headed a few blocks north toward the Pioneer Memorial Museum.

While the entire American West can rightly claim pioneer heritage of some variety, it is Utah that has cornered the Pioneer market with a capital P. As soon as I walked into the museum, a smiley desk attendant wanted to know whether my family had been pioneers, and when he had arrived. I sheepishly explained that I had gotten up that morning at home in Washington, DC, and arrived about three hours ago on a 737, alone. They were mildly crestfallen, but I was still allowed inside.

The Pioneer Memorial Museum is a multi-story building whose collection ranges from Pioneer clothing to Pioneer dolls to Pioneer fire engines to Pioneer flags to Pioneer maps to Pioneer medical implements to Pioneer musical instruments. Somehow, despite being such a big place, it manages to feel like one of those house museums where you can see everything in ten minutes. Maybe that's because everybody smiles so much. I spent perhaps an hour and a half wandering up and down the stairs and through the various hallways and side rooms.

Heading east from the museum, I meandered past the Utah State Capitol Building. Looking uncannily like its Rhode Island counterpart, this capitol is home to a nearly-opposite set of political priorities; Utah is one of the most consistently conservative states in the Union. What a miracle that a country so large can admit of such diversity in religion and politics and still manage to hold together as one.

The Second Sunday of Lent (two days before my visit to Salt Lake City, thus fresh in my mind that day) centers around the story of Jesus' transfiguration on the high mountain. Unlike most of the other stories in the Gospels, this one is really about the cessation of a miracle: For one brief shining moment, Jesus' humanity ceased to hide his divinity, and Jesus (who fulfills the Prophets and the Law) could be seen conversing with Elijah and Moses. In coming to Utah, I had come partly in search of a glimpse of that beauty, but I had no expectation of finding it in Temple Square, tour guides aside.

Instead, my search for beauty and goodness and truth sent me to the Cathedral of the Madeleine, a few blocks east of Temple Square, which is named for St. Mary Magdalene, first witness to the Resurrection, apostle to the Apostles, and (perhaps falsely) said to have been a reformed prostitute. The Madeleine is not only the seat of the Diocese of Salt Lake City and the site of Utah's only holy door, but home of one of North America's premier Catholic musical institutions, the Madeleine Choir School. A friend of mine, a Catholic man with a powerful non-tenor voice who'd grown up singing here, had advised me to come to Mass on a day when the girls' choir was singing, as they're regarded as being a finer ensemble than the boys' choir. I took his advice, and I came expecting musical radiance.

What I wasn't expecting was to be so overwhelmed with visual beauty...and visual truth! After I passed through the holy door, which was to the side of the main entrance, lined with a mishmash of multicolored decorations, and physically difficult to open, I came through the main center door and was afflicted with sensory overload. Here was a Gothic-revival church painted in bold blues, reds, yellows, golds, purples, browns; here were depictions of the angels worshipping Christ the Lord; here was the likeness of Christ crucified in his love for us sinners, surrounded by

Old Testament figures on one side and early Christian saints on the other. The cathedral's Spanish-influenced art drew my attention with its beauty, and then showed me goodness, pointing to the Truth.

A priest I know in Washington called this "one of the most 'correct' entrances I ever witnessed in person of a Cathedral, the baptismal font and confessional at the back near each other, centered on the Eucharist." Father is correct, of course; the entrance is at once a lesson in sacramental theology and a triumph of practical design. In order to approach the Eucharist, one must be baptized and in a state of grace. Baptism itself puts a soul in a state of grace, but that state of grace is damaged or lost through sin. Fear not: the soul can be made like new in the confessional, and the penitent (like St. Mary Magdalene herself) is then free to approach Christ in the Eucharist, that is, to be in Communion with Christ and the Church, in a state of grace.

But that's not all the teaching to be found etched into these stones. One element of the interior design is a pair of quotes from sacred scripture on the far left and far right of the front of the church. On the left, Christ is quoted speaking to his apostle Peter:

Thou art Peter and upon this rock I will build my church, and the gates of hell shall not prevail against it.

On the right, St. Paul is quoted from his letter to the Galatians:

Though we or an angel from heaven preach a gospel to you besides that which we have preached to you, let him be anathema.

I read each of these separately as I inspected each corner of the cathedral. Christ's quote to St. Peter is commonly found in Catholic churches, including one of my favorite parishes in Washington, St. Peter's, which has those same words in Latin around the top of its interior. But the St. Paul quote struck me as unusual, even unfamiliar, and I wondered why it had been chosen. And then, stepping to the back of the cathedral once again and beholding the whole display, I considered the two quotes together and realized the genius at work:

Mormonism was founded not by Christ and the Apostles whose acts and teachings are detailed in the Bible, but by a man named Joseph Smith, who claimed to have received the Book of Mormon – ostensibly containing a new revelation by God – from the angel Moroni near Rochester, New York, in 1830. Christ made clear that his Church would be founded on the Apostles, and particularly on St. Peter, a teaching that is fulfilled through the present day in the Petrine ministry of the popes in Rome and of the bishops worldwide; St. Paul warned the early Christians that there would be no gospel except the one he and the other apostles preached, even if an angel appeared as if from heaven with the new teaching. As a friend quipped to me, "This Cathedral is not only gorgeous but it is totally an evange-punch in the face of the Mormons."

This is why the Mormons have the clean-cut missionaries, their beautiful tour guides, their well-kept Temple Square, their massive choir and organ, their impressive world headquarters. They have beauty, and to some extent they might have goodness, but they do not have the fullness of Truth, as Christ proclaimed and St. Paul so plainly explained. Hilaire Belloc put it best: "The Catholic Church is an institution I am bound to hold divine – but for unbelievers a proof of its divinity might be found in the fact that no merely human institution conducted with such knavish imbecility would have lasted a fortnight." As one who works for the Catholic Church, I approve of that quote, and I'm suspicious of people, places, and institutions that seem a little too immaculate on the surface.

Against that backdrop unfolded the Holy Sacrifice of the Mass. The choir girls, as predicted, made the cathedral sound as beautiful as it looked. This happens here every day: a few dozen children from the minority Catholic population sing choral music as refined as anything three hundred adult Mormons can put together down the street, all in praise of Christ, all in communion with two thousand years of belief and liturgical practice.

Mass ended as the sun was going down that February day; my flight home wouldn't be leaving for six more hours, so I still had time for sightseeing. What, you may ask, does a person do for entertainment on a winter Tuesday evening in Salt Lake City? Well…quite conveniently, the Church History Museum was open until 9:00 p.m. So, leaving the oasis of beauty, goodness, and truth that is the Cathedral of the Madeleine, I walked back to Mormonville.

I don't remember much about the museum except for the docents. Here were more Mormons, older men this time, older than the ones who seemed so mesmerized by the beautiful tour guides. Their perpetual smiles creeped me out, and the warm, attractive, well-organized museum displays seemed paradoxically off-putting. I longed for beauty, goodness, truth, and knavish imbecility. This time I found some of those things at a restaurant with Sandbox cuisine, where I savored Moroccan lentil soup and chicken chwarma accompanied by Lebanese white wine.

Having gained perspective on Mormonism, having experienced a leading Catholic musical institution for the first time, having savored the crisp, thin winter air, and having tasted exotic food, it was finally time to retrieve my bag and make TRAX to the airport. The journey home was pleasantly boring, inasmuch as no planes were grounded by ice, and no trains collided with boulders.

#

Week Three: Lady On A Dolphin

My third Lenten pilgrimage destination of 2016 would be the one closest to home. It involved the earliest morning departure time of any of the five weeks and the latest non-redeye return flight, and thus the most time at the destination. By happy coincidence, the destination city would be America's largest and most exciting, none other than New York, New York.

This time, departure was so early in the morning that the Metro couldn't get me to the airport in time. If you're a savvy air traveler, you might know that there is a "shuttle" operation between Reagan National Airport on the Potomac River and LaGuardia Airport on the East River, with hourly flights, and you might object that I could have taken a later shuttle flight. But remember, mission rules require travel by train from the airport to the city and cathedral. LaGuardia (an airport like you'd find in a "third-world country", according to former Vice-President Joe Biden) is not connected to New York's wide-ranging rail network, though there are perpetual discussions about tearing up Queens and building such a connection. So I would have to fly to JFK today in order to connect to the subway system.

Emerging from the depths of the A-train, I found myself at Church and Murray Streets, in the midst of a Tuesday morning commute in lower Manhattan's financial district. Here was a corner of the world I first visited in the summer of 1990, a visit that was the subject of my first book, "A Trip to New York and New Jersey", written in early 1991 in Mrs. Burtch's second grade Writing Workshop. At the risk of sounding overly obvious, the neighborhood had been through some changes since 1990.

On that summer day in my childhood, my family had taken the express elevator to the top of Two World Trade Center and enjoyed the view from the outdoor observatory. Four years later, I became glued to CNN's coverage of the attempt to send one tower crashing into the other by way of a truck bomb in the underground parking garage. The Sandbox-based terrorists responsible were fortunately incompetent, but they didn't give up.

My last view of those twin towers came on Labor Day weekend of 2001, a couple weeks into my freshman year at Westminster Choir College. My mother had decided she was going to come visit me in late

#justpassingthrough

September, flying from Rochester to LaGuardia Airport; since LaGuardia isn't connected to rail transportation (have I mentioned this before?), I would have to come pick her up at LaGuardia. Being possessed of that newfound freedom of being away from home, I got wild that Saturday afternoon and took a "practice" drive from Princeton to LaGuardia and back. It was my first time to drive in New York City (those under 18 aren't allowed to drive in the city or Lawn Guyland), and I remember how those two boxy skyscrapers gleamed in the late summer sun.

The second time I drove in "The City" (as all the cool kids called it) was on November 11 of that year. I took two friends to a Choral Evensong in midtown where the guest speaker was Sam Waterston of 'Law and Order' fame; though I've since become addicted to reruns, I had no idea who he was at the time. Afterward, I drove us as far south along West Broadway as I could, stopping when the street became blocked by giant piles of ash and twisted metal; then, Lower Manhattan smelled of electrical fire, jet fuel, and burnt flesh.

Today, the 9/11 memorial on the grounds is fitting as could be, with the outlines of those fallen box-buildings forming memorials to those whose innocent lives were lost. Bravo to the decision-makers for avoiding the temptation to pave over the whole site with something newer, bigger, better. Today, the new One World Trade Center stands as a magnificent monument to a nation that defied the faceless bullies who attacked it, a fittingly post-modern complement to the art deco of New York's second-tallest skyscraper, the Empire State Building. When you get down to brass tacks, the new building is quite a bit more aesthetically pleasing than the old ones, those boxy things everybody hated until they were gone. So, too, the One World Observatory is at least as good as what came before it, enabling 360-degree views in the climate-controlled comfort of the great indoors. I'd picked a crystal-clear late-winter day, and I could see for miles in every direction. What a great city this was, where artists could get discovered, tall buildings could get built, immigrants from every corner of the globe could be welcomed, and even such a strange character as Donald Trump, then just beginning to look like a major contender in the presidential election, had the opportunity to make it big.

After visiting the Observatory, I descended past ground level to visit the National September 11 Memorial and Museum in earnest. You can discover and evaluate the contents of the museum on your own, if you've not already visited. It's well worth the journey and the price of admission, I promise. Just as memorable, to me, was the way the museum was built into the underground "bathtub" that had housed the original World Trade Center, thus solving (with hallmark New York ingenuity) the dual problems of where in crowded lower Manhattan to put a museum with high visitor traffic and what to do with the empty bathtub after the debris had been removed.

After this trip into the darker recesses of memory lane, I rode the subway back under the East River to Brooklyn, which is home to over half a million Jews, alongside immigrants and ethnic communities with roots virtually every place else in the world. My pilgrimage goal for the day would be the Cathedral Basilica of St. James, seat of the Diocese of Brooklyn, which includes all the Catholics in Brooklyn and Queens. (Manhattan, Staten Island, the Bronx, and seven New York State counties north of the city comprise the Archdiocese of New York.) Compared to the cathedral in Providence, this was a modest-sized structure; compared to the cathedral in Salt Lake City, this was no evange-punch to religious neighbors. Rather, the Cathedral Basilica is a simple neighborhood parish (not, I might add, in a terribly attractive neighborhood) that happened to be designated as the cathedral (seat of the diocesan bishop) and a basilica (important church recognized by the Vatican as such). And it was designated by the Diocese as the location of a holy door.

The holy door wasn't marked, and having come all this way to pass through it and gain the attached indulgence, I had to ask the custodian which door it was. The answer came in that particular isn't-it-obvious tone indigenous to New York City that the holy door was the central door to the cathedral, through which everyone had to pass on the way in.

Several of my sources agreed that Brooklyn is not the very center of good things in liturgical music; still, because the midday Mass is telecast, an organist and cantor took part.

One feature of the cathedral's art fascinated me: the baptismal font sits in an alcove off the south transept, next to the Paschal candle and the ombrellino (the Vatican-colored umbrella that sits in every Basilica, waiting to be put over the Pope's head in the event he drops in). Well, what really fascinated me was the mural beyond the font. Predictably, it includes the image of St. John the Baptist pouring water over Jesus in the River Jordan. Less predictably, that same River Jordan includes the likeness of a woman riding a dolphin.

Lunch was at a hole-in-the-wall burger joint with next to no seating. I managed to find a seat, though, and it was even next to a functional electrical outlet. After a morning of navigation, photography, and social media uploads, my poor phone appreciated the recharge, and so did I.

Next, on what was becoming a notably windy day, I walked about a half mile south to the New York Transit Museum. Located underground (notice a pattern in today's museums?), this museum makes use of an abandoned subway station to display a plethora of vintage rail cars in miniature and full-size, plus maps and explanations of how the subway got built (it wasn't easy), plus how the city recovered from the damaging floods of Hurricane Sandy in 2012.

Returning to Manhattan, I passed through Grand Central Terminal en route to the iconic Church of Our Saviour on Park Avenue. The parish musician there, my friend Paul, was my sponsor when I entered the Catholic Church in 2010, and also a college classmate. We were able to catch up on all the ecclesiastical goings-on along the I-95 corridor, which was a nice treat.

Continuing northward, I stopped briefly in St. Patrick's Cathedral, seat of the Archdiocese of New York. St. Patrick's is both magnificent and

Misericordes Sicut Pater

beautiful, but its greatest asset, its location on Fifth Avenue in the hustle-and-bustle commercial district near Rockefeller Center and Times Square and Grand Central, is its biggest liability. In most cities with a grand (neo-)Gothic cathedral, the cathedral dominates, but here, it is simply dwarfed by the modern office buildings and shopping centers that surround it. And it's often exceedingly crowded.

To your great surprise, I next entered an Episcopalian church, St. Thomas, just up Fifth Avenue from St. Patrick's Cathedral. Like the Madeleine in Salt Lake City, St. Thomas is known for its choir school, and I was here for Choral Evensong, the Anglican adaption of Evening Prayer (or Vespers) and Compline from the Liturgy of the Hours. In earlier times, the experience would have been the highlight of my month; as a Catholic, I've lost a great deal of my former interest in this sort of thing, but beauty is beauty and it points to goodness and truth. St. Thomas is a beautiful church, and the choir makes beautiful sounds.

These Tuesday Lenten pilgrimages, planned well in advance, turned out to be welcome mental respites from an unexpectedly demanding interim music directorship I undertook that Lent inside the Beltway. Still, getting up in the middle of the night, walking around a city for many hours, and then returning home late at night took its physical toll. As I sat listening to the men and boys singing Evensong, I was put in mind of a verse of the St. Thomas Choir School's hymn, also well-known at Westminster Choir College:

Come, labor on.
No time for rest, till glows the western sky,
Till the long shadows o'er our pathway lie,
And a glad sound comes with the setting sun,
Servants, well done!
(Jane Laurie Borthwick)

Pilgrimage, then, demands much of our bodily strength, but by putting us in fresh surroundings, it gives us the opportunity to contemplate things holy, in order to take those things home with us as we continue our larger pilgrimage toward heaven. My pilgrimage through life's long path had included serving the Episcopal Church through eight of my most formative years. There, I had been introduced to the workings of Christian liturgy rooted in pre-Reformation times. There, I had sung and played some of the greatest hymns and hymns texts, challenged myself organizationally and interpersonally, and made music of great beauty. As I came to realize that Catholic teaching carries the fullness of Truth, so I came to realize that my place within the Church founded on the rock of St. Peter would involve using my skills to make beauty a bigger part of Catholic liturgy in the places I would serve.

Having had my soul nourished foremost in the Eucharist at Mass, and secondarily through the beauty of Choral Evensong, I turned to bodily nourishment. Manhattan is one of the best places in the world for eating, having within its aquatic boundaries perhaps the greatest variety of cuisine of any territory on earth, including much of good quality; outside of Times Square, a lot of it is affordable, too. I found Matts Grill, at the corner of 55th Street and 8th Avenue, and enjoyed a simple chicken caesar salad with a Portuguese white wine.

Now came the journey home. I returned to Kennedy Airport by taking the subway to Jamaica Station in Queens, then the AirTrain to Terminal 8. Despite the late hour (it was past 9:00), the boarding area teemed with people. I circled the gate lounge looking for an electrical outlet to recharge my phone again, ideally with a chair to recharge myself, as at lunch.

And then I recognized a voice. Wandering around the boarding area until I could find its source, I found my friend Greg, with whom I've done a fair bit of singing at St. Matthew's Cathedral in Washington. At this point in the day, I was so delirious that it took me a moment to realize how odd it was to run into him here. Like me, Greg had come to

New York for the day; unlike me, he'd done so for work. I felt mildly awkward that I had been upgraded to First Class while he was stuck in economy, but the gate agent made it clear I couldn't upgrade him because we weren't flying on the same itinerary.

Through my Facebook posts, I learned that Paul and Greg weren't the only friends I'd seen that day. As it turns out, another college classmate, a countertenor named Jeff, sings in the choir at St. Thomas Church; if I'd realized this, I could've stuck around and said hello and thanked him again for the two times he died for me. You see, Jeff and I had been in the Westminster Choir together in the spring of 2005 when, after descending I-95 to Charleston, we'd served as the opera chorus, and, in fact, the title characters, in the North American premiere of a Walter Braunfels opera, Die Vögel ("The Birds"), at the Spoleto Festival USA. It's the story of a religious cult comprised of birds; at the end, the cult leader is unmasked as a fraud and the birds fly away. Well, most of the birds fly away, but I and a couple others were selected to die of shock at the revelation that we'd been had. At the dress rehearsal, my onstage death had been so convincing that the chorus master raced on stage and was about to call 911. Subsequently, I'd been nicknamed "ton of bricks", a name that, mercifully, didn't stick. Anyhow, at the second performance, I once again dropped dead in a realistic fashion, but I landed funny and probably broke a rib. I say "probably" because I refused medical treatment so that I wouldn't get sidelined for the rest of the Festival. After all, the usual treatment for a broken rib is to wait for it to heal, with or without medical bills. As a precaution, I asked not to have to die again, but to be allowed to drift off the set with most of the other chorus birds; the stage director insisted that somebody had to die in that location at that moment, so Jeff graciously volunteered to be the bird who died in my stead for the final two shows. That's Jeff. He died for me twice and I didn't even notice him in the midst of all that heavenly music at St. Thomas.

Once Greg and I and everybody else on the Embraer 175 landed at DCA, I quickly found Sylvia the Silver Sentra and drove home, arriving nineteen hours after I'd left. It had been a full day in nearly every respect, but at least unpacking didn't take long: I pulled my phone charger out of my pocket, plugged it in, and went to bed.

#

Week Four: What's in a Name?

The Fourth Week of Lent begins with Laetare Sunday, the one Sunday in Lent when penances are most relaxed and the liturgical color is rose ("It's not pink, it's rose!") instead of a severe deep purple. Whether it was intentional or not, my fourth Lenten holy door pilgrimage was the least demanding journey I would undertake, with the latest morning departure time, the earliest evening return, the least time walking around the destination city. After the New York City marathon the previous week, and in advance of what turned out to be the following week's itinerary, I didn't complain.

When I say "O'Hare", do you shudder? Lots of travelers do. Lots of people have horror stories of an airport with too many planes for its runways, too many planes for its gates, too many people for its security checkpoints, and so forth. Somehow, my experiences with O'Hare have been almost all good. Yes, Chicago has snowstorms and high winds and thunderstorms; yes, O'Hare is the major Midwestern hub for two of the world's three largest airlines.

O'Hare got its reputation the old-fashioned way. Until 2008, all but one of its six runways intersected with other runways; three pairs of parallel runways had been built, theoretically allowing for safe operation in just about any non-tornadic wind condition. The problem was that O'Hare's traffic volume requires a lot more than two runways for most of each day; not only is Chicago America's third-largest city, creating tons of local demand for air travel, but it is located in the middle part of country, nearer to the crowded northeast than to the wide-open west, making it a natural connecting point for traffic flows connecting from Boston to Albuquerque or from Buffalo to Des Moines or from Kansas City to Tokyo. When the sun was out and the wind was calm, Air Traffic Control used the interlocking runways to handle the traffic, but when visibility was reduced or surfaces were wet or the wind blew strongly, the FAA no longer allowed flights to land using converging paths to intersecting runways (an eminently reasonable use of federal regulatory power, in my opinion), and hours-long delays ensued while five runways' worth of traffic tried to squeeze onto two or three runways.

All that began to change with the implementation of the O'Hare Modernization Project. As aircraft design has improved, crosswinds are less limiting than they once were. So, over time, O'Hare has been closing some of its runways and opening new ones. Where once there were three pairs of runways in three directions, now the airfield has five parallel east-west runways. That means that, even in dense fog, up to three runways can be used simultaneously for arrivals, and at least two runways are always available for departures (departing flights require less separation distance than arriving ones, plus it's easier for a plane to wait in line on the ground than in the sky, so sometimes ATC assigns more runways to arrivals than to departures). Now, except when severe thunderstorms briefly make flight unsafe altogether, or when snowfall is so heavy that plows can't keep up, weather delays at O'Hare are quite rare.

In response, airlines began to schedule more flights, knowing that (absent unusually severe weather) flights would be able to land on time, even early, and queues for departure would be manageable. In turn, connecting passengers (who in the past might have favored connections in Detroit or Dallas or Denver) began to see O'Hare as more reliable than it had been, and demand went up. But do you see the problem here? While runway capacity had expanded, there were no new gates being built. Airlines sometimes schedule a flight to arrive at the gate five minutes after the previous flight departs; now that flights were arriving ten, fifteen, twenty minutes early due to the decreased airfield congestion, it became a common problem that landing flights had nowhere to park. ATC would send some planes to taxi in circles around the central terminal area until their gate opened up, leading to more ground congestion and wasted fuel and pollution.

Necessity is the mother of invention, so now flights that arrive early at O'Hare get to sit in the "Penalty Box", a slice of tarmac just off those circumferential taxiways where early-arriving planes can sit and wait for their gates to open. In the longer term, Chicago plans to expand the terminals and/or build new ones, but for now, the Penalty Box is the solution. It's not unusual nowadays to see a half-dozen or more planes sitting there shooting the breeze.

On this sunny March morning, the flight approached O'Hare from the east, allowing a great view of the Chicago skyline for those of us seated on the left side of the plane. When, despite an early arrival, the 737 skipped the Penalty Box and went straight to its gate, I knew this was going to be another good day.

O'Hare may have a reputation for being a sprawled-out monstrosity, but most gates have a fairly short walk to baggage claim and ground transportation; I was probably on the train platform within about ten minutes from when the plane door opened. Chicago's CTA trains are one of the oldest such networks in America; the Blue Line terminates at O'Hare station, located underground (yay for not having to brave the elements at the airport!) near three of the terminals and the airport hotel. Once you're on the train, it's a one-seat ride to downtown (known as "The Loop") in about forty-five minutes. For a good chunk of that distance, the tracks and stations are in the median of the I-90 John F. Kennedy Expressway, which also merges with I-94 closer to the city center, so Blue Line riders get to observe the traffic congestion and be glad their $5 is saving them time and trouble.

I disembarked at the Clark and Lake station, a major transfer spot, ascended to street level, and walked north to the Chicago River. In a week or so, the river would be dyed green in observance of St. Patrick's

Day, but not being one for parties, I was happy to enjoy the urban riverscape on this relatively tame Tuesday morning. The river was teeming with construction equipment repairing bridges and docks and so forth. I thought of a toddler nephew who'd love it here. As American cities go, Chicago is one of the few that rivals New York for architectural diversity; older buildings mingle with the new in a smörgåsbord for the eyes. Ambling east along the south bank of the river, toward Lake Michigan, I passed the Marina Towers, twin residential skyscrapers. Each tower is more or less circular in floor plan, with each residence possessing its own rounded balcony; the bottom fifteen floors, or so, constitute a parking garage, built as one spiral. The next block contains the glass-boxy Langham Hotel, and then, taller than the others, is the Trump International tower.

Walking east, I knew I wanted to leave the Chicago River at Michigan Avenue and cross the bridge to head north. How very helpful it is that the city puts labels on its bridges. This way, I could enjoy the view without having to stare at my phone screen to know where I was.

Chicago has some great museums: the Art Institute, the Field Museum, the Museum of Science and Industry, Adler Planetarium, and a few others come to mind. But the time and location of my visit limited me to the City Gallery in the Chicago Water Tower. I didn't know just how tiny an exhibition it would be, nor did I imagine that a temporary museum display could be so completely devoted to "Cards Against Humanity".

From the Water Tower, it was a quick four blocks' walk west to Holy Name Cathedral, the seat of the Archdiocese of Chicago, designed by the Irish-American immigrant Patrick Keely (1816-1896), the same prolific Catholic liturgical architect who designed the cathedral in Providence, among many other beautiful Catholic churches built in the eastern United States during that era. Boston's Cathedral of the Holy Cross, Charleston's Cathedral of St. John the Baptist, and even Washington's St. Dominic Church are among his credits.

#justpassingthrough

Here, at least, was a holy door embellished with the bright yellow and white crossed keys of the Vatican's Coat of Arms. The keys represent the keys to the kingdom of heaven given by Christ to St. Peter, the first Pope. Thus, Our Lord gave to Peter, and to his successors and to the whole Church, the means to open the gate of heaven by means of mercy. This being the Year of Mercy, and given that an indulgence was granted for pilgrims passing through the door to spring a soul from purgatory, the keys were precisely the right symbol.

The Cathedral of the Holy Name was dedicated in 1875, four years after Mrs. O'Leary's least-favorite cow burned down the old cathedral along with much of the rest of Chicago. The present cathedral at first appears to be "just" another impressive neo-Gothic cathedral, but it has several distinctive features, including stained glass windows that, while abstract, are identical to one another, the magnificent Flentrop organ in the west gallery, and the waffle-like ribbing on the ceiling vaults.

To my eye, the most important feature is the giant "IHS" on the ceiling about the cathedral's crossing, appearing above the crucifix. These three letters are a common cryptogram of the Greek name of Jesus (ΙΗΣΟΥΣ). The name is up there because, as St. Paul tells the Philippians, Christ "…humbled himself, becoming obedient to death, even death on a cross… God greatly exalted him and bestowed on him the name that is above every other name, that at the name of Jesus every knee should bend, of those in heaven and on earth and under the earth, and every tongue confess that Jesus Christ is Lord, to the glory of God the Father." So now, everyone who comes into Holy Name Cathedral – the homeless person looking for shelter, the pope making an apostolic visit, the affluent suburbanite coming to the city for Sunday funday, the Cardinal who might be tempted to place his own opinion and reputation over the requirements of safeguarding revealed Truth – can see through artistic beauty that the Holy Name of Jesus is exalted precisely because of Christ's humble goodness.

Speaking of Cardinals, Chicago has had quite a run of them. The College of Cardinals is an elite group of bishops from around the world, individually designated as such by the pope, who gather in the papal conclave to select a new pope when the Chair of St. Peter is vacant through the pope's death or resignation. Until 2013, the common practice was that certain archdioceses (usually those in the largest or otherwise most-important cities) would have their archbishop named a cardinal. But, as a balance on the power of cities and archdioceses, there would only be one voting-age cardinal (i.e. under 80) at a time per see. Since (arch)bishops have to resign at 75, this often resulted in a period during which the archbishop had to wait for his retired predecessor to reach age 80 or die, after which the pope would name the newer, younger man to the College of Cardinals. After age 80, the title of Cardinal is retained even though His Eminence is now too old to enter the papal conclave. When a Cardinal dies, his red galero (the Roman version of a Mexican sombrero) is suspended from the ceiling. A very non-dogmatic tradition holds that the deceased Cardinal's galero suspension fails and his hat falls to the floor the instant he is released from purgatory into heaven.

In the case of Chicago, the current Archbishop is Blase Cardinal Cupich. Their late Eminences whose galeri hang in the cathedral include Cardinals Mundelein, Stritch, Meyer, Cody, Bernardin, and George. I personally met Francis Cardinal George in his later years as he suffered through cancer with grace and humility, and consider him one of the great pastors of my lifetime. George Cardinal Mundelein's name will be familiar to many Catholics because of the seminary he founded, which is now the largest major seminary (i.e. offering graduate study) for Catholic clerics-to-be in the United States. Joseph Cardinal Bernardin is remembered for his "seamless garment" theory of Catholic social teaching, based on the premise that all human life is sacred and should be protected by law. It is used to tie together Catholic teaching and action against abortion, assisted suicide, capital punishment, euthanasia, and unjust war. While it is a useful key to understanding these strands of Catholic teaching and action, the "seamless garment" sometimes seems to lose sight of the fact that not all evil is of the same gravity. For example, abortion is to be vociferously condemned because it destroys the most innocent of lives, while killing in war is not inherently unjustified, but it is still problematic in slightly more subjective ways.

Among musicians, Chicago's cathedral is best known as the long-time workplace of Richard Proulx, a venerable church musician and composer whose death in 2010 was being mourned just as I entered the Catholic Church. He is responsible for volumes of responsorial psalms and choral music, but his most widely-use contributions are his English-language congregational Mass Ordinary settings, principally "A Community Mass" and secondarily "Mass for the City".

As I wrapped up my photo shoot in anticipation of the midday Mass, I was joined by my friend Esther, a fine concert pianist who returned to her native Chicago after earning a degree in Washington. Here was another serendipity-through-travel: For some reason, nobody ever seems to want to sit with me at Mass, which maybe has to do with my tendency to sit on the organ bench. At any rate, it's somewhat rare for me to attend Mass in the near company of anyone I know, and this was quite a treat, in addition to being briefly reunited with an old friend. After Mass, we had lunch at an Armenian restaurant, taking full advantage of the opportunity to catch up on mutual friends, career development, travel plans, and so forth.

Speaking of O'Hare, after I walked with Esther to where she practices piano downtown most days, it was time for me to head back to the airport. Yes, I told you this was a short pilgrimage day! It wasn't entirely easy, though. One of the hazards of being an itinerant liturgical musician (or, I suppose, any freelance/independent contractor/self-employed worker) is that sometimes your paycheck gets delayed. No, a delayed paycheck is an annoyance; the hazard is when multiple paychecks get delayed and you're just supposed to be able to deal with it. Well… the night before the Chicago pilgrimage, I very nearly canceled when two or three paychecks still hadn't arrived. Looking at my accounts, I realized that I would be down to precisely $10.00 available for spending on the Chicago visit. Taking stock of my anticipated expenses, I realized that I had enough DC Metro fare to get to and from the airport in Washington, and that I'd be fed breakfast and dinner on my flights. That left just lunch and CTA fare of $10. I grabbed the $50 gift debit card I'd gotten as a Christmas gift, planned to spend the $10 on an all-day CTA pass, and hoped for no serious problems.

I was awfully glad to get home that night and find one of the missing checks in that day's mail. I had traveled with no backup plan, but I hadn't needed one. God's providence gave me just what I needed for the journey, and literally not a penny more. For that I was thankful.

#

Week Five: Keeping It Weird

For the fifth week of Lent, I chose the farthest destination of the five: Portland, Oregon. As with the Salt Lake City visit, plans called for me to travel west early in the morning, arrive after noon, spend the afternoon touring the city, attend evening Mass, and then take the redeye home. The airline, as airlines sometimes do, changed my flight schedule in such a way that I wouldn't be able to attend Mass. I then called the airline and had them put me on PDX-SEA-MIA-DCA for the return journey, which had the dual advantages of allowing me to attend Mass in Portland (which is, after all, a main point of the journey) and netting more frequent flyer miles.

Pulling my roll-a-board suitcase behind me, I arrived at the Metro station to find it barricaded shut. Since the Metro is sometimes a little slow in the morning, as well as during the day, in the evening and at night, it seemed like nothing, but if this book were a fiction novel, my mentioning the closed Metro station would have constituted foreshadowing.

#justpassingthrough

My morning's itinerary would take me from DCA to DFW, and then up to PDX, including breakfast and lunch. For breakfast, notes indicate that I was served "egg-red pepper-broccoli strata, herbed roast potatoes, chicken sausage, mixed fruit, an apricot-raisin roll, and orange juice." Domestic First Class isn't the height of luxury, but it's better than Economy in the way that a night in a two-and-a-half-star roadside hotel with an Applebee's across the road beats a night on the couch with cold pizza. For no additional charge over the Economy fare I purchased, I'll take it.

Portland International Airport is famous for the carpet in its concourses; what at first seems like a random geometric pattern is actually the angle created by the intersection of two the airport's runways. While it's a cool concept, the carpet makes pulling one's roll-aboard suitcase a bit more difficult. This has to be another lesson about how dragging possessions around with you is a bad thing. In any case, PDX has a bag storage room; unlike the one at Seattle-Tacoma International Airport just up I-5, this one doesn't also store freshly-caught fish from Alaska, so there's a ten-point advantage for Portland.

Portland's public rail transit network is less a subway/heavy rail system like those of New York and Chicago, and more a trolley system like the one in Salt Lake City. The Metropolitan Area Express, or MAX, is a cheap, if not exceptionally quick, way to get from the airport to downtown.

I disembarked east of the Willamette River (downtown proper being to the west of the river, which flows northward into the Columbia River and then to the Pacific Ocean) with the intention of visiting Kidd's Toy Museum. The roadsideamerica.com review for this establishment describes it this way:

"Its exterior is a metal door with a peephole, smack in the middle of a windowless industrial building… its lone sign is a sheet of paper taped to the door. At its bottom is written, 'Please Knock.'"

Alas, when I arrived, I found a second sign tape to the door below the first:

"CLOSED for REPAIRS. Sorry for the inconvenience."

Darnitall. I'd been so eager to inspect their collections of vintage cast-iron mechanical banks (many of them now considered quite racist), Kewpie dolls, Winnie the Poohs (Winnies the Pooh?), and so forth. Another time, perhaps the place won't be CLOSED for REPAIRS.

Portland is awash with t-shirts, bumper stickers, and other forms of signage imploring anyone and everyone to "Keep Portland Weird". Though the slogan was apparently adapted from that of Austin, Texas, it fits here quite nicely. Seemingly every third person I passed had dyed his or her hair some unnatural shade of purple or green or yellow, or perhaps shaved it all off in favor of coloring with permanent markers.

Speaking of "awash", it was raining in Portland. I'd brought my umbrella with me, but that only did a limited amount of good. Below the waist, and especially below the knees, I was awash in Portland's famous rainwater; in hindsight, this was good preparation for Vietnam. Heading toward the cathedral, I walked across the historic Hawthorne Bridge, which is the oldest vertical-lift bridge functioning in America today, and a major thoroughfare for cars, buses, bicycles, and pedestrians. Despite the rain, I relished the experience of walking across, inspecting the lift mechanism from various angles, and then trying to photograph the entire bridge from a distance.

If this were a work of fiction, you can be sure the bridge would be a metaphor; this still being non-fiction, I can assure you it's merely a really cool bridge. That said, two things began to happen when I crossed the Willamette River:

First, I noticed that the bottoms of my feet were wet, indicating that my aging tennis shoes were no longer keeping the water out. And second, I was getting multiple messages on my phone about some sort of trouble with the Metro in DC. Mind you, I've had wet feet before, and the DC Metro has certainly had problems before, but this was getting interesting.

#justpassingthrough

On Monday there'd been a fire involving some underground cables, and the new management of WMATA was planning a systemwide shutdown of the DC Metro on Wednesday for inspections and repairs. This was remarkable, to be sure, but hardly unbelievable to those of us who regularly use the Metro and endure the planned and unplanned service interruptions. Still, so many people were contacting me, some of them twice when I didn't respond right away, that I grew concerned about my phone's battery life. I needed the device for navigation, photography, social media posts, professional communications, and whatever problems I might need to solve. And really, what did people expect me to do about the DC Metro closure from Portland, Oregon?

On further reflection, I realized that my friends were trying to be charitable and help someone they thought would become a stranded traveler. And I reflected on the false sense of intimacy that can be created by social media, wherein a post viewable to over a thousand people shows up in your news feed, and you think it's your problem to solve, your hurt feeling to assuage, your misunderstanding to correct. I tried to maintain that atmosphere of appreciation while conserving phone battery, and that wasn't easy; I simply didn't enjoy being asked for minute-by-minute updates on my thinking about how I would travel the last 8 miles tomorrow of a 3800-mile journey home. I'm a grown-up and a seasoned traveler; for their entertainment, I would post the details in nearly real time, as usual, but I didn't have time for lots of unnecessary personalized updates. To top it off, even the airline sent an e-mail about the Metro closure.

Salt Lake City might act like is has the "Pioneer" market cornered, but Portland was the destination of the Oregon Trail, made famous to my generation by the early computer game. How much of my childhood was spent deciding whether to caulk the wagon and float it across or to try to ford the river? And how many times did Betty Lou die of dysentery while we struggled with the implications of the caulk-or-ford decision? At any rate, the public displays around Portland reflected this (small-p) pioneer heritage. For example, Chapman Square is named for William Chapman, a Virginia native and lawyer who represented the Iowa territory in the U.S. House of Representatives before arriving in Portland in 1850, where he served in the Oregon territorial legislature. A statue of the Chapman family, with a wagon wheel backdrop, stands in the urban park made from land he sold to the city. Apparently none of them died of dysentery en route.

There are other statues in Portland. Perhaps the most famous is "Portlandia", a 38-foot high sculpture of trident-wielding woman kneeling sneakily above the entrance to the Portland Building near Chapman Square. One estimate states that the woman would be 50 feet tall if she stood up, making her the second-largest hammered copper statue in the United States. (If you're wondering, the largest is the Statue of Liberty, which I'd seen from the top of One World Trade Center two Tuesdays earlier.) Next to this is a plaque with a 1985 poem by Roger Talney:

She kneels down,
and from the quietness
of copper
reaches out.

We take that stillness
into ourselves,
and somewhere
deep in the earth
our breath

becomes her city.
If she could speak
this is what
she would say:

#justpassingthrough

Follow that breath,
Home is the journey we make.
This is how the world
knows where we are.

Perhaps you can read this poem and be filled with some insight to the enterprise of pilgrimage, but all I could think was "Keep Portland Weird."

It kept raining. I was soaked for the duration, so I decided this was just a small difficulty on a pilgrim's journey and pressed onward toward my goal. But first, as any book-loving pilgrim to Portland can tell you, would have to come the obligatory stop at Powell's World of Books. If you live in Portland, perhaps you visit Powell's to buy books, but if you're a visitor to town with no pressing literary needs, you might drop in just to gawk at the books. That's what I'd done four years earlier on the Aleatoric Road Trip. According to the store's website, Powell's "is the largest new and used bookshop in the world, occupying an entire city block and housing approximately one million books." It has "nine color-coded rooms and over 3500 different sections…" You get the idea. The place is huge, and it even has guided tours every Sunday. And it's true that they have something for every interest. There are many books on music history and geography, plus a maps-and-travel section that puts Barnes & Noble to shame. Funny thing, though: the "Christianity" shelf was empty, hidden behind yellow caution tape and a "pardon our dust" sign. Being a pilgrim and having to carry everything with me, I didn't need to buy anything; I'd learned my lesson three years earlier when I asked about the hymnal section on a visit to Hay-on-Wye, Wales, the self-styled used bookshop capital of the world, and ended up having to mail thirty hymnals home.

From Powell's, I walked a few blocks west, passing over the I-405 Stadium Freeway (not to be confused with the I-405 San Diego freeway in Los Angeles) on my way to the real destination. St. Mary's Cathedral of the Immaculate Conception is at least the third church to have stood on the site (the second having been destroyed by floodwaters in 1894, just nine years after it was built to replace the original, smaller structure).

Unlike the cathedrals of Providence and Salt Lake City and Chicago, Portland's cathedral is not widely known for its liturgical music. Rather, Portland's main contribution to Catholic liturgical music is through the Oregon Catholic Press (OCP) publishing house, which is responsible for the newsprint-quality "Today's Missal" and "Breaking Bread" your local parish might have in its pews, as well as hymnals such as "Glory and Praise", "Journeysongs", and "Flor y Canto", and the "Respond & Acclaim" psalter. Nearly all of these are throwaway paperback resources good for the current season or year only, guaranteeing a steady flow of business from pastors and music directors who want a packaged, ready-to-use resource for their parishes.

To my way of thinking, the variable musical quality here is the secondary issue, though still important. The main problem, at least with some hymnals from OCP and its main competitors, is the endless tinkering with tried-and-true hymn texts in the name of eliminating gender-specific or archaic language. Among many of us who want Holy Mother Church to serve better musical side dishes at the Eucharistic banquet, there was a hope that the 2013 appointment of Archbishop Alexander Sample to the see of Portland would lead to some improvement and/or house-cleaning at OCP; Sample had overseen some wholesale, back-to-basics liturgical music reforms in his previous assignment as Bishop of Marquette in the Upper Peninsula of Michigan.

After Mass I commenced the long journey home, but if I thought the train ride from Providence would be my only surprise on this series of Lenten journeys, I was wrong.

With the aforementioned changes to my return flight schedule, prudence allowed me only a brief few minutes for dinner. Since it was along my path back to MAX, I chose to eat at Sizzle Pie, diagonally across from Powell's, which Google described as a "vegan-friendly pizzeria with late hours". Their menu includes items such as "Napalm Breath" and "New

Maps Out of Hell" and "Six Degrees of Kevin Bacon" and (most audaciously) "It's Always Sunny in Portland". I chose a slice of "Spiral Tap", consisting of "creamy caramelized onion spread, house marinara red sauce, and a light dusting of nutritional yeast". Being soaked to the core and hungry and in a slight rush, I'll admit I chose this pizza based on its distinctive appearance, with the onion spread and marinara forming concentric circles on the display pie. I washed all this down with a beer. I don't like beer. I dislike beer so much that, one Lent, as a penance I took on drinking beer at the times when I might normally drink wine or a cocktail. Today's experience did nothing to change my opinion.

Solid and liquid penance fuel having been consumed, I rode MAX back to the airport and retrieved my overnight bag from the storage shop. Instead of heading to my usual airline, I found the boarding area for the Alaska Airlines shuttle service to Seattle. Alaska is the leading carrier within the Pacific Northwest, and offers about 25 nonstop flights every day just between Seattle and Portland. My flight, like most of the others, was on a Dash 8-Q400 propeller plane. Whatever drying of my clothes might have happened while I sat in the terminal studying the weird carpet was undone during the walk from terminal to boarding door. The flight itself was quite bumpy, which is what happens when a small plane flies at low altitude through a rainstorm near mountains.

The transfer back to the regular airline at Sea-Tac involved lots of walking at a time when I would surely have preferred to be in bed. Settling into my First Class seat on the 737 heading to Miami (status-based upgrades for the win!), I began to get that sinking feeling that something was amiss. While I tried valiantly to stay awake despite the effects of vegan pizza and beer in my belly and despite the thorough sogginess of my feet, the clock ticked well past the scheduled 11:15 p.m. departure time. By 11:45, my connection would be in jeopardy and I might miss my planned flight to DCA. Given the Metro closure and the fact I had a Wednesday evening rehearsal I shouldn't miss, this was not a situation I wanted to leave to the airline to solve. I took out my secret pilgrimage weapon – my smartphone – and checked out my other options to get home.

One option would be to walk off this plane and get on another one heading east (say, through Chicago or Dallas or Charlotte), but this was the last redeye departure with seats available, so I'd need to stick with the flight I was on. Next, I looked at later connecting flights from MIA to DCA tomorrow, and saw one leaving Miami at 12:55 p.m. A quick phone call to the airline's special reservations line for top-tier elite flyers (at that time of night, the notoriously competent Honolulu office was taking the calls) quickly got my reservation changed from the 9:20 a.m. MIA-DCA departure, which I'd likely miss, to that 12:55 p.m. flight. As I hung up, I remembered from a previous visit the convenient location of a Payless shoe store in downtown Miami, and made a mental note to pick up a new pair of shoes while I was there. Isn't it odd what we remember in our final moments of wakefulness?

The plane did eventually take off from Seattle. I removed my soggy shoes when I heard the double-ding at 10,000 feet, and was conked out by 12,000 feet. Awakening an instant later, I saw the Everglades out my window.

After a cool, rainy day in Portland and a short night's sleep, sunny South Florida was a shock to the senses in every wonderful way. Landing time was such that I might or might not barely have made the original connecting flight, but that was rainwater under the lift bridge. Next stop was the airline's business lounge, where I took a shower and replaced my rain-soaked Portland clothes with some dry ones, and grabbed a light breakfast from the buffet. Heading downtown by the Miami Metro's orange line, I found my way to that Payless shoe store, exactly where I remembered it from last summer's day visit (not otherwise described in this book). They had the size and style of supportive tennis shoes I wanted, just like the ones I'd been wearing except without the leaks that had soaked my feet.

#justpassingthrough

After a brief stop at the Gesu to pass through the holy door (which I would do again in a few months when, this time en route to Brazil, I would again find myself unexpectedly loose in Miami) and perhaps also for Confession, it was time to return to the airport and to Washington.

My flight (which, happily, included lunch, meaning that the airline had now provided 4 of my 5 meals on this pilgrimage) parked at DCA around 3:00 p.m. If the Metro had been running, I would have ridden it home to Little Rome, ditched my bag, and headed back downtown to St. Matthew's Cathedral in time for 5:30 p.m. Mass and then the evening's choir rehearsal. With the Metro out of operation, my plan was to splurge on a taxi ride home, get Sylvia the Silver Sentra, and drive to St. Matthew's.

However, I wasn't the only one with that type of backup plan, and the line of would-be taxi customers extended in the door and around the baggage claim area, meandering like a suitcase that had been sent to the wrong airport. Next, I considered which of my area friends or family might like to pick me up on the beautiful spring day whose warm sunlight was coming in through the terminal's floor-to-ceiling windows. Finally, I looked at the brand-new shoes on my feet, and decided that since this was a pilgrimage and pilgrimages are supposed to be hard, I would walk.

Pulling my roll-a-board suitcase filled with rainwater-soaked clothes, I exited DCA's Terminal C and walked north past the end of the terminal and through the employee parking lot. I kept moving past the mini-airliners parked just a few feet away behind a tall fence covered with signs threatening the swiftness of the terrible swift sword of justice for anyone who so much as thinks about trying to get through. The walk-and-bike Mt. Vernon Trail then took me along the George Washington Memorial Parkway past the approach end of Runway 15, where one of those mini-airliners flew about 50 feet over my head. What a rush!

The path winds its way into a grassy park known as Gravelly Point, directly under the final approach path for Runway 19, the main runway in use on nice days with winds from the south. I may have paused a few minutes to enjoy the unique atmosphere of outdoor fun and games that's punctuated every minute or two with the roar of low-flying jet engines. This place is top-notch free entertainment for humans of all sizes, including some small ones in my extended family.

After Gravelly Point, the Mt. Vernon Trail enters a wooded area along the Potomac River, more distant from the roar of road and air traffic. It continues under the series of bridges carrying the Metro's Yellow Line (well, not today…), Amtrak, Virginia Railway Express, and freight trains, I-395, and US 1 across the river. The last of these bridges also carries the walk/bike path, and that was my route back into the District of Columbia. The trail winds behind the Jefferson Memorial and the Tidal Basin. In a few weeks, this place would be packed with tourists trying to get that perfect shot of the cherry blossoms, a gift from Japan that just keeps on giving each year.

It's possible that my arms might have been getting sore from wheeling my bag next to me, and it's also possible that the clothes I'd so happily donned in Miami were becoming soaked with sweat. But I didn't care. This was what I had to do to make it to work on time, and it came with the bonus of a slow-motion tour of some beautiful places.

My path took me across the National Mall just west of the Washington Monument, past the White House, up 17th Street, through Farragut Square, and finally up Connecticut Avenue and around the corner to St. Matthew's Cathedral. I carried my suitcase up the steps where the remains of President Kennedy had entered for his funeral Mass 53 years earlier, passed through the holy door, and slipped into a pew just as the celebrant entered for 5:30 p.m. Mass. The walk from DCA had been nearly five miles, and the timing had worked precisely to the minute.

It was only after Mass, when I left my suitcase in the choir room to find dinner nearby, that I reflected on my journey of the past thirty-six hours (through five states and DC, through three holy doors, through rain and sun). I gave thanks for the providence that had led me home from Providence and the grace that led me safely home to DC despite the best efforts of my airline and WMATA. But mostly, I focused on the liturgical music that my colleagues and I were preparing for the upcoming celebration of Our Lord's great pilgrimage into Jerusalem for his Passion, Death, and Resurrection the following week.

Mistakes

One cold March night in 2015, after a rollicking good time of a choir rehearsal in Little Rome, eight or ten of us went for an even more rollicking good time after rehearsal at a new local eating and drinking establishment. The service was pretty incompetent: orders were messed up, waitstaff disappeared for significant periods of time, and water glasses went unfilled for far too long. You've had that kind of experience at some point, no doubt.

At long last, the server appeared with a pitcher of ice water. Standing directly behind me, she paused to ask a question of someone at the other end of the table. In so doing, she forgot about the full pitcher of ice water in her hand. Fortunately for her, it wasn't full for long, because most of its contents were now on my head, down my back, and in my denim-clad lap. I tried to enjoy my friends' company while soaked with ice-cold water, but this was no longer a rollicking good time for me. After a few minutes, I excused myself to walk the three blocks home.

Sodden and shivering despite what I'd thought would be more-than-adequate bundling, I had to stop and wait for a signal to change so I could safely cross the street. Like any self-respecting American in such a situation, I whipped out my smart phone and scrolled through Facebook, and I couldn't quite believe what I was seeing: my airline was offering Business Class tickets from Washington to Beijing for $462.00. This was utterly incomprehensible. Transpacific business class costs between two and ten thousand dollars. What was the catch?

Just before the walk signal illuminated, I read far enough in the Facebook post to see the words "mistake fare". Apparently, somebody who wouldn't be working for the airline much longer had been entering new business class fares for various U.S.-to-China markets and forgot to type all the digits before publishing the fares and clocking out for the day. Mistake fares notoriously don't last very long, for obvious reasons, and suddenly the cold wind blowing on my soggy clothes wasn't my primary impetus for hurrying home.

Within a few minutes, I'd booked myself a ticket from Washington to Beijing for a few days during the Easter Octave. My calendar was tight, and since I'd be there for only about 36 hours, I wouldn't need to get a visa, as my understanding was that China would let Americans in for up to 72 hours visa-free. Except when I looked into this further, that visa exemption only applies when you're arriving to China from one country and departing to a different other country within 72 hours. So, if I'd booked the trip with a connection on the way home in, say, Japan, I would have qualified for Transit-Without-Visa, but I didn't. Oops.

If you have ever had a "special case" requiring multiple visits to the Department of Motor Vehicles, you have the experiential knowledge to understand what a royal pain it was to get a Chinese tourist visa. The application requires you to list your profession and your employer. It would seem the Chinese don't like visitors who are freelance workers because they think we're either unemployed and taking advantage of the welfare state, or else we're spies, as if the CIA wouldn't furnish a better cover story. And they definitely don't like unmarried men in the employ of the Catholic Church because we're probably in the business of religious subversion of the atheist Communist Chinese government.

So after being turned away once because the photo on my application didn't meet the requirements, I was turned away from the Chinese consulate on the outskirts of Georgetown a second time with instructions to return with a letter from a priest stating that I would not be going to China as a missionary.

Ponder that: They don't trust the Church because it's subversive, but they'll trust you're not being subversive only if the Church says so.

An amused priest was gracious enough to sign such a letter. After enough visits to the Chinese consulate that the security officer started allowing me to bypass his checkpoint, I was the proud holder of a ten-year, multi-entry tourist visa for the People's Republic of China.

Mistakes

(On my way home from Brazil a little over a year later, I lost the passport containing this visa. The passport was replaced with moderate time and expense, but I can only imagine what would happen if I tried to obtain a new Chinese visa when there's another one unexpired out there somewhere.)

#

As it would turn out, Easter Sunday and Easter Monday were two of the most upsetting days of my life. I came face to face with a grave evil and needed to make difficult and potentially costly decisions about how to proceed. In that light, departure on Easter Tuesday for my lifetime first transpacific trip, with the hours of in-cabin detachment from the outside world it would afford, was fortuitous. I could have the time I needed, unbothered by anyone, to contemplate what I'd encountered and discern what to do next.

That sunny Tuesday, I boarded the 737 at DCA, taking my place in the jet's First Class cabin. Though I had booked a Business Class ticket at the mistake fare, I quickly applied upgrade certificates to First for the entire journey. The hop to Chicago went quickly; after a three-hour layover, the flight to Beijing boarded from O'Hare's Gate K19, a gate I've used a few times, and dubbed the "Widowmaker" gate after the 2002 Harrison Ford movie about a bad day on a Soviet nuclear submarine.

As I took seat 3J aboard the Triple Seven, I marveled that this First Class cabin was considered out-of-date and would soon be replaced. The seat swiveled through three positions: straight forward for takeoff and landing; angled toward the tray table and TV screen for relaxing and dining in flight; and facing away from the aisle toward the window and a small desk, office-in-the-sky style. And yes, of course, it reclined into a fully-flat bed. There was in-seat power, but these cabins were so old that they had DC power outlets, like the cigarette lighter jacks in your car. I'd brought my phone's car charger for just this reason.

#justpassingthrough

The 6580-mile flight from Chicago to Beijing passed fairly quickly, considering it was the longest flight of my life to date. Departure was Tuesday at 5:20 p.m., unusually late in the day for a North America-to-Asia flight. Due to the marvels of time travel and with the assistance of the International Date Line, arrival was scheduled for 8:10 p.m. Wednesday. Thus, dinner service was a protracted and central part of the experience.

First, there was a beverage service with warm nuts. At this point I pulled out my personal television screen, whose programming was helpfully prefaced with a video describing how to pull out my personal television screen. The appetizer was ginger beef with enoki mushrooms (skinny things you might mistake for midget squids) and cilantro pesto. Next came the creamy kale soup with parmesan croutons, which was definitely the tastiest thing I've ever had with "kale" in the name. The salad was seasonal greens with hearts of palm and sweet and spicy pecans and poppy seed dressing. Somehow I still had room for the main course, a grilled beef filet with thyme jus, blue cheese potato gratin, sautéed spinach, and mushrooms, and then for the fruit-and-cheese plate. Each course was washed down with an appropriate beverage. About three hours after takeoff, as the faint light of day illuminated the snowy shores of Hudson Bay, I changed into the inflight pajamas (provided to all First Class passengers) and turned my seat into a bed for a few hours' sleep.

I woke up in time for the mid-flight meal service, a Tuscan turkey sandwich with penne pasta salad and fresh fruit, and then slept another couple hours. Before arrival, a third meal was served, Char Siu duck with lo mein noodles, salad, and a piece of red velvet cake. Yes, somebody had really screwed up by publishing this mistake fare, but if I hadn't had the water dumped all over me by mistake, I wouldn't have been able to enjoy this trip; two wrongs don't make a right, but two lemons can certainly be made into strong lemonade. And as I sat up and changed back into my grown-up clothes for arrival, the sun set brilliantly over the Gobi Desert of Mongolia.

Mistakes

Deplaning, I was nervous about passport control, but the officer just flipped through my passport book, saw that I had a valid tourist visa, and placed a PRC entry stamp in the armpit of the Statue of Liberty. Like many cities, Beijing has an express train running from the airport to connect with the subway system in the city center. Taking that express train to Dongxiemen Station, I easily found my way to the correct train to take me to Tian'anmen East station, and from there it would be a short walk to my hotel.

As with most of the city-center hotels I've used around the world, I chose this one using online search tools, with regard for price, location, wi-fi availability, and little else. In this case, I would only be there two nights, so ease of access from the airport was paramount. Since there hadn't been time to learn to speak Mandarin, and certainly not to read it, I took the extra precaution this time of carrying a printed Google map of the hotel's location on the same page as its name and address in English and Mandarin. This would have been useful, for example, in case my flight had arrived several hours late and the subway had shut down for the night and I'd needed to take a cab to my hotel whose driver spoke no English – all difficulties within the realm of possibility and experience.

So, on my first visit to Asia, in my first Communist country, in the darkness of evening (it was after 9:30 p.m. and the streets were mostly quiet), I confidently strode off the subway at Tian'anmen East, my lone piece of luggage rolling behind me. Surfacing and taking a moment to get my bearings, I walked east along the north side of Chang'an Avenue to the location pinpointed on my paper map. And there was no hotel.

I continued another couple of blocks through darkened, almost-placid Beijing, and then returned to the subway station to try again. Did I have the right subway station? Yes, the English signage there confirmed it. Had I correctly selected found east after surfacing at night? Yes, because the street pattern wouldn't have matched any other orientation. And then I realized Google was one of the websites blocked by the Chinese government, so whoever plotted the hotel at that location had done so from outside China. Oh, boy.

Having little to lose, and not getting any particular sense of danger from my surroundings, I approached the taxi stand nearby. The first man spoke to me in Mandarin, and I shrugged to indicate my unfamiliarity with the language (openly admitting such a vulnerability to a stranger is a calculated risk travelers must sometimes take) and then showed him my printout. He looked at it quizzically for a moment, and then his face lit up: "AH!" He gestured for me to follow him, and he led me past several idling taxis to his bicycle rickshaw.

The enterprising man pedaled me, and the bag on my lap, about a mile east along Chang'an Avenue, right to the gate of the Capital Hotel Beijing. I made sure to tip him well. The clerk who checked me in spoke no English, but this was no trouble that wasn't solved by presenting my passport and a credit card. It really IS amazing how much business can be transacted with gestures and props and a little bit of motivation!

The room was as comfortable as most I'd stayed in, but I wondered whether I was being spied upon. You laugh, but it's reported that the Chinese police monitor hotel rooms for illicit activity. I wasn't involved with drugs or prostitution or overthrowing the government or converting everybody to Catholicism, so I didn't really worry, but if friends at home sometimes wondered whether I was engaged in some sort of espionage work, it wasn't so far-fetched for the Chinese government to think so.

What I did know is that the Chinese government bans Facebook in its territory. I paid for a VPN, supposedly a way to circumvent such restrictions and assure the outside world of my existence, but it wasn't working. I didn't necessarily mind being out of contact, but since I'd assured friends and family I would have Facebook access, I didn't want anybody contacting the U.S. Embassy and having them try to visit me at my hotel. That could have gotten pretty awkward pretty fast.

Yes, staying incommunicado had serious potential to go downhill, so I sent my sister a text message, and she dutifully posted the message to my

Mistakes

Facebook wall to reassure any nervous-nellie types that communication was my only unexpected challenge, and that I would post photos on my return to the USA.

#

Despite having flipped my body clock, I was ready for bed and slept a good five or six hours. When I awoke, I did what every tourist does on his first full day in atheist, Communist China. I went to Mass.

The Catholic Church in China is a curious thing. The government officially bans it, and there are priests and bishops living (metaphorically or perhaps literally) underground and ministering Christ's sacraments in real fear of arrest, torture, and execution. It's not that the Communists find the doctrine of the Trinity, transubstantiation, absolution, or whatever, so distasteful; it's the matter of allegiance to the Holy See that's a bee in their bonnet. Along those lines, there is a Chinese Patriotic Catholic Association (CPCA). Its bishops are appointed by the state, and its activities are monitored by Big Brother.

The tricky part, for the Catholic visiting China, is figuring out whether the CPCA's sacraments are valid. Being officially out of Communion with Rome, the official answer would be that, no, CPCA's sacraments are not valid. But it's an open secret that many of the CPCA's clergy are, in fact, validly ordained and in clandestine communion with Rome and the apostolic succession that connects today's bishops (and those they ordain as priests and deacons) to Christ and the twelve Apostles. As a visitor, you just can't tell which ones those are.

What is generally agreed is that, as a Westerner, if you somehow learned the location of a clandestine Catholic church in communion with Rome and you went there, you would be endangering lives and the Church's mission. So if you want to attend Mass in China, you go to one of the state-sanctioned churches and hope the sacrament is valid, which it might very well be.

#justpassingthrough

With those parameters in mind, I decided I would attend Mass at 6:00 a.m. at Beijing's Cathedral of the Immaculate Conception. It would be celebrated in Latin, in the Extraordinary Form. Since the Ordinary Form options were in Mandarin, this seemed like the most sensible choice to me. Much ink has been spilled about the glory of the Extraordinary Form, or else its dated repugnance, and I don't mean to wade far into that diabolical war here. Suffice it to say that on those days when I understood virtually no spoken or written communication in the local language, I was glad for the universality of the Traditional Latin Mass. It truly was Home away from home.

#

Easter Thursday having been celebrated with such extraordinary solemnity, I began an ambitious one-day sightseeing itinerary. Until departure day, I had planned to spend half of today walking myself all over Beijing and a half day visiting the Great Wall of China via bus tour (with the bus ride creating a natural break in the walking), but the tour organizer e-mailed while I was in the air to cancel my reservation because of some holiday or another, so rather than scramble to find another ride to the Great Wall I decided Beijing would supply all the necessary diversions for one day. I knew I would be flirting with collapse due to fatigue and jet lag, but I could spend most of tomorrow in First Class, so it didn't matter so much. I just had to push through.

Disembarking from the subway at Tian'anmen East once again, I used the pedestrian tunnel to cross under the street and join the queue for entrance to Tian'anmen Square. There was a maze of security lines to get in, and I patiently waited my turn. Now, I've been through security lines to get into airport concourses, sports arenas, government buildings, museums, and so forth, but until today the only public square I'd entered that required a security screening was the vicinity of the Western Wall in Jerusalem.

Mistakes

In contrast to that relatively compact place of prayer, Tian'anmen Square is distinguished chiefly by its size: it's supposed to be the world's largest urban outdoor gathering place. Most non-Chinese became familiar with it in 1989, when a large group of student protesters staged demonstrations in the square. What were their grievances? The students were protesting inflation, inadequate education, restrictions on political engagement, and the one-party rule of the post-Mao Communist Party. Up to a million students gathered in Tian'anmen Square that June (did I mention it's a big place?), and the Chinese government wasn't having it. Premier Li Peng called the students terrorists and counterrevolutionaries, which always a great way to convince people you're not a totalitarian dictator, and persuaded the Politburo to crack down on them with military force. From there, it got pretty messy, and the People's Liberation Army tried to roll into Tian'anmen Square in the wee hours of June 4th. Students formed roadblocks; troops shot at them and killed more than a few. Civilians heretofore uninvolved attacked the troops, and the government used those military casualties as an excuse to escalate further against the students, and so on and so forth.

The most famous image from that tumultuous period – indeed, one of the most famous news images of my lifetime – was taken on June 5, 1989, as the protesters were leaving the Tian'anmen Square. When a column of tanks left the square, more or less pushing the protesters, a lone young man stood in front of one of the tanks, forcing the vehicle (much less maneuverable than a human pedestrian) to stop for a conversation between the brave blocker and the tank's driver. I later learned that this incident had taken place on Chang'an Avenue, where I had ridden the bicycle rickshaw the previous night.

Today, Tian'anmen Square was much more orderly and peaceful. Groups of tourists, mostly domestic if appearances were any guide, huddled here, there, and everywhere. In the middle stands the Monument to the People's Heroes. To the west is the Great Hall of the People, housing China's National People's Congress. This 2924-member organization is the largest legislative body in the world, with the power to make laws, oversee government affairs, and elect major government officials. One thing it lacks is the power to say no; in its entire history, nobody can remember the National People's Congress voting down a government proposal.

On the east flank sits the National Museum of China, which I would have visited given another day or two in town. To the south is the Mausoleum of Mao Zedong, founder of the People's Republic of China. The line to get in was quite long, so I didn't bother.

I spent a few minutes wandering amidst the crowds, taking it all in. Tian'anmen Square is ginormous, but once you get past that, it's really just a bunch of concrete surrounded by ugly buildings where ugly things are done.

Turning my back on Chairman Mao in his mausoleum, something I only got away with because he's dead, I walked north toward a gate. Over the gate hung a giant portrait of... Chairman Mao! So really, you can't turn your back on Mao in Tian'anmen Square, not because of the laws of men, but because of the laws of geography and geometry. If the Chinese ever do take over the world, it will be by sheer cunning, of which this was a fine example.

Mao's portrait hung over the central portal of the Gate of Heaven ("Tian'anmen") and in front of that portal stood a solitary PLA soldier. I paused for a few moments to wonder how that soldier got picked for that duty. Was it a look-a-like contest? A lost bet? An honor stemming from family connections? A punishment? I would probably have a more interesting story to tell you if I'd just wandered up and asked the guy, but he didn't look like the extroverted type who was into casual conversation about stuff like that.

Passing through the Gate of Heaven (how often do you get to begin a paragraph with words like that?), I was next confronted with an array of ticket-purchasing booths for groups, individuals, pre-purchasers, or walk-ups, all labeled in Mandarin. I guessed correctly on the second try, forked over some yuan, and continued on my long march. There was the opportunity to rent an audio guide in any of thirty-five languages from Finnish to Esperanto, but I opted against it. Continuing across bridges and up some ramps, soon I was in the heart of the Forbidden City. Given the sheer size of the crowds here, I wondered whether "Forbidden City" might be euphemistic or downright ironic, and then I puzzled over whether "Gate of Heaven" might be in a similar category. This was, for my western mind, a great leap forward in understanding China.

On the Forbidden City's 180 acres sit nearly a thousand buildings. Here, from 1420 to 1912, reigned the emperors of the Ming and Qing dynasties. Here, too, had lived their families, and from here had all of China been administered and ruled. Now officially the Palace Museum (part of whose collection went to Taipei in 1949 with Chiang Kai-Shek and the Nationalists), this is one of the world's most-visited tourist attractions. With 16 million visitors in 2016, nearly as many people visited here as entered Walt Disney World's Magic Kingdom. And at a tiny fraction of the price!

On passing through the second gate, or Meridian Gate, I found myself in the open-air Outer Court. It's not as big as Tian'anmen Square (literally no place is), but it could hold many thousands of people who came to witness imperial coronations and royal family weddings. You might call it the Westminster Abbey of the Ming Dynasty. Towering over the Outer Court is the Hall of Supreme Harmony, instantly recognizable to movie watchers worldwide. It houses the ceremonial throne room used when the emperor wanted to be seen reigning. Leading from the Outer Court up to throne level are two staircases flanking a ramp in the center. You might guess correctly that the ramp was reserved for use only by the emperor; you might be surprised that it is still off-limits to the public today, even though there's been no emperor for over a century.

After battling the crowds for a glimpse of the throne, in which my height was to my advantage, I walked back down a staircase and continued behind the Hall of Supreme Harmony. The Forbidden City is constructed primarily of wood, ornately carved and painstakingly bracketed together without screws or nails. Most of the roofs are painted yellow, a color reserved for the imperial family. Of course, fire is a particular danger when buildings are made of wood (see: London in 1666), and the imperial architects surrounded many of the buildings with giant, ceremonial-looking water jugs that functioned as fire hydrants.

Shortly, I came to the Hall of Central Harmony, once called the Hall of Central Extremity (I'm still scratching my head at that last one… what's a central extremity?), used by the Emperor to rest before and during ceremonies. Over the throne hangs an inscription that translates:

Doing Nothing

Leaving behind the central palaces and the great throngs of tourists with their selfie-sticks, I meandered east to the Hall of Clocks and Watches, and wondered how there came to be such a place. The answer lies in the fine art of diplomacy. In former times, when an ambassador was posted to a new foreign capital, the custom was to present a gift to the host monarch. Apparently word got around Europe that the Chinese emperor thought fancy clocks were the bee's knees, so all the European diplomats tripped over one another to bring His Imperial Majesty the biggest, best-looking, most creative clock of them all. I wandered among mechanical clocks disguised as a sunflower, a rock with ducks swimming in a pond, a lamp carried on a serving-boy's head, an imperial litter, a chest of drawers. All told, this one little museum holds about 300 clocks of Chinese, Japanese, British, French, Swiss, and American origin (among other nationalities).

The Forbidden City is overwhelming in nearly every respect, and after a while I began to feel exhausted from it all. Continuing out the back of the palace complex, I passed through the Imperial Garden, which was in bloom that April day. A sign warns that a certain pile of rocks is "Perilous Hills". The entire area is surrounded by a moat that was built more for fire protection than as a defense against invasion.

#

Just off the northwest corner of the Forbidden City's moat, I came to the gate of Beihai Park, which surrounds the "Northern Sea". (Actually, "Beihai" means "Northern Sea", just as "Beijing" means "Northern Capital". Congratulations! You just learned Mandarin!). This former imperial recreational park was meant to evoke the scenery and landmarks of other parts of China; built as it is around a small inland lake, you'd be forgiven for making the comparison to EPCOT Center. Mercifully, again, the admission price was much lower. Here there is an expanse of ornately manicured gardens with an emphasis on brightly colored flora, accessed by pleasantly wide, smooth walkways. There is abundant signage (including signs in English that say "NO SMOCKING") for those who prefer not to stare at their phones to navigate during their stroll in the park. Men in blue coverall maintenance uniforms make their rounds with brooms to keep the walkway clean. If I hadn't gotten so hungry from all my walking (perhaps six miles of it already, and it was only about noon), I might have stayed longer to enjoy the people-watching.

So far, I've described the stark vastness of Tian'anmen Square, the ornate construction of the Forbidden City, and the splendid beauty of Beihai Park. What I haven't mentioned was how difficult it was to breathe in Beijing. The air quality there is simply horrible. Between the traffic congestion and the heavy industry, thick smog is everywhere. In fact, many people walk around wearing surgical masks, and as the day wore on, I began to understand why. The polluted air burns the throat and makes the eyes water.

Still, I hadn't come this far to sit and cry about something as inconsequential as dirty air poisoning my body. Exiting Beihai Park, I continued northward along Longtoujing Street. I was now in a Hutong, a term that technically refers to a narrow street or alley lined with houses. Given the rapid pace of government-directed development, this sort of neighborhood without soulless high-rise buildings and arrow-straight ten-lane avenues is becoming a rarity, so much that tourist guidebooks suggest "touring" a hutong (defined as the neighborhood rather than just one alley) to get a feel for old Beijing.

Maybe I was in the wrong hutong, but this seemed less like a tourist activity and more like a pleasant walk in the neighborhood. Here, laundry hung on clotheslines and kids rode bikes and people could rest on park benches next to propaganda statues of PLA soldiers. The government can't put human eyes on everyone, I reasoned, so they figure people will be cowed into submission with a few smiling seated statues.

Speaking of submission to the Communists, I next happened to go past the Chinese Patriotic Catholic Bishops' Conference headquarters. At home in Little Rome, I live a few blocks from the United States Conference of Catholic Bishops, where there's a famous statue of Jesus outside; he's supposed to be extending his hand to give a blessing, but really just looks like he's hailing a taxi. There's no such statue in Beijing.

By now, I was seriously feeling hungry, and this mainly residential neighborhood didn't look like a promising place to do anything about that, at least until I walked past a building where two people appeared in the doorway and greeted me with, "Beef?"

I guess I wasn't blending in very well with the locals. So much for being a spyvangelist.

They used gestures to invite me inside, and showed me a rudimentary picture menu with prices. Pointing to one picture, I decided to trust but verify: "Beef?" "Beef!" came the response. A few minutes later, there appeared on my table a plate piled with small pieces of thinly-sliced beef, cooked medium or so, salted, with a side of cheap wooden chopsticks. Rather more difficult was obtaining a bottle of water. After several frustrating attempts at verbal communication, I gestured toward the refrigerator and they opened it to allow me to take the beverage of my choice.

I paid and then said thank you in every language in which I could remember the word (Mandarin not being one of them), smiled, and left. Hunger problem solved.

And in about a half mile, I finally boarded the subway and returned to the hotel for a little rest, staying for about an hour and a half to sleep and breathe some slightly less polluted air.

#

My feet and legs were still quite sore when I awoke, but at least my mind was refreshed and I could stay alert for the rest of the day. The trouble was deciding what to do with about three hours until dinner time. Having spent the first part of the day north and west of the hotel, now I would aim for geographic diversity and ride east and south a couple miles to the Temple of Heaven.

The Forbidden City is and was many things: imperial capital, imperial family residence, gathering place for imperial spectacles. But it was not designed as a place of worship. The emperors of China were regarded as "Sons of Heaven", in effect vicars of heaven on earth, with dominion over all earthly matters on heaven's behalf. In addition to the roles of prophet and king, the Ming and Qing emperors fulfilled a priestly role, offering sacrifices to heaven on behalf of the people for this or that intention.

In my description of the emperors' religious function in Chinese society, you might have noticed that I interpolated Christian terminology into a decidedly non-Christian story. Mostly, that's just how I relate to things. But partly, to my way of thinking, that points to the universal trueness of Truth (Jesus being the Way, the Truth, and the Life) and the reality that Truth, if truly true, can be discovered in sundry ways. In other words, in needing a representative of heaven, the Chinese imperial social/religious structure pointed to the human need for Christ and the Church.

(Note: this is not the same as the universalist heresy, which maintains that there are many forms of truth and that all religions lead equally well to heaven.)

Here at the Temple of Heaven, the emperors performed annual sacrifices for good harvest. Just before winter solstice each year, the emperor and his entourage left the Forbidden City and made a pilgrimage through Beijing to camp on the grounds of the Temple of Heaven, abstaining from meat all the while. On the solstice itself, the emperor would enter the Temple of Heaven and perform the sacrifice, which he was required to do perfectly or else the harvest would be bad that year. No pressure.

At the Forbidden City earlier that day, I had noticed that all the buildings were rectangular, and often strictly square, in their layout. So, too, here at the Temple of Heaven complex (which, at a mile or so square, is about the same size as the City of London), most of the layout was squared, both the buildings and the paths in the surrounding parkland. The Temple building itself, however, is round. That's neither an accident nor a coincidence, since in traditional Chinese thought, heaven is round and limitless while the earth is square and finite. The round temple on the square pedestal thus symbolizes the meeting of earth and heaven, almost like a launch pad.

The micro-design reveals more symbolism than I had time to comprehend: months, days, weeks, the emperor, etc. were all represented in the number of columns here or the number of steps there. Like the buildings in the Forbidden City, the Temple of Heaven's structures were of wood without nails or bolts, brightly colored, and impressive to behold. The elevated plaza, paved with stones, leads to the Temple of Heaven for a half mile. The center walkway was reserved for the emperor, while the sides could be used by common folk. It wasn't precisely clear to me how commoners were supposed to get to the other side. Maybe they never did, not being chickens.

Mistakes

In the surrounding park, locals gathered in small groups for picnics, games, and general relaxation. As the sun got low in the sky, I wandered slowly around the area, not eager to return to the inhumanly-scaled boulevards and their clusters of cars spewing toxic fumes. There was a ton more I wanted to experience of Beijing (museums, food, neighborhoods) but this one day had been quite the eye-opener, even as my jet-lagged body struggled to keep up with my mind.

#

In hindsight, after a brief respite in the hotel, I should have gone to explore another part of the city for dinner. But at the time, I was so completely bushed that I dined in the hotel's restaurant on some sort of chicken-and-vegetable stew. Or maybe it was a stir-fry. I don't remember.

Thursday night was a fitful one, sleep-wise, despite the amount of exercise I'd had, and despite the comfort of my room. I often find this to be true when I travel: the first night I sleep like a rock because I'm so exhausted from the journey, and then the second night my better-rested body realizes it's not sleep time at home and puts up more of a fight. Short of using some kind of pharmaceutical product to induce sleep (alcohol doesn't help either, by the way), I've found no way around the problem except to eat well, get sunlight, exercise my muscles, and be patient.

#

Friday morning dawned bright and smoggy, and I once again attended Latin Mass at the Cathedral of the Immaculate Conception. This time, the lack of the customary photo of Pope Francis bothered me, not because I'm so personally enamored with Francis, but because it points to the difficult state of affairs for the Church in China.

#justpassingthrough

From there, I rode the subway and the airport express line back to Beijing-Capital International Airport, the world's second-busiest for total passenger traffic after (you guessed it!) Atlanta. If this statistic surprised you, remember that in terms of raw population numbers, China's domestic population is four times as large as America's. India's population is set to surpass China's, but Indians are in general less affluent than the Chinese and travel less; their country is also somewhat more compact, meaning that rail and road journey times more often compete well with air travel. Depending on how you measure, three of the world's ten largest airlines are Chinese. On top of all that, Beijing is the world's seventh-largest metropolitan area; of the six larger metropolises, three more are in China and another is nearby Tokyo. In the context of the larger Asian air travel market (Korea, Japan, India, Indonesia, Vietnam, Thailand, Malaysia, the Philippines, and so on), and given that Beijing-Capital is the only commercial airport serving Beijing, it begins to make sense that this should be one of the world's busiest airports. But it doesn't really seem so busy when you're traveling First Class, which is a significant part of why one might choose to travel that way.

After using a dedicated check-in line in which I waited behind nobody, and passing through priority security screening and passport control with similar waits, I was ushered into the lounge and served a breakfast of Nasi lemark (Malaysian chicken curry with rice – yum!), plus a croissant and orange juice. I'm not sure about the curry and orange juice pairing now, but I guess it worked okay.

#

When I boarded the Triple-Seven, I was greeted by the same crew, in the cabin and in the cockpit, as those who'd staffed my flight to Beijing 36 hours earlier. I thought about how tired I felt having flown halfway around the world for a day and a half. Then I thought about the people who kept that same schedule once a week or so and had to be on their feet working the whole time I was enjoying the First Class treatment. What a life that must be.

This was one of the few times in life when I was glad to be breathing the air on an airliner. The reality of Beijing's air pollution problem became clear as the giant plane turned left onto the runway for departure. Looking out my left-side window, I couldn't see the other end of the runway. It was sunny day outside and the airport is about fifteen miles from the Forbidden City, covered in grass where it isn't paved, but because of the wicked smog visibility was less than the two-mile length of the runway.

It's sometimes interesting to compare the in-flight food on a flight departing a destination country versus the meals on a flight departing the airline's home country. How thoroughly I've enjoyed, for example, a couple different curry dishes out of London (a city chock-full of Indian immigrants), or the chicken biryani I was served on that hours-late flight out of Kuwait.

On today's flight from Beijing to Chicago, dinner started in a fairly Chinese way, with an appetizer of Peking Duck spring rolls with leeks, cucumber, and balsamic glaze, and service continued with hot and sour soup. After a couple spoonfuls of the soup, I realized I was supposed to pour the "Chinese vinegar" into the main bowl; the caterers left the vinegar on the side because, as with that ex-London curry sauce, not everybody likes it full-force. I ate it full-force and still remember that soup three years later. Salad was a more familiar seasonal greens with carrot spaghetti and tomatoes, all in a honey mustard lime dressing. The main course was more normal still: grilled beef filet in port wine sauce, with potato gratin, asparagus, and carrots. I washed these down with a New Zealand sauvignon blanc and then a Rhone valley red. Dessert was the least Chinese of all, vanilla ice cream with butterscotch sauce and pecans, doused with cognac. It was the best meal I've ever had for $0 plus tax, and it made for a nice culinary transition from East to West.

#justpassingthrough

After a few hours of sleep, waking up someplace over Manitoba, I made that difficult decision I needed to make in the wake of Easter Sunday and Easter Monday. There was breakfast followed by arrival at O'Hare. It felt good to breathe the relatively clean air of Chicago, and even better to take a shower in the lounge. And unlike that night in the restaurant a few weeks earlier, the water was hot.

Atlas Roads

Three weeks later, I dragged my luggage through the DC Metro to my favorite little airport by the river. Having enacted the difficult decision I'd made over the Canadian tundra on the way home from Beijing, I now felt much lighter. It was time to take a whole week off from the burdens of liturgical music – yes, including a Sunday! – to explore a corner of the world not choked by pollution and Communism.

As my Yellow Line train passed over the Potomac River into Virginia, I checked the upgrade list for this first flight to Miami, where I had no plans to spend the night. It was a silly, unthinkingly reflexive thing to do, since all my upgrades for this outbound journey had already cleared, to Miami and off the continent. The airline's app, like the monitors at the gate, displays the names on the upgrade list with the first three letters of the flyer's last name, comma, first initial. So, when my name appears, it's "MUE, M." Today, as I mindlessly scanned the list, I saw a traveler named "RUB, M." near the top of the list. What were the odds I would be on the same flight as Senator Marco Rubio, the young-ish Cuban-American Floridian who was running for the Republican presidential nomination next year?

Pretty small, I figured, and I forgot about Sunshine State politicians as I dealt with the mind-numbing inanity of checking in for a multi-leg, multi-carrier itinerary. Yes, I'm really flying three segments touching three continents. Yes, I'm really traveling without checking bags. Yes, I meant what I just said: packing clothes for warm weather destinations doesn't require much space.

I got past the Blueshirts, arrived at the gate, and despite being ticketed in First Class and holding the airline's highest status level, my boarding had to wait until Senator Rubio made his way aboard, stopping to smile and wave briefly at the rest of us. When I took my place in seat 4F, the good senator was getting comfortable in 6B. This was the same treatment I'd seen another airline give Bill Gates on a flight to Boston a few years earlier, an aisle seat in the back row of First Class where nobody could see him.

Nobody, that is, except a guy in 4F with his phone camera in selfie mode. Being the respecter of privacy that I am (stop snickering…the man chose to run for president!), I posted such a picture on Facebook. Within a few minutes, someone had incorrectly identified the woman in 5E as Carly Fiorina (another candidate for the same nomination), and a short while later, a frequent-flying priest commented that he'd been on a flight with Sen. Rubio from Los Angeles earlier that week. Isn't social media wonderful? No doubt Sen. Rubio was heading home this Friday afternoon for a weekend with his family after a long week of legislating on Capitol Hill.

(The following year, I would stand in line to vote for Sen. Rubio in the DC Republican primary election. There aren't many of us Republicans living and voting in Washington, but most all of us turned out to vote against Donald Trump in that primary contest. Rubio won the DC primary, but without my vote: after two hours in line, I still hadn't even made it into the building, and had to abandon the election in order to make good on a commitment to sit on an organ bench in the suburbs.)

A couple hours later, the view out my window was of sun-baked I-95 in Miami. This would be the most humid stop on my itinerary, but not the warmest. I high-tailed it to my connecting gate, and fell into seat 9A, in the Business Class cabin of a Triple-Seven just like the one on which I'd ridden in First to and from Beijing recently. A transatlantic flight in this so-called "angle-flat" product wasn't as restful or as luxurious as that last flight had been (the seat reclines to be flat like a bed, but not level with the floor, so it's rather like sleeping on a jammed⌐ seesaw), but it was still tons better than economy. After a four-course meal featuring saffron gnocchi in tomato sauce, and a few hours' sleep, the Triple-Seven landed at Madrid-Barajas Airport. As in Miami, the sun shone brightly; in Spain, the rain was mainly off the plane.

The home airline at Barajas has a fine Business Class lounge with a breakfast buffet, wi-fi, and showers, and I took full advantage of all three. And within a couple hours, I found myself aboard another plane, my first visit to Spain now concluded. On this flight, the view was at first of the blue skies, puffy clouds, and slightly dry land of the southern Iberian peninsula, until it gave way to the bright blue of the Mediterranean. There was the Rock of Gibraltar, an imposing presence, I'm told, to those who view it from land or sea, but even with my camera zoomed all the way in, it wasn't much to behold from cruising altitude.

Once you fly south across the Strait of Gibraltar, you're over Africa. This was my first time in African skies, and I watched the Moroccan Atlantic coast roll by. If you've ever looked due east across the Atlantic anyplace between Virginia Beach and Cape Canaveral, you were looking not at Europe (which is further north than most Americans seem to realize), but toward Morocco. Morocco is a substantial country, physically slightly larger than California, with about eighty-six percent of the population.

Landing on Marrakech Airport's two-mile-long runway, I could see it was a beautifully sunny spring afternoon here, too. Deplaning was by airstairs, and walking out the door was like walking into a brick oven: the air temperature was 102 degrees here at the far western edge of the Sandbox. Thirty-five hundred miles of Sahara and Arabian deserts stood between me and the Arabian Gulf I'd visited fourteen months prior, and although the Arabic language and the desert climate and the Islamic religion were in common, I immediately sensed a detachment from the problems of the Middle East. That ought not to have been a surprise, since I was as far from Iran as New York is from London. Here I was where the cultures of Africa, Europe, and the Arab world meet, and this was going to be an eye-opening visit!

#justpassingthrough

Wheels were a necessity here, so after breezing through immigration and customs I picked up a rental car. This would avoid the cost and hassle of a taxi ride. Safety was a consideration, too; because my body was tired from overnight travel and not used to the heat, a quick and direct drive in air-conditioning would be helpful throughout my stay.

Finding the hotel was easy this time, inasmuch as the Moroccan government does not ban Google and the dot on the map precisely matched the location of the hotel. And what a hotel: Four stars, with restaurant and full service and powerful a/c, within walking distance of the souq and restaurants, with free parking, for all of $34 per night. Check-in was quite a ritual; instead of standing at a desk and filling out forms and so forth, the clerk invited me to sit at a coffee table and transact the business of checking-in over a cold drink. No, I was not allowed to wheel my own bags through the hotel.

I spent an hour or so in the cool darkness of the room marked 007, drinking lots of bottled water. Yes, there was a perfectly functional tap in the bathroom, but one of the cardinal rules of traveling overseas is not to drink the water. Even in places where the locals drink the tap water safely, it still contains different sorts of pathogens and pollutants than the tap water you might drink at home, so spending a few dollars per day on bottled water to avoid shocking your digestive tract is any traveler's first and most important budget line.

By late afternoon, with the sun getting lower in the sky, I was restless and eager to make my first pedestrian exploration of North African territory. Hydrated and rested, I set out for the medina of Marrakech, which contains its souq, about a half mile away.

#

Marrakech is a city of over 900,000 people, the fourth-largest city in Morocco. Founded in 1062, it has been a center for commerce, imperial government, Islamic learning, and (most recently) tourism. Originally, it consisted of the walled city toward which I was walking; as more modern neighborhoods sprawled outward, the original walled city became known as the medina. That same word is the proper name of a city in Saudi Arabia; while in English it has been defined as the "walled Arab or non-European part of a North African city", in Arabic the word simply means "town".

Promenading past trees with stunning purple flowers, dodging the apparent chaos of traffic circles, I found an archway leading into the medina and was almost immediately transported into a place long ago and far away. Here, in alleys barely eight feet wide, shopkeepers and salesmen jostled for position with small children, big children, entrepreneurially-minded teenagers, stray cats, goats (both butchered and ambulatory), motorbikes, and vats of spices. The salesmen are extremely aggressive: they corner you, they pull at your heartstrings, they try to embarrass you, they speak a few words of the language they think you understand. Passing a shop with shiny metal lamps and other vessels, I half expected Aladdin to come swinging around and Abu to relieve me of my wallet.

At one point, for the fun of it, I allowed myself to engage with a man selling various brightly-colored cloths, clothes, and sundry pieces of fabric. By playing to my desire to please the "special lady" in my life… wife…daughter…seester…girrrrrrlfrond… he persuaded me to buy two pieces of cloth too big to be handkerchiefs and too small to be non-decorative scarfs, all for a "very good price", good, that is, for him. Why I succumbed, I don't know. Chalk it up to not having lain in a real bed since before I saw Marco Rubio, plus the shock of the heat, plus that vague sense of embarrassment I always feel as a comparatively wealthy westerner wandering through such an otherworldly place as the souq of Marrakech. I still have the two cloths in a bag at home if anybody wants them. I'll give you a very good price.

Needing some air, I came into the square known as Jemaa el-Fna. If I was expecting tranquility, I expected wrongly. Here, dinner was getting into full swing, and I was stopped in my tracks by the aromas of roasting chicken, lamb, and beef, mixed with cumin, saffron, and cinnamon. I can't imagine that the wedding feast of all eternity smells better than this, even if by definition it has to.

Ambling reluctantly back into the narrow alleys of the souq, I passed a vegetable stand with potatoes, onions, cucumbers, peppers, and carrots laid neatly on a blanket at ground level. Pests would not be a problem for this vendor, primarily because the vegetable stand was staffed by a bored-looking cat.

Although I was not the only tourist in the souq, it was definitely a "real" place where locals conducted commerce, and not an institution maintained just to impress visitors.

After perhaps an hour of wandering through the medina and its souq, it was time to return to the hotel, though this was easier said than done. According to Tolkien, not all who wander are lost, but I was, because the medina's alleys follow no discernible pattern or orientation. Shrugging and under no special deadline, I followed an alley until it spat me back out an archway into the twenty-first century. Happily, this turned out to be the side of the medina facing toward my hotel. I strolled through a beautiful park with lots of shady spots; here and there, young lovers could be spotted in the shadows enjoying each other's company, and groups of children frolicked in the fountains to get some relief from the heat.

By the time I got back to my room, connected to wi-fi, and uploaded the afternoon's photos to Facebook, the outside temperature had dropped to a much more comfortable 99 degrees. Having exhausted myself thoroughly with the medina expedition, I opted for dinner at the in-hotel restaurant. First course was Moroccan salad with various nuts and beans, and the main was red meat and seven vegetables in saffron couscous. This was accompanied by a Moroccan red wine that, while definitely not the sort of wine that comes from California or Australia or France or Italy, was quite drinkable and matched the local food flavors nicely.

Yes, I'd chosen this destination very, very well.

#

When I awoke from my long, deep, first-night slumber, it was Sunday morning, the Fifth Sunday of Easter. That meant, of course, that I would attend Mass. If I'd been in London or Paris or even Beijing, there would have been a plethora of options to choose from. Here in Marrakech, I could attend 10:00 a.m. Mass at Holy Martyrs, or I could drive to another city. I chose Holy Martyrs, conveniently located just a couple blocks from the hotel.

Actually, as I rounded that corner, I did see some options. Among the buildings glowing in red stone were outposts of three religions: the Catholic parish, a mosque, and secular consumerism as represented by the Coca-Cola sign.

On the plus side, the parish had a cross on top of its tower; if you recall from my visit to Kuwait, not all Muslim countries allow this. Outside the front gate, though, stood a solitary police officer, quietly watching people file into the church. A casual observer might have figured that the cop was there to protect the Christian minority from the sort of radical Islamic bomb attacks that had begun to plague the Middle East and North Africa. The reality is more sinister: Despite Morocco's reputation as a "moderate" and Western-friendly Islamic country, it is still illegal there for a Muslim to renounce Islam. Indeed, the crowd inside was mix of sub-Saharan types, religious brothers and sisters, European expats, and a very few tourists. The common spoken language seemed to be French, as was the primary language of the liturgy. Also sung at Mass were English and an African language I couldn't identify. Notably absent were Greek, Latin, and Arabic. The music was a bit of a mess, but Jesus was really present despite all chaos around Him.

After Mass, I stopped for lunch at a neighboring chain restaurant, where I ordered from the French menu (not the Arabic one) the mixed kabobs. Soon, a plate arrived with skewers of beef and chicken in aromatic spices, accompanied by a pile of just-right fries, a small salad of lettuce and tomato and onion, a basket of olive bread, and a large bottle of water. That did the trick all around, and now I was ready to take a Sunday afternoon drive.

Passing through central Marrakech with its congestion, I drove east on the N8 suburban arterial road, then made a right onto the N9, a high-quality two-lane road that took me away from the city toward the High Atlas Mountains, away from Franco-Arab civilization into the rural lands inhabited by the Berbers, away from the coastal semi-arid climate toward the bone-dry Sahara regions. Actually a series of distinct mountain ranges, the overall effect of the Atlas is to separate the coastal Atlantic/Mediterranean areas where most Moroccans (and Algerians and Tunisians) live from the harsh wilderness of the vast desert of North Africa.

As I drove, the road became less straight and less flat, curving in and out of Berber towns, sometimes tracing the crooked path of a small river, and eventually entering a long series of steep switchbacks ascending to the Tizi n'Tichka Pass (Berber for "it's difficult"), which allows vehicular access between Marrakech and Ouarzazate. Predictably, I found myself behind a double-decker truck full of goats and sheep moving at seven miles per hour uphill; the four-legged passengers of that vehicle looked just as annoyed to be there in front of me as I was to be behind them.

From a few different observation stops, the panorama unfurled. This was truly rugged terrain, with jagged mountain peaks as far as the eye could see. Some of those peaks still had winter snow on them, and the runoff generated under the spring sunshine fed forests and green fields along some, but not all, of the slopes. The road itself was a snake-like path that disappeared around more bends than I could count. Villages were made of the same red clay on which they sat, making them seem to be camouflaged.

Here I was, on the afternoon of the Fifth Sunday of Easter, standing in a mountain pass in North Africa, breathing fresher air than Beijing will ever know, enjoying the type of scenic panorama most Americans don't know they're missing. There's a reason the English language has us talking metaphorically about a "mountaintop experience", and on several levels, I was having one.

I couldn't stay up there forever, so presently I drove back down the mountain with all its twists and turns, arriving back in Marrakech just as the sun set. Dinner in the hotel restaurant tonight would be lamb shanks with herbed vegetable confit in olive oil, accompanied by a Moroccan wine known as "Terre Rouge" – red dirt, like I'd been seeing all day in the countryside – followed by an orange-mint crème brûlée.

#

In the morning, once again I set out by car. This time, I stayed in the valley to the northwest of the Atlas, driving east-by-northeast for about two and a half hours. Here again, the road was mostly of good quality, taking me past fruit groves, semi-arid brush land, small towns made of red clay, and as I got closer to my destination, rolling hills.

Reaching Ouzoud, I found a few of the trappings of a tourist trap. Having come to see the Cascades d'Ouzoud, a waterfall fueled in springtime by runoff, I had to pay to use one of the town's abundant gravel parking lots.

In the first world, this is when you approach a ticket kiosk and you pay and you're given a map of the place and you're told what you should do first and you do all the things and at the end you're dumped into the gift shop. Here in Morocco, out of reach of that sort of development, I was approached by Samir, a Berber man about my age or perhaps a little older, who offered me a particular price for his services as my guide, which would include lunch by the waterfall. The price seemed reasonable, so we shook hands and he led me away from my car toward the swift-flowing water, pure and clear.

Samir led me along a path that was about to be paved but currently consisted of large, loose stones, walking on the wooden edge of the path with arms extended for balance the way children walk on a curb. He led me through olive groves and down a steeply-sloped dirt trail. When at length we reached the bottom of the gorge, Samir pointed out a creature known as a "petit frog". Samir was pleasantly surprised to learn that, even though I'm American, I know some French. We conversed in a mixture of English, French, and gesticulations, which was illuminating for both of us. I learned that we were surrounded by pomegranate trees, cedar trees, almond trees, argan trees, mint, and lavender. Yes, the smell was powerful.

Having crossed the river upstream of the falls and come down the right bank downstream of the falls, we would be able to see the falls only by crossing once again to the left bank. The narrow river was full of rocks, such that two separate bridge segments were required. These were not concrete-girder spans, but the sort of pre-fab bridge made by laying out two parallel logs and affixing planks across the gap between them and then laying the whole assembly across the water with each end resting on the rocks. Samir must have been used to spoiled Western visitors being afraid of the simple bridges; being sure in my knowledge that the laws of physics applied just as well in Morocco as in the USA, and figuring that any construction flaw likely would have revealed itself long before I arrived, I wasn't concerned for my safety as I crossed the river. Nevertheless, Samir made a big point of assuring me that this bridge was of American construction, and that I should cross without fear. It was only when I was standing on the left bank once again that Samir decided to mention that the second span of the bridge was Chinese. If he wanted a reaction, he didn't get one. I'd seen the Forbidden City a few weeks before and didn't doubt Chinese construction know-how.

Samir instructed me that the part of the river we now beheld was known as the "piscine naturelle", a natural swimming pool. Indeed, the water looked tranquil even as the falls cascaded in the background, and I could see why the spot would be popular with swimmers. As we sat by the piscine admiring the splendor of nature, Samir summoned a freshly-squeezed glass of orange juice, which was thoroughly appreciated.

We crossed more rocks. Samir used my phone to photograph me on a boulder mid-river near the falls; he also used it to photograph me getting down from the boulder, which seemed to amuse him. Soon it was lunchtime, and Samir ushered me to my patio seat at a restaurant overlooking the river. I was served a simple but scrumptious meal of roasted chicken skewers, some fried potatoes with ketchup, and a Moroccan "salad" (not the careful mixture we call a salad, but a lettuce-less plate of sliced and chopped vegetables with dressing poured on top), plus some freshly-baked bread.

On the way up the steps back toward the parking lot, we passed a family of monkeys. Mommy monkey was feeding her babies while Daddy monkey stood guard; the spectacle of a parent feeding a child was quite similar to what I often observe among humans. I'd been to zoos and seen monkeys in captivity, but this was different: the monkeys were not caged, so in effect this was their turf more than it was mine or Samir's. They did what they had to do, and we didn't interfere.

As I thanked Samir for his first-rate services, I reflected that today's entire outing, including gas, parking, the tour, lunch, and a portion of rental car costs, cost me about $90, and practically none of it was for make-believe.

Driving back "home" on Monday afternoon (how quickly we reorient ourselves!), I knew Marrakech was getting close when I began to share the road with trucks, one of them carrying an upright tree of the same variety as the trees lining the road, which was slightly confusing. Morocco's roads aren't just for cars and trucks, though; they're also used by motorcyclists, bicyclists, adult pedestrians, child pedestrians, and various groupings of escorted or unescorted animals from dogs to goats to cows. In other words, you have to pay close attention in order to avoid causing carnage.

#justpassingthrough

There is another type of road hazard in Morocco, one with which I shortly became familiar. It begins with two officers of the Gendarmerie Royale standing by a four-lane suburban road at the beginning of evening rush hour, causing traffic to slow to a crawl. The first officer eyeballs each car and driver while the second one points a radar gun at traffic. The first officer spots a rental car with an obviously foreign driver, and the second officer points his radar gun at that car, which is moving at a snail's pace through the artificial traffic jam. The first officer then gestures at the foreign driver to stop his rental car on the shoulder, informs the driver that he was detected traveling at 68 kph in a 60 zone, and demands to see license, registration, and proof of insurance. When the first officer disappointedly finds that the paperwork is in order, he demands immediate payment of 300 dirhams (about $30 US). When the driver happens to have that much cash on his person, the officer is further disappointed not to be able to add more fines for failure to pay on time, wishes the driver "bonne route", tears up the citation, and pockets the cash.

It's highway robbery, and it happened to me. Fortunately, I'd done my homework and knew this was a common practice, so I carried enough cash to satisfy the officers and drive away with a good story. If you don't carry cash you can be taken to the police station, and that's an adventure I didn't need to have.

The rest of the day was quiet. I uploaded photos, went to Mass, found some pizza for dinner, did some planning for the next day, and called it a night.

#

Tuesday was, you'll be shocked to learn, hot and sunny in Marrakech. In fact, though, it was the coolest day of my visit, with temperatures barely reaching 90 degrees. Today my rental car would remain parked, somewhat reducing the chances I'd be cited for speeding, and I would take advantage of the milder weather to explore Marrakech on foot.

Parts of the city are quite picturesque, so much so that Hollywood frequently shows up to film movies here when they need a ready-made "Sandbox" backdrop. In fact, Morocco features in such a diversity of films as *13 Hours, Spectre, American Sniper, Sex and the City 2, Sahara, Black Hawk Down, Lawrence of Arabia,* and *The Man Who Knew Too Much*. This makes sense, as Morocco has lots of desert, mountain, and coastal landscapes. It has a variety of cities from modern, bustling Casablanca to weird Fes to old-souq-in-the-medina Marrakech. It's a stone's throw from the comforts of Europe. And it has little of the violence that plagues many parts of The Sandbox; take note of the modern war movies on the list above.

Consequently, Marrakech is on the radar of the Hollywood social set. A friend told me to drop into a hotel called La Mamounia to gawk at its level of luxury, so when I passed it Tuesday morning on the walk into the medina, I tried to go inside. However, nervous-looking armed guards blocked the door to anyone who wasn't a registered guest. Later, when I saw CNN playing in a restaurant, I learned that Bill Clinton had been in town for some conference of an international aid association, and figured he was staying at La Mamounia on the dime of the Clinton Foundation.

The day's real first stop would be the El Badi ("Incomparable") Palace, constructed in the late sixteenth century by the Moorish Sultan Ahmad al-Mansur. Sultan Ahmad had some spare money on his hands, inherited from his late brother, the former sultan Abd Al-Malik, whose army won a battle against the Portuguese (whose loss was so politically and militarily catastrophic that for sixty years Portugal suffered the indignity of being ruled by the Spanish), but still managed to die during the battle.

Little brother played his hand magnificently, constructing a palace of hundreds of rooms made from gold and onyx and Italian marble, with splendid courtyards and outbuildings of various sizes and descriptions.

#justpassingthrough

The ravages of time and politics have not been kind to El Badi Palace: when the Saadian dynasty (to which Sultan Ahmad belonged) fell from power, a new sultan removed the precious building materials for use in constructing his new palace elsewhere. Thus, my tour today was a walk through ruins.

On arrival, I was once again greeted by a man who would be my guide. He showed me first through what had been the palace's private mosque. There, the walls contained three stacked rows of cubbyholes. The guide explained that the top row was for lanterns, the middle row was for Korans, and the bottom row was for the storage of shoes, which may not be worn in a mosque. Very practical.

From there, we wandered through the ruins. The guide informed me that the palace was constructed with 365 bedrooms so that the sultan could keep one wife for each day of the year. (Perhaps February 29 was his quadrennial day of rest?) Incidentally, the birds nesting on top of the remaining walls were storks. One level below the royal harem's quarters was an also-extensive prison; the sultan liked to keep his friends close and his enemies closer.

In one corner, I was invited to ascend a restored marble staircase for a panoramic view of the palace and its surroundings. Looking outward, I beheld what passes for a skyline in Marrakech: roofs crowded with gardens and small pools and satellite dishes and antennas and billboards, minarets, palm trees, cell towers masquerading as palm trees, and the faint trace the Atlas for a backdrop. Looking inward, I saw the floorplan of great halls alternating with courtyards full of orange trees. In one of the courtyards, my guide pointed out a temporary platform being erected for some upcoming VIP event (perhaps involving Bill Clinton and friends). "Not for me, not for you," he observed.

Having enjoyed the ruined palace about as much as one can on a warm spring morning, I ambled a few blocks west to a place marked "Tombeaux Saadiens". Here were the tombs our friend Sultan Ahmad built for his mother and himself. Unlike the palace, the complex of tombs is intact and in a good state of preservation. This seems fitting since the Sultan's place of bodily residence (and his mother's) has been here for far longer than the opulent palace he built for himself and his year's worth of wives. You can write the moral of the story for yourself without my help.

The tombs complex is doubly prone to crowding compared to the palace; not only are the walls intact, but they're closer together. I had the good fortune to arrive at the same time as a group of several dozen German tourists. Since there were so few Americans in town, it's safe to say this group of sombrero-sporting, camera-toting, t-shirt-wearing, loud-speaking, all-the-space-occupying affluent northern Europeans was the biggest annoyance around. It was literally impossible to enjoy the view of anything in the beautiful grounds without including part of their conveyor-belt method of moving through. It was also impossible to cross from one side of the path to the other because they formed an impenetrable line the whole way through the gardens. If the last few sentences didn't make it clear, this tour group's oblivious presence really annoyed me.

But for all that, the opulence and care with which Sultan Ahmad built his mother's tomb (she died in 1591, he in 1603), suggests that the leaders of the religious wars, on both sides, sincerely believed they were destined for something greater than all the riches and comforts of this life. Faithful to Islamic tradition, the art here is completely abstract, depicting no living thing. The flowers are real, but the tiled surfaces around the flower beds are colorfully geometric. Inside the mausoleums, one is confronted with a dizzying array of different kinds of arches, rectangles, diamond shapes, starbursts, blues, greens, browns, oranges, yellows, carved wooden gates, Carrara marble, and stone paths. The building containing Sultan Ahmad's tomb includes a prayer room (complete with prayer rugs), a central room with the main tomb, and a "Hall of the Three Niches" where younger princes are buried. His mother's building, though smaller, is more ornate; here, the arches holding up the gilded ceiling panels are of a jaggedly complicated, though always symmetrical, shape.

Palace intrigue here did not end with death. While Sultan Ahmad prepared places of honor for his mother, his princes, and himself, about 170 lesser officials and their wives are buried in the ground outside. In the middle of the seventeenth century, Sultan Moulay Ismail of the Alawite dynasty was now in charge, and in order to solidify his position in the minds of his subjects, he barricaded the Tombeux Saadiens shut. It worked for quite a long time; only with the advent of aerial photography were the tombs re-discovered in 1917, restored, and opened to the public again.

Once the Germans let me out of the tombs, I high-tailed it back past the El Badi palace ruins to the Bahia Palace. This had been built in the 1860's as a residence for and by Grand Vizier Si Moussa (a vizier being a principal advisor to the monarch), and elaborated at the end of that century by Abu "Bou" Ahmed, a former slave who was then the vizier himself. Under some monarchs, the vizier has default control over many day-to-day matters, so it was important to impress, not to say intimidate, visitors with the opulence of one's office. If you needed a legislative favor, you came here. If you were in legal trouble and needed a thumb on the scales of justice, you came here. If you were competing for a government contract and needed to make a sales pitch, you came here. You waited for the vizier (and by implication if not always in physical reality, the sultan) in these courtyards with their brightly-colored tile patterns, lush vegetation, and rows of bedrooms occupied by the girls of the harem.

But not even the powerful vizier was master of the kingdom, and the sultan's power was recognized in several ways. Here, notably, Sultan Sidi Mohammed Ben Abderraham was accommodated with extra-wide arches, not for some symbolic reason, but because he was an exceptionally obese man. What an awkward moment it would have been if the sultan had come to check on things and he didn't fit through the front door! Today, though, as I was admiring the extra-wide entrance, it revealed its unintended modern use: Letting in that same crowd of German tourists, two and three abreast.

Despite the Teutonic stampede, I still managed to find details to admire, though the Islamic calligraphy around some of the art would mean a lot more to me if I understand the slightest thing about written Arabic. As I stood to the side fighting against some decision my camera phone had made for me, I inspected the pattern of tiling in the wall. Here was a relatively simple blue-and-white pattern, ostensibly designed to be like plain wallpaper that doesn't distract from the main attractions hanging on the walls. But there, in the midst of the pattern, was one brownish-orange diamond piece perhaps an inch high, that ought to have been a deep blue like the surrounding pieces of the same shape and size. As I expanded my view, I found a couple other pieces that were the "wrong" color in no discernible pattern, assuming at first that these were shoddy repairs. But the guide pamphlet told me that these imperfections were a feature, not a bug, designed to remind the sultan that not even he is perfect.

As I pondered the nature of royal imperfection, I stepped into the throne room, where my effort to take a beautiful picture of sunlight streaming through the sultan-sized arches was thwarted by a lone German tourist who'd wandered away from his flock into my frame of view in order to pick his nose. Being fed up with that particular crowd, I snapped the picture anyway.

Despite the warmth of the noontime sun, there was shade and a breeze in the royal and vice-royal chambers of the palace, contrasting with the heat of the area where visiting supplicants would wait for admission. All the windows and doors were carved quite elegantly in some sort of matching wood and painted brown.

Needing a break from former and current royal residences, walking, the building heat, and German tourists, I found lunch in a nearby restaurant where I once again ordered from the French-language menu. There was a tomato-vegetable soup served with delicious bread, followed by a couscous with chicken, beans, and vegetables, plus bottled water. Always bottled water.

Lunch having been consumed and lunch break having been enjoyed, I once again penetrated the commercial heart of the souq. After several days living in and around the center of Marrakech, I no longer found the geography of the souq to be quite so disorienting, and having slept a few nights and gotten used to the way micro-commerce is done, I managed not to be guilted into buying anything for non-existent female relatives. Also, there were no Germans in my way.

My destination this time was the Musée de Marrakech, where I was greeted at the door by a bored security guard and a sign that read as follows:

"The culture, the music, and help to some one give us some happiness and like says Voltaire a big French writer 'I decided to be happy because it's good for my health'. The president and personal of the museum wish you welcome to this historic place."

Unable to resist such a gracious and eloquent welcome, I went into what was once the Mhnebi Palace, home to Defense Minister Mehdi Mnebhi around the turn of the twentieth century. The palace had also been home to a girls' school before being turned into a museum. This history highlights an interesting problem in a city like Marrakech, which was a royal capital for so many centuries: everybody who's anybody wants to build a new palace, and nobody wants to live in somebody else's old palace. What do you do with perfectly nice old palaces that happen to have been built by those no longer in power?

I spent perhaps a half hour wandering past all manner of tilework, painting, pottery, sculpture, and the other sorts of treasures one finds in an art museum that isn't quite at the level of the Met or the Louvre or the Uffizi. There was, though, a nice exhibit on Arabic calligraphy, and even a calligrapher ready to make beautiful wall posters with the transliterated name of anyone you chose. I picked several names, paid a fee significantly less than what I'd paid for driving in a traffic jam the previous day, and walked out with the sort of souvenir one simply can't get closer to home.

Atlas Roads

Looking at my notes and photographs for the rest of the day, it's not clear exactly what I did after mid-afternoon. It's likely that I drank bottled water. Perhaps I also avoided the hottest part of the day by sitting in my hotel room answering professional e-mails. I would likely have attended Mass at Holy Martyrs.

Oh, yes, Mass at Holy Martyrs. I walked past the police officer whose job is to help keep Moroccans Muslim. Mass itself was, I'm sorry to say, quite a liturgical mess, with various paraliturgical (a.k.a. illicit) texts and actions thrown in, such as a consecration-by-all-present. I think the sacrament was still (barely) valid, and I wasn't about to drive to Casablanca just for a different experience that might turn out to be just as bad. Afterward, before I could leave the church, I was approached by a man who explained in broken English that he was from Mauritania and needed help buying drugs. I'd noticed during the liturgy he didn't seem to know what was going on; it's one thing not to know the words in a particular language, but it's another thing not to know the motions. It wasn't clear whether the help would be financial or linguistic or what, nor for that matter what sort of drugs he wanted to buy. He was appealing to what he assumed would be the guilt of a rich white guy, I think... most people there were considerably darker-skinned, and many were in religious habits (i.e. they have no money). I try to help people when I travel, say, by assisting a fellow airline passenger with baggage or giving directional aid, but this didn't pass my smell test. I watched the man approach one other individual, who also turned him down, and then leave, his efforts at who-really-knows-what having been confounded. Out of an abundance of caution, I waited a while in the church and then left at the same time as several other people.

#

Wednesday's plan called for me to be at the airport not later than noon, and to spend the morning mopping up any unvisited destinations in central Marrakech that I hadn't managed to visit. Despite the best efforts of a certain crowd of Germans who, by the way, were staying at my hotel, I'd seen all the main attractions I'd meant to see. So at the crack of dawn, I checked out of said hotel, loaded my bags in the trunk of the rental car, and headed for the hills once more. My destination was Toubkal, the highest mountain in Morocco, the Atlas, and North Africa generally. No, I had no intention of climbing to the 13,671-foot summit. I did, however, want to see the Atlas one more time and to breathe a little fresh air before the journey home.

On my previous two road trips ex-Marrakech, I'd headed east through lots of suburbs, but this was different. Within a few minutes' driving south from the hotel, I was on a rural road with little traffic. In the sleepy town of Asni, the morning sunlight reflected brilliantly off the minaret of the local mosque; as on my drive to Ouzoud, the towns were built of clay so that they blended into the surrounding hillsides. From Asni, a still windier road with even less traffic took me along the narrow river valley, or in Arabic, "wadi", a canyon, almost, to Imlil. At Imlil was the end of the road for drivers, and the beginning of the trail for climbers.

As at Ouzoud and El Badi, I had scarcely parked when a young man appeared and offered to be my guide. He tried to interest me in a multi-hour hike up the mountain to such-and-such a location. I declined. He persisted. I don't recall whether I used English or French to impress on him that time would be limited because I had a flight to catch, but he caught on and our adventure commenced.

At any National Park in the United States, you're instructed via dozens of signs not to stray from the path, not to feed the bears, not to walk backward next to a cliff while using your selfie stick, and so forth. Railings compliant with the building and environmental codes keep you isolated from any topographical danger, and omnipresent park rangers make sure you comply with all the rules, which have the force of federal law.

Not so in Morocco. Here, it's you and the wilderness and whoever you happen to pay to be your guide. Mohammed the Berber led me away from town, up a trail, and directly across what amounted to the lip of a waterfall up a series of rock islands in the stream that carries winter runoff to the coastal plain and the Atlantic; somehow, my feet didn't get drenched. This is an experience you won't have at Yosemite! Mohammed and I posed for a photo in front of a thundering cascade about 25 minutes into our hike, and then he turned us around and led me back to town by a somewhat different route, ending predictably, yet still jarringly, at a gift shop.

Having climbed part of one more mountain and forded one more stream, I could now depart Morocco in peace. Seldom had I so enjoyed myself in a foreign country. Seldom had I encountered so few surprises. The weather, climate, geography, road system, languages, royal palaces, nasty public restrooms, and even the contrived speed trap were as I had read before my trip. Seldom had nearly everything gone so smoothly from a logistical and transportation point of view.

The trend continued as I returned my rental car, checked in for my three-segment return trip, and cleared security and exit immigration. Having time to spare, I retired to one of the least luxurious business class lounges I've ever encountered. Scrolling through my Facebook feed, I clicked on an impressive article about the organ project at St. Matthew's Cathedral back in Washington. Such are the vagaries of human memory that even now, three years after the fact, it's rare that I hear the organ at St. Matthew's without thinking of Marrakech, Toubkal, and that business class lounge.

#

A couple hours later, I was a world away from Morocco, riding an air-conditioned subway into central Madrid on a pleasantly (and merely) warm spring afternoon. The flight schedule was such that the only flight

#justpassingthrough

from Marrakech arrived after the last flight to North America departed, so I was forced to stay overnight in the Spanish capital. That was perfectly fine with me, as I'd never been to Spain before this trip and welcomed the opportunity to soak up some Madrid-ness.

I wanted to make the evening Mass at the Cathedral of the Almudena, but first I needed to check into my hotel and drop my luggage. Surfacing from the Metro at Opera, I expected to do (at most) a 360-degree turn and see the hotel where I'd made a prepaid reservation. Unfortunately, the location where Google displayed a red marker appeared not to be a hotel. Worse, there were no bicycle rickshaws around.

I walked around the block, dragging my luggage across the uneven cobblestones and feeling in every step the morning's exertions at Toubkal. The situation officially became an awkward moment when I saw a building with the same numbered address as my hotel and wandered into the bar with no priests or rabbis. I used my relatively basic Spanish skills (compared to the French I'd been using all week in Morocco) to ask, "¿Por favor, donde esta [my hotel]?", but the bartender had never heard of the place. Perplexed, I wandered back outside and found the hotel directly next door to the bar. Google hadn't been wrong about the location of the hotel's rooms, but the entrance was at the other side of the block on a completely different street.

Dumping my bags in the room, I skedaddled to the nearby cathedral, known officially as Catedral de Santa Maria la Real de la Almudena. Begun in 1883 and consecrated by Pope St. John Paul II in 1993, the Almudena is one of Europe's newest cathedrals. Artistically, its overall shape and Gothic-style arches connect it firmly to the more distant Catholic past, though the smaller-scale decorative elements such as mosaics and murals are in a decidedly more modern style. The icon, or image, of the Virgin of Almudena is the patroness of Madrid. Given the Spanish Catholic influence over so much of the western hemisphere, I'm embarrassed to say I'd never heard of that title before I visited Madrid. I didn't even have any idea where Almudena is.

As it turns out, Almudena isn't a city at all, nor is the word even particularly Spanish. In fact, it's a corruption of the Arabic word (you won't believe it…) "medina", referring to what was once the smaller and geopolitically much less important walled city of Madrid. As the story goes, 8th-century Christians hid the image of the Virgin (of Almudena) inside the city walls to protect it from the Muslims who were taking Iberia by storm (a full eight centuries before Abd Al-Malik lost his life defeating the Portuguese and left his money for his brother to build a palace for himself and 365 wives). Then, in the 11th century, the Castilians reconquered Madrid but couldn't seem to remember where that image of the Virgin of Almudena had been hidden. They prayed and prayed for divine assistance in finding it, and eventually one section of the medina's walls came a-tumbling down, revealing the hidden image.

I don't know about you, but for me that story is almost as good as the one from Aparecida in Brazil where they fished a statue out of the water. Our Lady pops up everywhere.

Back to 2015. After the delay in finding my hotel, I slipped into the cathedral's Blessed Sacrament Chapel just as Padre began Mass with the Sign of the Cross. I don't remember the day's readings, and I'm sure I didn't understand much of the homily, but I do remember the look on Padre's face right after the same person's phone rang for the third time. It was not the face of God's mercy.

The cathedral sits next to the Palacio Real, official residence of King Felipe VI, and after inspecting the outside of both buildings, I continued into a well-populated pedestrianized area teeming with both locals and tourists shopping, eating, drinking, and generally enjoying the exquisite spring evening. Searching for dinner, I decided on a pizzeria, and what a pie I consumed: the Pizza Tartufo came with thin black truffle slices, fresh boletus seasoned with garlic oil and brandy, mixed wild mushrooms and a creamy mushroom sauce, sliced grana Padano, roquette, and black truffle oil, and I paired it with a glass of Pata Negra Verdejo Rueja. Wow, was that ever tasty, and was it ever different from the Moroccan meals I'd been enjoying all week!

After dinner, stopping at Chocolateria San Gines, I ordered the only item on the menu, six churros and hot chocolate, for which I paid a grand total of €3.90.

Somehow, on this trip, I found the two least expensive hotel rooms I've ever stayed in. This room, too, cost under $35 for the night. Tonight's lodging was more basic than I'd enjoyed in Marrakech, but it was a bed and a bathroom and a small space to walk from one to the other. Unlike many hotel rooms, it didn't come with bottled water or other beverages in a minibar. Since I was only staying one night, for some reason it didn't occur to me to fully unpack and stock the room with essentials. And that's where I made one of the dumbest mistakes of my traveling life.

#

It was 1-something in the morning when I woke up. Between yesterday's climb at Toubkal, the flight from Marrakech to Madrid, dragging my bags around looking for the hotel, wine with dinner, and my walk around town afterward, I'd gotten a little dehydrated. Being groggy, and facing a long travel day and thus wanting to get back to sleep, I did what I always do at home when I'm dehydrated: I got out of bed, grabbed a glass from the shelf, went into the bathroom, turned on the tap, and downed a few swigs of water. Then I went back to bed, not fathoming the manner in which I had just made my journey home so gut-wrenchingly unpleasant.

#

In many cities, the cathedral is the star of the ecclesiastical architecture show. Not so Madrid. While the Almudena is a "correct" traditional design and not at all unpleasant to behold, there are a good many churches more ornate, more dazzling, more classically Catholic-looking. At the crack of dawn, I checked out of the cheap hotel and made my way to La Iglesia de San Manuel y San Benito. Here was a domed church from the twelfth century with ample mosaic work, statues everywhere, simple stained glass letting in just enough light, and a pulpit accessible only by stairs in another room. The exterior of the church, like that of so many Romanesque-style buildings, bears an uncanny resemblance to a mosque: the bell tower looks not at all unlike the minaret that had caught my eye driving through Asni the previous morning.

At the airport, the check-in agent told me to go through the special premium-class security checkpoint, where there was no line and everyone is treated courteously. Well, I quickly became a pawn in the ongoing feud between Madrid's airport security agency and my airline. Apparently, the notation on the boarding pass indicating a seat in Business Class isn't enough for priority screening (as it usually is in most places); the airline is supposed to distribute a special pass to eligible passengers. The agent who checked my boarding pass demanded to know where my special pass was. I shrugged, and after one of the most cutting eye-rolls I've ever seen, she informed me that next time I was to obtain a special pass. I made that mental note, and continued on my way.

Despite the turf war in the terminal, Madrid was firmly on my "must come back" list. The food, weather, architecture, and general atmosphere of Madrid definitely agreed with me; the tap water, however did not. Meal service across the Atlantic was delicious and wide-ranging, including warm nuts, mixed drinks, a Lebanese appetizer plate with hummus and pitas, a green salad complete with lettuce, chicken in a jalapeño cream sauce (how cool is it that they worked in a Spanish-sounding menu item!), sesame potato wedges, green beans, wine, an ice cream sundae, and Sherry. And about ten minutes after the last bit was cleared, I was in the bathroom. By the time we entered Canadian airspace, I'd been to the bathroom adjacent to the cockpit enough times that one of the flight attendants was giving me a worried look, and the 767 was still a long way from Dallas. I was

#justpassingthrough

one of the first people off the plane at the end of the eleven-hour flight, but I'm pretty sure I was the last one from my flight to get through passport control en route to my connecting flight back to DCA. It was then and there, in the DFW international arrivals bathroom, that I resolved never, ever to go to bed in a foreign hotel room without a handy supply of bottled water.

The Americas

A few months after the Sandbox adventure involving Bahrain and Kuwait, another good international mileage run fare popped up, this time from Dulles Airport to Georgetown, Guyana.

Now, stop right there. Do you know where Guyana is? Do you know what continent it's on, or what hemisphere(s) it's in? Do you know anything about its history or its economy or its people? Don't worry – you're not alone. Being a certified (certifiable?) map nerd, I was familiar with Guyana's location on the northern coast of South America, bordering Venezuela and Brazil and Suriname, but I couldn't have told you much more than that.

Guyana was an insignificant enough place that none of the major U.S. airlines flew there. I'd be flying on a Panamanian carrier, which was just starting thrice-weekly service to Georgetown, and crediting the miles to my "home" airline. In fact, the flight schedule was such that the flight from Panama City to Georgetown departed in the morning before the first arrival from Dulles landed at Panama City, so I would be required to spend a night in Panama on the outbound trip.

The necessary research told me no visas or special immunizations would be needed, so there I was making the pre-rush hour trek to Dulles on a beautiful, if slightly chilly, October morning.

Never having flown a Panamanian carrier before, nor really having had anything to do with anyplace between Tijuana and Buenos Aires, I showed up at Dulles far too early and ended up spending over an hour in the business class lounge of a certain German airline, known as the finest lounge at Dulles. So, for a few minutes, there I was in suburban Virginia eating German breakfast food next to a clock showing the current time in Hong Kong while I waited for a flight to Panama, and it wasn't disorienting at all.

#justpassingthrough

You might have the idea in your mind that Panama, being on the Pacific side of the Americas, is someplace south of California. But if you flew south from San Diego looking for Panama, you'd run out of fuel somewhere southeast of Hawaii and nobody on land would see the splashdown. In fact, Panama is almost due south of Washington, DC, and the flight gave me great views of the Carolina coastline, and then of the Bahamas and Cuba. En route to the tropics, I had my first taste of guava-pineapple juice before being served arroz con pollo, or rice with chicken.

Panama, of course, is the textbook example of an isthmus, a narrow strip of land connecting two larger lands (in this case, North and South America), and my flight's approach path went from the Caribbean Sea (which is officially part of the Atlantic Ocean) to the Pacific side of Panama in only ten or fifteen minutes. Just to make you a little more confused, I'll mention that the Pacific Ocean is actually east of Panama City (though also south), while the Caribbean/Atlantic is most immediately to the north and northwest. Don't you believe me? Look at a map.

At Tocumen International Airport, the Panamanian airline operates flights all over North and South America as well as the Caribbean, so that a person can fly from San Francisco to Santiago, or Lima to Montreal, or Havana to Mexico City, or Washington to Georgetown, in a day's travel on narrowbody airliners, with a hassle-free, security checkpoint-free, passport control-free connection in Panama City that compares favorably to one in Charlotte or Salt Lake City or Houston. There's often a downside, though, to an efficient connecting hub, in the form of a sub-par experience for local arriving and departing passengers. If you don't believe me, try being an originating passenger in Atlanta during the morning rush hour and see if you get through the security line in less than half an hour. At Tocumen, the substandardness showed itself in the half hour I spent in line for passport control in a subterranean hallway with poor ventilation.

The Americas

Just after Panama gained independence from Colombia in 1903, it got an official currency called the Balboa, named for the explorer who, according to one rather audaciously-worded website, "discovered the Pacific Ocean in 1513." (I discovered the Pacific Ocean in 1995 on my first visit to San Francisco. Will the future People's Republic of California name its currency the Mueller?) Anyway, the Balboa is pegged at 1:1 with the U.S. Dollar as a way of insulating Panama's economy from inflation and other forms of financial unpleasantness. In practice, Panama's currency is the U.S. Dollar, so the greenbacks in my wallet were just as good after I flew IAD-PTY as they had been in the German airline lounge in Virginia. Not needing to exchange for dong or dinars or dirhams, I picked up a rental car and made a beeline for my one and only planned tourist stop in Panama: the Canal.

#

Panama City, with a metropolitan population larger than 1.5 million people, is about five hundred years old, but its boom time began in the mid-nineteenth century, in the years between the California gold rush and the completion of the U.S.'s Transcontinental Railroad. Even before the Panama Canal was built, it was easier to get from, say, New York to San Francisco by sea than by land, and the 30-mile-wide isthmus was soon spanned by the Panama Railroad to make the journey even easier.

Like so many cities, Panama City has a problem with traffic congestion. To ease the pain for those needing to get between the east side of the metro area (where Tocumen Airport is) and the west side (near the Panama Canal), there are two separate tollways. One on the coast, south of the urban center, is known as Corredor Sur, while the one on the inland side of town is the Corredor Norte. Being firmly in possession of more than enough dollar bills, I got on the Corredor Norte and headed west.

#justpassingthrough

This went very well until I got to the first toll booth. I aimed for a lane marked "tarjetas", Spanish for "cards", where, as a savvy and linguistically sophisticated traveler, I'd knew I'd be able to pay with a credit card and save my cash for something else. That turned out to be a bad plan because "tarjetas" in this instance refers to a special rechargeable toll payment card which a driver can tap in this toll lane, or refill here using cash. Unfortunately, this was not the location to purchase a new tarjeta, and the drivers in the line of cars behind me let me know about it with longer and longer sonatas for various sizes of car horn ensemble. Presently, a police officer arrived to begin a rather impassioned monologue in Spanglish about what the "tarjetas" lane is and is not for. After a few tensely awkward moments, my contrition for misinterpreting the sign was reckoned as righteousness, and I was allowed to pay for a new tarjeta with cash, hand-delivered with a smile by the highway patrol with no markup. At the next toll booth, I found the tarjetas lane and swiped my tarjeta all by myself, like a big boy, glad that I had mastered the art of paying a Panamanian highway toll.

The Corredor Norte unceremoniously dumps its traffic into a bowl of asphalt spaghetti a couple miles from the Pacific end of the Panama Canal. From here, I managed to find my way to what had been from 1903 to 1979 the American-controlled Panama Canal Zone.

Opened in 1914, the Canal itself is one of the greatest engineering projects in the history of the world. It contains six three-lane locks to get ships from sea level up to Gatun Lake, whose surface is about 85 feet above sea level, and back down to sea level to enter the other ocean. Ships transiting the canal between the North Atlantic and the North Pacific save up to 7,900 miles of travel versus going the long way around South America. Transit takes about ten hours, though ships sometimes must wait as long as a day for permission to enter the Canal given the high demand for passage. Tolls for a fully-laden container cargo ship can be as high as $450,000, but I'm not sure whether or not that can be paid with a tarjeta.

Unfortunately, the long line at immigration and then the tarjeta drama delayed my drive just enough that I missed the last entrance time at the Miraflores Locks visitor center. Signs around the visitor parking area warned: "Cuidado posible presencia de cocodrilos en la acera", so with the clock ticking toward sunset I took my wounded pride and left without seeing any ships in the canal, nor even any water in the canal, but also without encountering any crocodiles.

All was not lost, however. I wound my way back southeast toward the Pacific coast and drove across the Bridge of the Americas. This magnificent mile-long cantilever truss bridge carries commuter and long-distance traffic in and out of Panama City across the Pacific mouth of the Panama Canal. This spontaneous adventure took me over the bridge, around a curved ramp, and under the bridge along a 2-lane local coast road. Panamanians were out in large numbers eating picnic dinners while watching the ship traffic. I passed restaurants and parks and a shooting range, and the whole thing was pleasantly un-touristy. This could just as easily have been the Carolina coast I'd overflown that morning. If I'd been local and had a family, I'd have found some food and had a picnic, too, perhaps away from the shooting range.

But since I was a foreigner and a bachelor and quite exhausted, I made a U-turn and headed back across the Bridge of the Americas toward the city center. Part of my route was the cinta costera, literally "coastal beltway", a 2-mile causeway built just off the coast of Casco Viejo and the historic district (an ingenious way to get around the problem of needing to build a road from one side of a protected archeological site to the other, if you ask me), providing first-rate views of the old and modern skylines. In my semi-delirious state at the end of a long day of travel, I mused that as a city built on a major trade route, Panama City was just like Kuwait City, except instead of minarets it has humidity. By this point, all I wanted was to get some dinner and then go to sleep. And all that stood in my way was rush hour traffic.

#justpassingthrough

Rush hour in Panama City is unlike rush hour I've experienced anywhere else, a list of places that includes New York/New Jersey, Washington, Sao Paulo, Los Angeles, Milan, London, Amman, Paris, Atlanta, Tel Aviv, Kuwait City, Buenos Aires, and goodness, let's not forget about Marrakech. Here, it's not the limited-access Corredor tollways that are the problem; it's the city streets, many of which intersect without any particular form of traffic control. I guess the idea is people are supposed to take turns (without necessarily actually stopping, so just like a four-way stop at home), or that the more major route gets priority. But, at least at rush hour, in many places three lanes of southbound traffic fights three lanes of eastbound traffic for use of the intersection, without a break, all evening. Block after block after block gets filled with such congestion, and the quick result is gridlock in which nobody moves more than what seems like a few feet a minute. The last couple miles to my hotel took well over an hour. And then when I spotted the sign, I was just past the entrance to the parking garage and had to spend another twenty minutes or so going around the block for another landing attempt. It was a nice warm-up for Paraty.

If I'd been delirious before, now I was just plain done with Monday. And that's when there was yet another surprise. While the clerk was processing my check-in, I looked around the lobby and spotted some unusual decorations: organ pipes. Except they weren't just decorations. Yes, a vacationing American organist had chosen the Continental Hotel and Casino in Panama City, Panama, for its convenient location and reasonable price and reliable parking availability, and somehow ended up in one of a small handful of hotels in the whole world with a theater organ in its lobby and bar area, a theatre organ with pink lights, no less. No, I didn't offer to play a free concert. I went to the hotel restaurant, ate a steak, retired to room 007 – yes, again – and was neither shaken nor stirred until morning.

#

Morning came too soon, and after Mass at the nearby Iglesia Nuestra Señora del Carmen, I was back in the car heading for Tocumen International Airport. This time, my route made use of the Corredor Sur, a more or less direct route to the airport from downtown near the Torre Trump. Now, as I approached the toll booth, I confidently chose the tarjetas lane, having left my tarjeta in the ash tray in the car door. When it was my turn, I picked up the tarjeta and waved it in front of the scanning device and waited for the gate to go up…and waited and waited and waited. This time, the responding officer pointed out that the Corredor Norte tarjetas don't work in the Corredor Sur toll booths, and vice-versa. So, after forking over another wad of green paper for another tarjeta I'm unlikely to be able to find if I ever need it again, I was on my way once again toward the airport. On the bright side, for some reason there was no traffic on the road ahead of me.

The business class lounge at Tocumen is a far cry from the Teutonic luxury I'd enjoyed the previous morning at Dulles, but it was a place to sit and ponder why they'd had to put a sign next to the toaster explaining that bagels must be split before insertion. The airport also has a properly Catholic chapel dedicated to Our Lady of Loreto, who (according to the airport website) is the patroness of fliers.

#

The morning's flight headed east from Panama City, passing over the Caribbean Sea, Colombia, and Venezuela (where I could see the flames of oil refineries beckoning like the volcanoes of Mordor) before entering Guyanese airspace. Landing at Georgetown's Cheddi Jagan International Airport from the south, the view was of little besides rainforest and the Essequibo River and the tall midday clouds of these tropical lands. Never had I landed in place where I had so little idea what to expect when I got off the plane.

#justpassingthrough

But before even that much could happen, several law enforcement types came on board. Having been upgraded on this segment and thus being seated in row 1, I heard snippets of their conversation, which was in English, with the flight attendants, including the words "spraying" and "deportation". Flights on a foreign carrier are exceedingly few at Cheddi Jagan, and I got the impression these border officers were scrupulously following their prescribed procedures for avoiding occupational boredom.

The terminal had no jetways, and in fact only one gate for all arriving and departing passengers. In front of the terminal was enough parking for several mid-size jets to load and unload, and after a short walk I found myself in what might have passed for a suburban office building at home, the kind with a dentist's office and an SAT-prep center and maybe a post office branch. It had only one story, a couple of baggage belts, and perhaps a half-dozen booths staffed with immigration officers. After that, there was an arrivals hall about the size of your middle school cafeteria with currency exchange and bathrooms and little else, and then the taxi stand. It made the famously compact Ronald Reagan Washington National International Airport look genuinely huge.

Catching a taxi for the 25-mile ride to Georgetown, I reflected on what I'd read about Guyana and what I saw out the window. Guyana is the only mainland country in the western hemisphere where traffic moves on the left; as you probably guessed, that's a legacy of British colonial rule, just as it is on a number of islands in the Caribbean. So is the use of English as an official language, the only such country in South America. The two-lane road passed along the Demerara River, whose regular habit of flooding can make access to the airport a little dicey. I guess when the road is closed, either you ride to the airport in your private helicopter or you just don't leave Guyana. In a few places, I saw evidence of a much-needed widening project, adding another two lanes to this badly congested roadway, which should help spread the flooding over a wider area.

Guyana might appear on a map to be a South American country, and there are paved road links with neighboring Brazil and Venezuela through sparsely populated Amazon rainforest areas. But really, its geographical isolation and British colonial heritage (independence came only in 1966) make it more Caribbean than Latin American in most respects. The population is quite diverse, including the descendants of Africans, Indians, Amerindians, and various other groups. Along the way into the city, I saw religious buildings of various Christian denominations, but also Hindu, Muslim, and Buddhist establishments. If you've heard of Guyana, it might be because of the Jim Jones cult that committed mass suicide here in 1978 by drinking the non-proverbial Kool-aid. Somehow that particular religion seems to have been filtered out of modern Guyanese society.

By the time my cab driver got us into Georgetown, my low expectations were undercut. This place was a dump. Since much of the city lies just below sea level, there's no place for sewage to flow out. And since many of the streets have pools of sewage on either side, why not just throw the trash there, too? Many of the buildings looked flimsy, like something out of a low-budget high school musical scenery shop. When I arrived at the Halito Hotel (I remembered the name by thinking of bad breath) and opened the taxi door, I was hit by the stench of a city with sewage running along its streets. Mercifully, the interior of the hotel was free of this problem, and the room came with some bottled water. In contrast to the otherworldly excitement I would feel the following spring getting to Marrakech, the Halito Hotel felt something like a prison.

I'd arrived in Georgetown for a three-night stay with relatively little idea what to do there, and even less idea when I'd do it. Partly that's because there's not a lot of tourist infrastructure, and partly that's because the few such establishments around didn't bother to maintain even a 1996-grade website listing their hours and admission prices. Even though this was 2014, I planned the remaining two days by opening an actual paper phone book for the first time in a decade in order to call and ask humans voices my questions. How utterly retro!

After a brief stroll around the neighborhood, I returned to the Halito Hotel and ordered dinner in the restaurant. The cuisine on offer mirrored the ethnic and religious diversity I observed on the ride into town. The starter was salmorejo soup, a Spanish-derived dish featuring diced tomatoes and bread crumbs in a clear broth. For the main course, I settled on "Bam Bam Beef Steak", in which the roast piece of cow meat was doused in "a thick Asian marmalade of black bean sauce, red wine, fresh ginger, and cilantro", alongside baked potato slices and what passed for a salad. I had no complaints about these courses, nor about the banana split that functioned as dessert.

The Halito Hotel served its guests breakfast in their rooms each morning (there has to be a halitosis joke in there someplace, right?). My "continental" one consisted of a small muffin, an even tinier banana, a can of orange juice, a napkin, two slices of wheat toast, and a foil-wrapped slab of butter, but no knife with which to spread the butter on the toast. After I figured out how to eat that, I made a self-guided walking tour of downtown Georgetown.

First stop was the National Library, begun with Carnegie money and housed in an unusually sturdy-looking building bearing the industrialist-philanthropist's name. Inside, the collection was on par with what you'd expect in, say, an American city of 25,000 people. There was organization in theory, but also quite a bit of messiness in practice, and the building could have used another room or two to house everything in a more accessible way. For some bizarre reason, I decided to check whether this was a good library or not by trying to find a book I knew a good library must have: Jane Austen's "Pride and Prejudice." There was no gap on the shelf near "Mansfield Park" and "Persuasion", so maybe "Pride and Prejudice" isn't part of their collection.

One display in the library did satisfy an area of curiosity: Guyana's eye-catching flag. It's worth quoting the caption in its entirety:

"The National flag of Guyana is called 'The Golden Arrowhead'. It bears five colors: red, black, yellow, white, and green. The flag has the unique design of two triangles (one within the other) issuing from the same base. The outer triangle is gold-colored (arrow-shaped) with a narrow border of white along two sides. The inner triangle is red with a narrow strip of black bordering the sides. The background of the flag is green, representing the agricultural and forested nature of Guyana. The white border represents the rivers and water potential. The golden arrow represents Guyana's mineral wealth and the black border, the endurance that will sustain the forward thrust of the Guyanese people. The red of the flag represents the zeal and dynamic nature of nation-building which lies before the young and independent Guyana."

A few blocks away sits the Guyana National Museum, in a more typical building with iffy lighting and some open windows for air-conditioning. The exhibits here focus on natural history through the art of taxidermy.

Weary from a half-day spent in a city the smells like sewage, I retreated to the comfort of my room at the Halito Hotel to upload photos to Facebook, read a spy novel, answer e-mails from home, and look up numbers in the phone book in preparation for tomorrow's big outing.

Then, as the sun began to move off to the west, I made my way to the Cathedral of the Immaculate Conception, which is staffed by Jesuits. About 7% of Guyana's 773,000 people are Catholic (working out to roughly 54,000 Guyanese Catholics), and this cathedral is their headquarters. Known informally as the Brickdam Cathedral (after the road by which it stands) to distinguish it from St. George's Anglican Cathedral a few blocks away, the building is of vaguely Gothic proportions in a tropical style. Unlike most churches around the world, this one is surrounded by a moat, probably to collect rainwater and guard against flooding of the cathedral; it also acts as a decent security perimeter and repository for any garbage people might need to discard before entering. Instead of windows, there are ventilation slats near ground level that seem always to remain open to allow a "fresh" breeze.

After Mass, it was time for dinner. Despite having spent over 24 hours in Georgetown, I had yet to detect a full-service restaurant (as distinct from a number of fast-food joints like Burger King and Church's

Chicken) other than the one in the Halito Hotel. So back to the hotel restaurant it was, this time to enjoy Thai chicken curry with rice and steamed vegetables. In the morning, breakfast again showed up in my room. This time, there were two packets of butter and still no knife with which to spread it.

#

In the time I'd spent in the Halito Hotel with the phone book Wednesday afternoon, I'd managed to arrange what everybody most wanted while visiting Georgetown: a trip out of town. About 6:00 a.m. Thursday, as some local boys played soccer in the empty lot across the street, a taxi arrived to drive me to the offices of a domestic airline offering daytrips to particular locations in the Amazon interior of Guyana. I was betting about $200 – and my life – that they do airplane maintenance better than they do website design. It was simply impossible to book online, or even get a good idea of the tour schedule, but my old-fashioned phone call had answered all my questions.

After our payments were taken by credit card imprint or by cash, ten of us including a pilot piled into a large van and set out for Cheddi Jagan International Airport. Arriving there, we were ushered past the security checkpoint and exit passport control (since Cheddi Jagan has no scheduled domestic service, the entire terminal building is designed for international arrivals and departures) and across the sun-drenched apron to a waiting twin-engine propeller aircraft, a Britten-Norman Islander with precisely ten seats, including two for the pilot and co-pilot. Our group was a mix of adventure-traveling couples from Canada and oil-industry workers on holiday from Trinidad and two Guyanese men and me.

By dint of the fact I was a solo traveler, I was asked to sit in the co-pilot's seat. Instantly, this became one of the best days of my life, and not just because I was getting out of stinky Georgetown for a few hours.

The Americas

You don't realize just how big a commercial airport's runway is until you see it from a low angle, as I did that morning. At 150 feet, the standard width for runways at international airports, it's half as wide as a football field is long. Our pilot taxied to the end of one of the runways, hot-rodded a U-turn, opened the throttles, and took us into the sky.

Viewing the landscape two days earlier from six or seven miles up, the rainforest of Guyana's interior had looked rather boring, all green except for the occasional river. Today's flight was at 4500 feet (assuming the altimeter in front of me was accurate) with the windows open for a brisk breeze. Even at mid-morning, the cumulonimbus clouds were starting to build, and I watched as the pilot deftly steered us around the fluffy hazards like a driver avoiding DC potholes. Looking out and down, I spotted mud airstrips used by the mining industry, alongside mines themselves. I saw streams and ponds. And then, as we turned around another cloud, suddenly we were flying up a river valley – no, a river canyon – carved by the Potaro River. Just as suddenly, there was Kaieteur Falls, and still somewhat suddenly, we landed.

The (actual) pilot pulled us off the runway, which had grass growing through hundreds of cracks in its surface, onto a dirt parking space and cut the engines. The quiet was otherworldly. Here I was with nine strangers, only one of whom knew how to fly a plane, at an airstrip with no lights, no control tower, no fuel source, no mechanics, and just a park office for a terminal. As some of the others formed a gaggle and talked about Guyanese politics, I wandered over to the runway and took a few pictures standing on it. This was truly the middle of nowhere, and it smelled nothing like sewage.

Our pilot led us along a trail for about a quarter mile, whence we all got to see the world's tallest single cascade up close and personal. This was tropical paradise worthy of an Indiana Jones movie backdrop, in which water plunged 700 feet and released great quantities of spray all over the place. We were cautioned not to get too close to the edge of the trail, as the rocks might be surprisingly wet. We were shown some of the distinctive flora and fauna: a plant whose leaves are so soft that the indigenous peoples use them for toilet paper, and a species of golden frog small enough to jump into one's nostril if it were so inclined. In case you were wondering, I didn't test either one.

This was the dry season, so the volume of water over the falls was not great, and the river at the top was quite shallow. One of our group members, a Guyanese man with pink shorts and lots of opinions about Guyanese politicians, waded into the river about fifty feet from the precipice. After lunch in the only building within eyeshot, during which a great deal of discussion took place on the upcoming Guyanese elections, we boarded the plane.

I wondered briefly what might happen if the pilot couldn't get the engines started, or if there'd been a fuel leak or something. We were the only people and the only plane there. There was no cell service. There was no road in or out, and the river from Georgetown was blocked by a 700-foot waterfall surrounded by single-ply rainforest and tiny frogs. I'm sure there was some method of calling for help if we'd needed it, and another plane could have gotten there in an hour, but I did entertain thoughts of the ten of us getting out and pushing a disabled plane off the runway so that our rescue flight could land.

No matter. The engines started just fine, and within a few seconds of takeoff we were making figure-eights above the gorge so that passengers on both sides could get one last view of Kaieteur Falls as we departed. From here, it was an epic ride straight down the canyon and up into the clouds. Landing was on the same runway at Cheddi Jagan where I'd landed two days earlier in a 737, though it looked a little different from the co-pilot's seat than it had from Clasa Ejecutiva. When we got into the terminal, we all just walked through an unmanned passport control lane, got into our van, and headed back for the sewer, er, Georgetown. The day's outing had completely changed my outlook on Guyana: in some countries, the big city is a main attraction (think of Paris or Beijing or Rio de Janeiro), but in Guyana, Georgetown is just a barely-necessary evil.

The Americas

The real riches were hidden deep in the jungles of the world's fifth-least-densely-populated country. (Only Mongolia, Namibia, Australia, and Iceland have fewer people per square mile; Canada and neighboring Suriname are the next two countries on the list.)

And the riches aren't just for the eyes. According to the Guyanese government's investment website, Guyana's undeveloped interior is home to "gold, diamonds, and bauxite", as well as "industrial minerals such as kaolin, silica sand, soapstone, jyanite, feldspar, mica, ilmernite, columbite-tantalite, and manganese; base metals such as copper, lead, zinc, molybdenite, tungsten, and nickel; ferrous metals, of which iron as magnetite and laterite is the main type; uranium; and semi-precious stones such as amethyst, green quartz, black pearl, agate, and jaspar," amid other substances auto-correct doesn't recognize.

As a visitor from a powerful and affluent nation to the northwest, it boggles my mind how a land so rich in resources could be home to a nation so poor that they can't afford a proper sewer system in the national capital city, or else don't care to install one. Maybe greed, the thirst for power, and the vestiges of colonialism have something to do with it, but all those things are factors in American society, and have been since long before 1776, yet even our smallest, backwoodsiest towns have provisions to deal with sewage. This is a great mystery.

At length, the van arrived back at the airline/tour company's office in Georgetown. The taxi driver who'd dropped me there early in the morning had agreed to return, but he was nowhere to be seen, so I decided to walk the couple miles back to the Halito Hotel in the faint hope of seeing something beautiful or at least mildly interesting. Other than the fast-food joint where I stopped to buy a bottle of water (it turns out you sweat a lot when you walk a couple miles on a sunny afternoon in the tropics), the best I could find was the cemetery. Here, all the bodies are "buried" in above-ground boxes. Georgetown is, after all, below sea level, and floods happen from time to time.

#justpassingthrough

#

For the third night in a row, still having found no other restaurant I had the slightest desire to patronize, I sat down to eat in the Halito Hotel's restaurant. Memory is fuzzy writing four years later, but I don't recall that there was ever another patron in the restaurant at the same time as me. This time, I went for the beef bourguignon with baked potatoes and mixed vegetables, and as before, I was not disappointed.

For my final meal in Guyana the next morning, I splurged and ordered an omelette instead of the continental breakfast. It came to my room with toast, butter, and a single pathetic-looking slice of tomato, plus – wonder of wonders! – a butter knife.

Having a few hours to burn until the thrice-weekly plane from Panama arrived to carry me back to civilization, I set off to explore more of Georgetown. Just north of where I'd found the National Museum and National Library sits an area one online reviewer had described as "posh". Nothing I'd seen so far in Guyana came anywhere near fitting that description. To be sure, here were some grander houses, but the main difference between this and other neighborhoods was the presence of multiple public trash cans, each quite full. It's a wonder other parts of the city don't invest in a few of these so that they, too, might become posh.

Approaching the northwest corner of Georgetown, where the Demerara River empties into the Atlantic Ocean, I came upon the Georgetown Lighthouse. I'd hoped to be able to climb the lighthouse for a high-angle view of the area, but it was closed to visitors that day. Actually, some recent history involving the Georgetown Lighthouse begins to shed some light on the questions I raised above, regarding why such a mineral-rich country is so poor.

The Dutch built the first lighthouse here, of wood, in 1817 (they colonized Guyana and neighboring Suriname before ceding Guyana to the British) to help ships at sea find the river entrance. In 1830, the British designed and built the present brick structure, crowned with an iron

The Americas

gallery and a thousand-watt lightbulb visible for thirty or forty miles out to sea. So far, so good. The problem came when an international hotel chain bought the "corner" coastal real estate a few blocks downriver from the lighthouse: Midway through construction, somebody realized that the ten-story building would stand directly between the 103-foot lighthouse and the sea. One can imagine at least two problems arising from this arrangement: Firstly, guests in the rooms on one side of the hotel might find it difficult to sleep with a thousand-watt bulb shining in their windows from two blocks away. Secondarily, guests in rooms on the other side of the hotel might have their slumber interrupted by ships running aground because sailors couldn't see the light. For several years, the hotel stood on Guyana's choicest real estate, half-finished, until someone had the bright idea to mount a new light on top of the hotel.

Turning right to walk east along the shore, I found myself in a grassy park area with a number of cows grazing, just like you find in capital cities around the world. Climbing up a berm of perhaps ten or twelve feet, suddenly I found myself at the beach breathing fresh air that smelled nothing like sewage. It was marvelous to see the sea, and to have risen above sea level. You might wonder how a coastal city in the tropics can sit below sea level and not be destroyed every five years by some passing hurricane; I sure did. The answer is simple: Hurricanes don't go here. If a wave comes out of Africa and turns into an "organized" storm over the Atlantic, the prevailing winds always steer it northward toward the lesser Antilles and then maybe Puerto Rico or Hispaniola or Cuba or the Bahamas or Florida or Jamaica or North Carolina. But never does such a storm hit South America.

#

The taxi ride back to Cheddi Jagan International Airport was as mind-numbing as the other three trips I'd made on that road during the week. If ever there were a city/airport situation where mass transit could be justified, this looked like it. One envisions a rail line with two or three stops in Georgetown, a few in the towns along the river, and a terminus at the airport. In contrast to many cities, not least the sprawling metropolises of the United States, here the traffic was really crowded along one skinny corridor. I don't want to assume that the government didn't perform a cost-benefit analysis of building a railroad versus four-laning a congested two-lane road (especially not a government that allowed the construction of a tall hotel seaward of a lighthouse), but I wonder whether adding more lanes will really help improve journey times that much.

Cheddi Jagan is a small airport despite being the only commercial gateway to and from Guyana; all I can add to that picture is that my 3:10 p.m. departure to Panama City was the second-to-last flight of the day, and maybe also that the best lunch I could buy consisted of a candy bar and a bottle of water.

Georgetown is not a place I'd recommend to an American looking for an exciting urban getaway; in fact, I wasn't aware of any other Americans there. Seeing the waters of Kaieteur, though, and the experience of flying there in an unpressurized little plane, ranks as one of my favorite adventures ever. Isn't it funny how sometimes you have to pass through the ugly and the distasteful to reach the truly beautiful? And doesn't the memory of such purgatorial unpleasantness make the good places seem even more heavenly?

To Invade Normandy

No plan of operations extends with any certainty beyond the first contact with the main hostile force.

So wrote Field Marshal Helmuth Karl Bernhard Graf von Moltke, and he ought to have known about such things, for he was Chief of Staff of the Prussian military for three decades in the nineteenth century. Such is the nature of planning most anything, actually, whether the "hostile force" is a great army, a workplace conflict, an election, the weather, or even a technological malfunction.

An experienced travel planner might think of two opposing ideals: One is the internet-enabled, detailed-oriented itinerary designed to make the very most of the time and money available. The other is the open-ended plan that allows the traveler to make spontaneous decisions, take advantage of serendipitous opportunities, and work around unforeseen challenges. Online personality quizzes sometimes reduce this to an either/or proposition, but the mature travel planner – indeed, the mature human being – knows that most situations call for a balance of the two poles, tending in one direction or the other based on the circumstances at hand.

For instance, when I arrived in Guyana I had no firm plans on the ground because the information with which I could have made those plans was not available online, and because even the phone numbers I could have called to ask weren't there. When I visit a city, whether it's a pit like Georgetown or a treasure trove like London, detail-specific planning tends to end once I've made flight reservations, picked a centrally-located hotel, and figured out how I'm getting from one to the other. Back in 2012, I spent three weeks on an "Aleatoric Road Trip", leaving home only with clothes, maps, enough money for three weeks of hotels and food and gas, and enough CD's for three weeks of driving across America, choosing the route as I went.

On the other hand, when I'm trying to cover lots of ground and see lots of places, it can make sense to spend more time planning a tight itinerary, accounting for the opening hours of places I want to see, likely traffic patterns, sunlight angles for driving and sightseeing, and of course the Mass times at particular churches. Having a shorter visit in the destination area mitigates toward careful planning in order to make the best use of limited time; when I plan to spend more than a couple days in a place, my body needs rest times, so spending an hour or two each day planning as I go ends up being a good way to force myself to take that respite.

Many of the journeys I've described in this book arose due to particular opportunities occasioned by particular airfare sales. When one does a lot of travel, one looks for the chance to visit someplace new and exciting without breaking the bank. There's less pressure to make a given trip the journey of a lifetime when one is likely to go overseas again several times in the next year.

But for October 2017, I was planning the journey of a lifetime. I've always been fascinated by the Second World War, its origins and philosophical underpinnings, the military and political history of the war itself, and the profound effects it had on all of human civilization. Earlier that year, I'd gone to Hiroshima, and a couple years earlier I'd been to Pearl Harbor. I'd seen the War Rooms in London, visited Hitler's mountain lair in Bavaria, and driven through towns in (formerly East) Germany where bomb damage from the war still went unrepaired in 2004.

And now, with careful planning of my own, I would tour the sites in Normandy where Allied resolve had fueled so much careful planning, and where so much of that great battle plan was tossed out the window at first contact with hostile forces. Along the way, I would visit London and Paris and Reims, and I would make my pilgrimages to Mont St-Michel and St. Thérèse's adopted hometown of Lisieux.

To Invade Normandy

#

Occasionally I'll sign onto Facebook and read that so-and-so has begun packing for a trip next week. This makes me scratch my head. Do people store their toothbrush and their phone charger in their suitcase for a week? For my part, I usually pack in the hour before I leave for the airport, having made sure the laundry gets done a day or two earlier. I check the destination and en-route weather forecasts and pack the right types of clothing in the right quantities, and maybe an umbrella. I pack my toiletries and then remove the toothpaste and shaving cream to a clear plastic bag in an outer compartment to ease passage through the Blueshirt checkpoint. I toss in the relevant guidebooks, my professional calendar book, and, if there's to be a rental car, a travel case of CD's. (No, I no longer take a Bible because it's heavy and can be accessed easily online.) I stuff in copies of my itinerary, and then phone chargers for wall plugs and car outlets, plus a plug adapter if necessary. My pockets contain my passport, a pen, a pencil, a pack of chewing gum, my wallet, keys, my phone, and my rosary. The whole process seldom takes a half hour.

What made packing a challenge today was that I would be gone for ten nights and would not be checking luggage; a quirk in the way I'd booked my plane ticket meant that checking luggage was likely to be a recipe for trouble, so I eliminated that risk factor entirely. Thus, everything would need to fit in my roll-aboard bag and a smaller "personal item" bag. I'd never crammed so much into such a small space, but a practice run several weeks earlier had proved it was possible. One of the shirts I packed was old and unraveling; my plan was to wear it one day and then throw it out in order to make room to carry souvenirs on the journey home. Yes, this was a meticulously well-planned trip.

When I left for the airport just after noon that Monday, I had the itinerary in both bags and in my shirt pocket to prove exactly what I planned to do, and when, and how, and in what order. Little did I know how quickly my great plan would come tumbling down like the walls of Jericho in the face of small first-world problems.

#

 This time, my belt was holding up my pants as advertised, so the connection at Dallas-Fort Worth did not involve becoming shocked at the price of anything. Instead, I went to the lounge and gawked out the window at my chariot, one of the airline's flagship Boeing 777-300ERs. These birds fly all the high-profile routes; next to the aircraft I would shortly be boarding for London were the planes headed to Hong Kong, Sao Paulo, and Tokyo. On board are seats for 8 First Class guests, 52 Business Class customers, and 248 Economy Class sardines. Tonight, I would be in a state-of-the-art Business Class suite with three windows, direct aisle access, a personal TV screen, noise-cancelling headphones, multiple storage drawers, two individually-controlled lights, an oversize tray table, a small flat workspace, and a seat that could be customized as a recliner or converted into an actually-flat bed. No, I didn't pay the upper four-figure asking price, but used the last of my one-way upgrade certificates.

 After takeoff, the flight path bent to the west and, looking out my right-side window, I could see the hostile force that required the detour: a line of thunderstorms extending from Oklahoma to Iowa. The jagged lightning was a thrill to watch from sixty or eighty miles away.

 I'd chosen to backtrack through DFW on this trip so that I could actually get some rest on the overnight flight. The five-course meal service wrapped up someplace near Toronto, and then I slept until Ireland. After landing, I was able to take a shower in the arrivals lounge at Heathrow (the kind of shower that entails a continuous flow of hot water at the discretion of the shower-taker) before boarding the Heathrow Express and minding the gap to board the Circle Line at Paddington. Feeling more mobile after storing my stuffed-to-the-gills luggage at Kings Cross station, I hopped on the Victoria Line and made for Westminster Cathedral, where I unburdened myself further by taking advantage of the Eucharist and Confession. Waiting in line, I was somehow reminded of Isaac Watts's hymn-paraphrase of the 23rd psalm, which would stick in my mind for the rest of the trip:

> *My Shepherd will supply my need:*
> *Jehovah is His Name;*
> *In pastures fresh He makes me feed,*
> *Beside the living stream.*
> *He brings my wand'ring spirit back*
> *When I forsake His ways,*
> *And leads me, for His mercy's sake,*
> *In paths of truth and grace.*

Having shed both my physical and spiritual baggage, I rode the Tube back as far as Holborn, then zigzagged at street level to the British Museum. Here, in contrast to my previous visit a year and a half earlier, there was an elaborate security queue set up in a giant tent in the courtyard, a reminder than Britain (like any country that stands up to certain kinds of tyranny) is not quite as safe a place as we'd all like to imagine.

The British Museum, according to Google, is "A historian's treasure trove." And that's pretty much all there is to say about a place that houses the Rosetta Stone and stuff from King Tut and artifacts from every world culture the British ever ruled. That's a lot of cultures: A popularly-circulated map depicts the 22 countries (out of about 200 in today's world) that British forces have never invaded or occupied. Naturally, as many of the former colonies and adversaries have become independent nations, some of their governments, or else groups of concerned citizens, have demanded that the United Kingdom return what amounts to a big pile of stolen property. So far, Her Majesty's government has not accepted such invitations.

#justpassingthrough

The British Museum is one of those places one should never try to "finish" in one visit. An attempt to do so would leave one with the intellectual equivalent of an ice cream headache, to say nothing of the bodily equivalent of really sore feet. Mercifully, admission is free, so there's no sense of needing to get one's money's worth on a given visit. Instead, I'm seeing it little-by-little whenever I'm in town and have a half hour to kill. This time I sauntered through a couple galleries, noting a bust of King George III, who inspired some of Thomas Jefferson's best writing. There was also a wood carving of St. Catherine trampling the head of some unfortunate emperor.

One of the best things about being in London is that you're in London; from the British Museum, I made good use of the fall sunshine and strolled through Russell Square and eventually across Euston Road into Kings Cross station. As I retraced my earlier steps back to the luggage storage place, I noted the curious phenomenon whereby a large group of people, including some children but mostly young adults, waited dutifully in a rope queue that seemed to lead to a gift shop called "9 ¾". Upon closer inspection, it became clear that in between the rope queue and the gift shop was a brick wall labeled "Platform 9 ¾". Here, Harry Potter fans took turns donning Gryffinclaw and Slytherpuff scarves and posing for pictures as if they were on their way to Hogwizards School of Witchery and Wartcraft. At least as long as I was watching, nobody actually attempted to run through the brick wall.

#

Having avoided becoming the patronus of a visiting muggle, I retrieved my – UGH! – luggage and crossed the street to St. Pancras International station. Instead of flying to France, I'd booked the train from London to Paris. In fact, this had been a bucket-list item ever since 1991 when Mrs. Burtch had told us second-graders that the Chunnel was under construction.

To Invade Normandy

The Chunnel was first brainstormed as early as 1801, though construction began in earnest in 1988, with the first service starting in 1994. The idea is on the surface quite simple: to connect the extensive British rail network with the mainland Eurasian rail network, allowing the free movement of people, their cars, and all manner of freight between Great Britain and the mainland of Europe. Like NATO, the European Economic Community, the European Union, and other such internationalist projects, it was a sign that by the end of the twentieth century Europeans would be bound by what they had in common and war between their countries would be unthinkable. Of course, some in the United Kingdom thought the Chunnel was a bridge too far, that its construction would surrender the one insurmountable advantage that had kept their islands free from continental domination since 1066. The jury is still deliberating on that front, for sure.

Unlike most journeys I've taken by rail, this one involved passing through a metal detector and having my passport stamped by French police officers even though I was still firmly on British floor tiling. With those formalities out of the way, the train ride itself began well enough. Announcements were made in English and French, and the people around me spoke a mix of the two languages. The platform gave way to the rail yard, and the rail yard gave way to the suburbs, and the suburbs gave way to England's green and pleasant land. So far, so good.

One of the supposed advantages of rail travel is the it's a more communal experience than riding in the privacy of one's own car. Another is that you get to see the landscape from a human vantage point as opposed to viewing it from cruising altitude. I wasn't passionate about any of this; each mode of transport has its comparative advantage and its drawbacks, and thus its place in the panoply of options available to the traveler. My interests today boiled down to timely and efficient transport for point A to point B, and then perhaps bragging rights to having used one of the marvels of the modern world. That's why I had booked my nonstop ticket from London to Paris on the Eurostar.

As for the social aspect of intercity train travel, there was indeed some worthwhile people-watching to be done. Just across the aisle sat four American women, perhaps in their 60s and 70s, around a table. I could tell they were American by listening to their accent, and so, no doubt, could the people three train cars away. After a short time, I learned that in addition to being American, they'd been on a daytrip to London from Paris, and that they were quite drunk.

Meanwhile, on the other side of me sat a French woman, sixtyish, trying to read a novel but putting it down every page or two to sigh loudly at the drunk Americans, as if to implore someone to do something (stop the train and toss them overboard, maybe?) to keep those vile creatures out of her culturally pristine homeland.

After a few minutes of this, the drunk ladies began to doze off, an arm hanging off the seat there, a stray leg blocking the aisle there. The French woman on my left began to calm down, but then a cell phone rang in the purse of one of the American ladies. And it rang and it rang and it rang. By now, I was about ready to use some choice words in French myself, and the ladies just sawed their logs while the rest of us suffered in quiet. A few moments later, the caller tried again, and this time the phone's owner woke up to answer it using that voice you use when you can't tell how loudly you're speaking because you're wearing headphones, except without the headphones. The conversation went on for a couple minutes, and I sensed there a small but potent French missile could be launched just above my cranium at any given time. Certainly, I dared not choose this moment to examine my passport, lest I be added to the target list for the sake of thoroughness.

All this was great fun and games, but then I noticed the Kentish countryside was passing at quite a slow pace, and eventually it came to a stop entirely. This was supposed to be a non-stop train to Paris, and we were quite still in England, yet we were stopped. After a few moments, a voice came over the intercom to explain that a freight train had broken down midway through the 30-mile Chunnel and would have to be towed out.

To Invade Normandy

We would have no choice but to wait while that mission was accomplished.

Now we were all facing a hostile force, the broken-down freight train, together. The drunk Americans were less obnoxious, and the French woman read her novel disdaining something else for a change. Thank goodness for the obstacles that put our differences in perspective.

Eventually I gave up on Eurostar's free Wi-Fi, having gotten what I paid for, and connected to the French cell data network to check e-mail. I had a message from a colleague, an organist named Paul (but not the same one I'd met in New York) saying that he wouldn't be able to do whatever thing I'd asked him to at home because he was out of the country, currently in Paris.

The train rolled into Gare du Nord nearly an hour late. I retrieved my bags from overhead – UGH! – and left the station for the pleasantly cool Parisian evening and ¾-mile walk to my hotel up the Rue de Dunkerque, named for the city associated with the largest evacuation from France in modern history. The hotel clerk was not amused that I didn't have a €1 coin with which to pay the tax on my otherwise-prepaid room. This was an odd thing, for sure; in a culture where sales tax is included in the advertised purchase price of anything, people checking into hotels who'd been in-country for fifteen minutes were expected to have change to pay a tax that wasn't included in the online booking price.

The clerk forgave me (maybe the French weren't all merciless, after all, or maybe he was less annoyed because I conducted the transaction in French) and I squeezed into the broom closet with my hefty baggage and rode it up to the third level. On emerging, of course, I still had to carry the bags up five steps or so before I found my room. Inside, I removed the shoes from my aching feet and discovered that the carpet was wet. Under other circumstances, I would have asked for a different room, but what was to say it would be any better? My shoes were off, so I took off my socks, too, and started to get ready for bed.

And when I realized I hadn't had any dinner, I put them back on.

As I had planned this trip so meticulously, I chose the hotel with the wet carpet on purpose. No, it's not that I like my feet to be wet when I get in bed, but I needed someplace I could find easily from Gare du Nord (mission accomplished) and someplace whence I could climb Montmartre before dawn.

By 1871, Napoleon III and the French had lost a war to Field Marshal von Moltke's Prussian armies and their battle plans. In the same period, there was a secular uprising in the Paris Commune, whose stronghold was here on Montmartre, during which revolutionaries had executed Archbishop Georges Darboy, making him another martyr upon the Hill of Martyrs. Darboy's successor, Archbishop Guibert, is said to have had a vision on this site in 1872, saying, "It is here. It is here where the martyrs are, it is here that the Sacred Heart must reign so that it can beckon all to come." Soon, social sensibilities were such that the Church was expected to play an important role alongside the government of the new Third Republic in rebuilding and renewing French society, and the land where Guibert had had his vision was requisitioned under what we might call "eminent domain" laws for the "public utility" of building a great church dedicated to the Sacred Heart of Jesus. Political, social, and economic forces delayed construction of the Basilica of the Sacred Heart of Jesus, and Sacré-Coeur was not consecrated until 1919, after a far more disastrous war with the great power to the east.

But in order to see any of this with my own eyes, I had to imitate Kaiser Bill and get up the hill. My plan called for me to leave no later than 6:35 a.m. to walk the one-third of a mile to Sacré-Coeur for 7:00 a.m. Mass. I confidently marched up to the park, but this time the hostile force was a locked gate. Welp… now what?

I headed first to the east, but the park fence went as far as I could see, which was not very far in the mists of the Parisian dawn. I gave up on

To Invade Normandy

this plan, and walked west instead. And here was a detail I'd somehow missed in all my months of planning: to ascend Montmartre, you use the Funiculaire (if you speak Pittsburghese, think "incline"). In fact, at this early hour, I was the only customer to use what is, despite its name, technically a double elevator. That is to say, instead of a conventional funicular design in which each of the two cars is the counterweight of the other, here each of the two cars has its own counterweight and thus operates independently of the other. I didn't learn this until I researched it for this book. At the time, I was glad to be able to reach the entrance of the Basilica without having to climb the 220 steps next to the Funiculaire. It's not a free ride; despite being unconnected to any other form of public transit, the Funiculaire is considered a line of the Paris Métropolitain, and the 90-second ride costs the same as a trip all the way across Paris with multiple transfers. And it's worth every penny.

The church is loosely Roman-Byzantine in style, and while the distinctive onion domes are visible from much of Paris, nothing quite prepared me for my first entrance into Sacré-Coeur. My planning had told me there was perpetual adoration of the Blessed Sacrament, but I assumed that was in some side chapel, away from the flow of tourists. No, here the consecrated host is enthroned in a monstrance front-and-center all day and all night. I walked in, saw that I was in the Presence of the King of the Universe, and was overcome with the majesty of it all.

Once I recovered from the initial shock, I surveyed my other surroundings. Above the altar and sanctuary, there is a mosaic of Christ in Majesty. Though the Basilica is only about a century old, this image is part of an iconographic tradition dates to the earliest years of the Church. In fact, one school of thought holds that the Pantokrator (Greek for "ruler of all", generally speaking) is an adaptation of the way the ancient Greeks depicted Zeus. On closer inspection, I could see the Holy-Spirit-as-dove and the partly hidden figure of God the Father. And unlike other Pantokrators I'd seen, this one included the Sacred Heart of Jesus, the original bleeding heart. This devotion is one of the most widely practiced in the world, revealed to the French nun St. Margaret Mary Alacoque, and calls to mind the Passion and Death of Christ in relation to his Divine Mercy. It is in this light that the mission and vocation of Sacré-Coeur involves perpetual Eucharistic adoration, confession, and holy Mass. As a place of pilgrimage, it is not a parish church.

#

The previous evening, my American friend Paul (not the same as the Paul I met in New York, but also an organist) had agreed to meet me this morning by St. Joan of Arc, one of the two large statues on the plaza in front of the Basilica (the other being King St. Louis IX, of whom there is more to be said shortly). About 8:00 Wednesday morning, that's where I found Paul, and after exchanging pleasantries we strolled off to Montmartre to find some crêpes for breakfast. Paul explained that he is a frequent visitor to Europe: every couple months, he flies to Europe and rides his bicycle for a week or two, then flies home to work for a while before returning to his bike. Rinse and repeat. This time, Paul had arrived in Paris a day or so before me, with the intention of taking a train to someplace in nearby Germany to pick up his bike from a friend and ride it to Scotland. Perhaps his plan involved a boat ride, too. The hitch was that Paul's German friend was away from home for another day or two, so Paul was stuck in Paris. I was overcome with compassion for poor Paul.

#

After catching up on life, riding the Métro for a while, and posing for a photo-op in front of Notre-Dame, I bid Paul farewell and continued a morning walk along the Seine. It was cloudy, but the temperature was mild and the tourists were relatively few, even in the courtyard in front of the Louvre. In the last half hour I'd strolled casually past two of Paris's three most-visited sites, and had no plan to visit the Eiffel Tower.

Indeed, I never even saw the Eiffel Tower on this visit, though on a previous weekend in Paris I'd waited in two hours of lines to get to the top and look at Paris through a cloud. Was I a jaded traveler?

No, just a focused one. Even as I posed for a selfie with the Arc de Triomphe as a hat, I was going over the complicated plans I'd set up for the next few days. I was to ride the train to Reims today, spend until Friday morning there gawking at the cathedral and tasting champagne, then pick up my rental car and drive west, arriving Saturday at Mont St-Michel and then plunging into the historical meat of my journey, the beaches and museums and monuments of Normandy, interspersed with a pilgrimage to Lisieux, visits to culinary and cheese-related sites, and (I'd appreciate this after all the war stuff) Monet's estate at Giverny, before flying home next Thursday.

Remember when I said, in the context of a daytrip to Chicago, that freelancers sometimes find that they haven't been paid on payday? A rash of that had occurred in the week or two before my impeccably-planned French odyssey. I'd managed to collect enough cash to fund the trip, but it was more complicated than that. I had credit card payments due while I was overseas, and each of those means a chunk of cash can't be spent but the credit doesn't become available for a day or two. I also knew the rental car would temporarily make funds/credit unavailable in excess of the final cost of the rental; then there were the fluctuations of the exchange rate, plus the perpetual possibility of the unexpected. I had flirted with cancelling the trip a few days before departure, but determined that with careful monitoring of accounts and tight control over discretionary spending (Do I really need that second glass of wine? Can I visit the castle with €10 admission and free parking instead of the one with €35 admission and parking by the hour?), I'd have plenty of margin for error. Besides, my trip home was funded by frequent flyer miles, and my balance in that account was enough to get me my airline's last available seat home from Paris, in any class of service, on any given day if some emergency were to take place. And with the phone in my pocket, I could summon help instantaneously from dozens of family or friends in an emergency. I wasn't just unworried, I was confident. I figured that if I could get home from Vietnam by going the long way around the world, and if I could drive safely through storms on I-95, and if I could walk away when the Washington Metro closed down unexpectedly, this trip would go just fine, too. And I certainly wasn't going to throw all my planning away like Chicken Little.

#

Checking out of the hotel with the wet carpet, I dragged my – ugh! – bags back down the Rue du Dunkerque, past Gare du Nord, to Gare de l'Est. Here, I found my way to the TGV (Train à Grande Vitesse, literally "Train of Large Speed") bound for Reims, just an hour away. On this ride, there were no drunk Americans, no tunnels blocked by incompetent freight trains, and in exactly an hour I stumbled off with my l – ugh! – gage and spent fifteen minutes trying multiple exits from the station until I found the one that led to my hotel.

Dragging overloaded bags three-quarters of a mile over old pavements is nobody's idea of fun, but taxi rides get expensive and this is a good way to survey the options for dinner later. And in that process, you just might remember that you're past due for lunch, too. It should have been a red flag that my focus on fulfilling my plans had caused me to almost forget to eat two of my first three meals in France.

#

After dragging my bags to a third-floor room, I made for the Musée de la Reddition, about a mile away on the far side of the tracks. The building was originally a school, and most of it still is today, but some upper rooms were commandeered by General Dwight Eisenhower in 1945 as Allied troops pushed through Germany to the east. The entrance is flanked not only by the Tricolor, but also by the Union Jack, the Stars and Stripes, and the Hammer and Sickle. A picture inside shows Eisenhower welcoming Winston Churchill and Gen. Charles DeGaulle.

In the first week of May, 1945, just after Adolf Hitler's suicide, Third Reich President Karl Dönitz dispatched Col. Gen. Alfred Jodl to Reims with instructions to surrender to the Western Allies, but not to the Soviets. This did not meet the Allied requirement for an unconditional surrender, and they told Jodl that Nazi Germany must surrender to all the Allies or none of the Allies. Allied high command did agree to allow a 48-hour delay for Germany to withdraw its troops on the Eastern Front so that they would not be taken prisoner by the Red Army. And so, on May 7, 1945, Jodl signed the official Act of Military Surrender to the Allied Expeditionary Force, represented by British Lt. Gen. Alfred Bedell Smith, and to the Soviet High Command, represented by Maj. Gen. Ivan Souslaparov, witnessed by Maj. Gen. François Sevez representing the host country. Gen. Eisenhower did not sign, and did not attend the signing, because he outranked Jodl. Visitors to the Musée today can see the conference room where the surrender took place, with maps covering the walls.

In a sense, visiting the Musée de la Reddition before seeing the beaches of Normandy was a plot spoiler, but the realities of geography dictated that my plan must be flawed in this way. In another way, this trip was turning out far better than I had asked or imagined: The dreary morning in Paris had given way to blue skies with fluffy white clouds. On my way back to the hotel, I paused for a while in a small park to admire the Tricolor against such a smile-inducing celestial backdrop. As with my photos in London the previous day, I noticed that my camera was producing slightly blurry or unfocused pictures. Since there was nothing to be done about it, I kept going.

#

#justpassingthrough

The quietly brilliant afternoon gave way to a near-perfect evening, so I settled into an outdoor dining area for what would be one of the best meals of my third visit to France. Round one was Salade de chèvre chaud ("salad of goat hot", to be overly literal). Here was a just-right pile of green lettuce, radishes, tomatoes, carrots, and onions, topped with two perfectly round cakes of warm goat cheese. Admiring it, I almost hated to destroy it with fork and knife, but the perfectly-sculpted salad did not long survive contact with the hostile forces in my hands. For the main course, I chose Sauté de beouf a l'oignons with a side of tagliatelle (beef onion stew with the consistency of a chocolate éclair) and I paired it with a red wine from the nearby Burgundy region.

I slept well that night.

#

Thursday was even more beautiful than Wednesday, the perfect backdrop for exploring the charms of Reims, but my first order of business on emerging from the hotel was to find breakfast. The glory of French cuisine is that the simple things are as good as the complicated things, and I eagerly devoured two croissants for the price of one. Why I received that discount I didn't understand, and I felt no compulsion to press the matter.

Next, I had to tend to a small emergency. No, my belt hadn't disintegrated, but my rosary had. I'd purchased it two years earlier at the cathedral in Mexico City, and now one end had become detached so that it was no longer a loop. Thus, I took the rare step of departing from my itinerary and entering Reims cathedral for the first time with a commercial purpose in mind. I don't know why (perhaps I was thinking in terms of frugality) but for some reason I emerged with the simplest black plastic rosary in the gift shop.

I couldn't help but spend some time gawking at the cathedral, and then made my way through the Palais du Tau museum next door with its

To Invade Normandy

exhibits on the history and construction of this place. Deciding to get back on the printed program, I walked just over a mile through Reims to my next appointment.

#

Come quickly! I am tasting the stars!

According to legend, these are the words uttered by Dom Pierre Pérignon, O.S.B. (1638-1715), the monk frequently (but falsely) credited with the invention of the sparkling wine that came to be known by the name Champagne. You've probably heard that, by law, only sparkling wine produced here can bear that name; the fine sparkling wines of California and Italy and other places cannot be called "Champagne", just as "Bordeaux" and "Burgundy" and "Côtes du Rhone" are used exclusively by wines produced in those reasons (and so with wines from Chianti in Italy, Rioja in Spain, etc.). This contrasts with the products of vintners in the United States and South Africa and South America and Down Under, among other places, where wines are known by the "varietal" of grapes used: Chardonnay, Cabernet Sauvignon, Merlot, Pinot Grigio, and so forth.

My mission Thursday afternoon was to take a tour of the Champagne production process at Champagne Taittinger. Among the top ten Champagne producers, all headquartered in Reims, in neighboring Épernay, or in other nearby towns, Taittinger (which ranks sixth for quantity of worldwide distribution) is the only family-owned business. In contrast to some wineries you might have visited in Napa Valley or elsewhere, Taittinger and its neighboring competitors don't age their products in the same place where the grapes are grown. Instead, these larger producers own farm fields that may be scattered all over the region and then bring the fruits to their in-town cellars for bottling, aging, and distribution. Thus, while I was visiting a winery, there were no vineyards in sight.

#justpassingthrough

Our tour group gathered in the lobby of the Taittinger facility, and after we showed our pre-purchased tour tickets to a functionary sitting at the desk, a young woman appeared and began to give us the pre-tour spiel. She conducted the entire tour in good, though obviously non-native, English. As things progressed, I was reminded that some people build an entire vacation around visiting Champagne and touring all the major production houses, then going home and regaling party guests with their advanced knowledge of Champagne. One couple, though, stood out as actually being knowledgeable, and later in the tour I overheard them saying they were vintners from northern California who decided to go on vacation to Europe because wildfires had forced them to evacuate their home.

With the formalities out of the way, our guide unlocked a door, and we all descended the stairs to a subterranean cavern filled with aging Champagne. Actually, the "cavern" was the remains of the Abbey of St-Nicasius, whose patron was a local bishop beheaded by either the Romans or the Vandals or the Huns (take your pick) and which was destroyed in the French Revolution. With dim lighting and cool temperatures, the Abbey's tunnels and passageways were the ideal environment for this stage of production. Along the way, we passed a set of heavy wooden sacristy doors decorated with symbols of Christ's Passion.

Like all wines, Champagne is produced after grapes are crushed and the resulting juice is allowed to ferment. After this, unlike non-sparkling types, the wine is poured into bottles, which are sealed, allowing a second round of fermentation. This has several effects:

First, Champagne has somewhat higher alcohol content than other wines.

Second, the gas produced in this second fermentation has no way to escape, so it remains (literally) bottled up, causing the high pressure that leads to the popping of the cork.

And third, as it waits in vain to escape the bottle, the gas forms Champagne's trademark bubbles.

To Invade Normandy

While most Champagne is sold in standard .75-liter bottles like other wines, it is also bottled and sold in other sizes, from the small ones you might be served on an airplane to larger, party-size bottles named Magnum (1.5 liters), Jereboam, Rehoboam, Methuselah, Salmanazar, and Balthazar, all the way up to the Nebuchadnezzar (15 liters). As we were led past a display of the different sizes of bottle Taittinger produces, our guide casually mentioned that the largest one is generally shipped only to the Riviera and to Russia.

When you book a Champagne tour, you're usually also booking a Champagne tasting. A large vintner like Taittinger produces different grades of product, some the vintage of particular years or grape varietals, others a mix of whatever is most available. The thing is, it's all Champagne and it all sparkles and it all tastes good and it'll all make you tipsy if you drink it in significant quantities. Sitting before a website an ocean away a month beforehand, I decided to go for a tasting of two mid-grade Champagnes, making sure that I would not have to drive later that day. Others can tell you how the Compte de Champagne Blanc de Blancs (a 2006 vintage made purely with Chardonnay grapes) has a more pristine taste than the Brut Réserve, but I can definitely assert that they both sparkle and they both taste good and they both make a pilgrim tipsy when said pilgrim drinks them in significant quantities.

It tasted like the stars.

#

Because I'm good at travel planning, I made sure my next stop was nearby, that it was easy to find, and that I could spend a good deal of time there recovering from the tour and tasting. I'm speaking of the second-largest church in Reims, the Abbey of Saint-Remi. Conveniently, the Abbey had an evening Mass that day, and the intervening hour and a half was just enough for me to undertake a detailed photography session, let the stars work their way through my bloodstream, and enjoy a long, slow, northern sunset through the stained glass pretty much by myself, with most of the artificial lights off.

St. Remi(-gius) (437-533) was known as "Bishop of Reims and Apostle of the Franks", and is most famous for having baptized Clovis I, King of the Franks, along with 3000 others the same day. Wikipedia summarily credits him as the founder of French Catholicism. Clovis was the first monarch to reign over what we now call France, and converted with some prodding by his wife, Ste-Clotilde. His relics rest here in an unsubtle block of stone behind the apse. The perimeter of the tomb is decorated with carvings of St. Remigius in various poses, rather like the outtakes of a selfie session.

As I continued to wander around the church, as the sun continued to set the west rose window ablaze, as the doubly-fermented local products continued to work their way through me, I couldn't help but slow down and gaze heavenward. This place was imagined, designed and built before the advent of CAD, forklifts, cranes, or jackhammers. The builders simply did their math, used their hands and a few simple tools, and took their time knowing that their individual labors were part of a process of building and rebuilding over a period of centuries. This was an act of faith, and an act of evangelism still at work in the hearts of schedule-bound Americans more than a millennium later.

And in this city of 180,000 people, St-Remi was only the second-ranking church.

#

Friday morning I arose well before dawn. I had a cathedral to tour and photograph, a rental car to pick up, a couple hours' driving to accomplish, a chateau to visit, and then another four hours of driving to put behind me in order to begin exploring Normandy on Saturday morning. It was perhaps the most ambitious day of my well-planned visit to France, and I was looking forward to nearly every moment of it.

To Invade Normandy

It may be that there's a place more grand, more royal, more Catholic, more historically significant, or more French than Reims cathedral, but I'm at a loss to think where that place might be. Being me, and having a schedule to keep, I was in the cathedral square before opening time with a few others, sitting on benches in the chilly moonlit morning, looking up at the majesty before me, thinking of all that had happened in this little corner of the world.

There was at one point a Gallo-Roman bath on this site until St. Nicasius founded the first church here in 401 or thereabouts. It was in that church that, about 95 years later, Clovis would come to be baptized by St. Remigius, beginning the widespread Christianization of what we now call France. In the ninth century, after Pope Stephen IV crowned Emperor Louis the Pious, the Emperor decided to have the church rebuilt because of its poor condition. By now, it was the seat of the Archbishops of Reims, making it a cathedral. When that thirty-year project was finished, the cathedral was decorated with all the latest art work, including tapestries, statues, gilding, mosaics, and so forth. Over the next couple centuries, kings and clerics left their mark on the Carolingian-era cathedral, adding substantially to its size, but also giving it beautiful stained-glass windows and bells.

Beginning in 1027, most of the Kings of France were crowned in Reims Cathedral, putting yet more focus on the building. In the twelfth century a new Gothic-style east end (apse and choir) was built, with a matching west façade, while the body of the nave and the transepts remained in the earlier Carolingian style. However, in 1210, the cathedral was destroyed by a fire whose origins were never specifically determined. Not to worry, for the archbishop was oddly well-prepared with plans for a new cathedral, and construction began the next year on the present Cathedral of Our Lady of Reims. The first part to open was the apsidal chapel, the easternmost part of the cathedral, in which I would shortly attend Holy Mass.

#justpassingthrough

The rebuilding committee decided the new cathedral needed to be larger than the old one in order to accommodate the crowds that gathered every time there was a coronation, so new land was obtained to the west of the old cathedral's footprint. This may have been the start of a struggle between the cathedral's chapter and the people of Reims, which was fought in the realms of legal jurisdiction and tax status. From 1233 to 1236, things got so bad that the clergy all left town, forbidding any sacramental celebration in their absence. Still, it took until 1299 to purchase lead for the nave's roof, and even then it only happened because the king allowed a tax break on the material. The façade that towered before me took several more decades to complete.

The French Revolution did less damage here than at other French cathedrals, but funds for the repairs were not authorized until 1860.

No sooner had that been accomplished than the Great War broke out. In an effort to preserve their treasured cathedral, the French declared it a hospital and therefore off-limits to German bombing. The Germans didn't initially get that memo, so a Reims municipal worker went to the German gun position four miles away and politely asked the gunners to please stop firing on the large Gothic hospital in the middle of town and, being gentlemen, the Germans complied for a while. But eventually some other indignity offended the Germans, and they once again began shelling central Reims. Some wooden scaffolding caught fire, one thing led to another, and the roof lead which had once been the subject of a royal tax loophole melted, flowed through the gargoyles, and destroyed surrounding buildings including the Bishop's Palace. In turn, pictures of the devastation were circulated by the French government as evidence of the Germans' utter depravity, and so it went. Repair work continues today.

#

At long last, a maintenance worker unlocked the small side door and I entered the nave. The hordes of tourists were still a few hours away, and

To Invade Normandy

just as I'd witnessed the sunset through stained glass across town the previous evening, so I got to experience the quiet majesty of sunrise in one of the world's greatest churches virtually undisturbed. As the sun rose in the east, its light entered first through Marc Chagall's 1974 stained glass windows over the apse chapel, a modern-era replacement for those destroyed in the Great War. Here, as in so much of the Church's life, new creativity was necessarily bound into the old framework.

At Mass under those great windows, I was able to join effortlessly in the chanting of the Sanctus and Agnus Dei because they were in the Church's universal language, exactly the same as I'd sung in Beijing and so many other places around the world. My fear is that the widespread use of the vernacular, evangelically well-intentioned as it may be, is contributing to the balkanization of Catholicism, in which North Americans can visit Africa or Asia and have little in common with the local religious practice. By maintaining even these small bits of unity, the stranger is welcomed home thousands of miles from the address on his driver's license by way of a familiar tune in a strange dead language.

After Mass, as the sunlight poured through more and more windows, I admired the grand organ with its Baroque-era casework sitting over the north transept door. It is here that generations of organists, the most famous probably being Nicolas de Grigny (1672-1703), have filled this majestic building with fittingly majestic music. Nearby sits the chapel where the Blessed Sacrament is reserved; plaques indicate that this is the altar where St. Jean Baptiste de la Salle celebrated his first Mass on April 10, 1676.

In addition to St. Remigius, who is depicted over the west door holding his own chopped-off head, the most famous saint associated with Reims is King St. Louis IX, who was crowned here as a twelve-year-old in 1226. His mother ruled in his stead for several years until he was old enough to assume the full duties of kingship.

Now, as a red-blooded American, I'm trained to look skeptically at monarchy and monarchs, but the fact of Louis' canonization got my attention, so I dug into his life story a little more. Would you believe that history turns out to be a little more complicated than "monarchy is bad"?

Louis married Margaret of Provence, and together they had eleven children, of whom nine made it to something like adulthood. During his reign over France, then considered the "oldest daughter of the Church", Louis dealt with his share of political controversies, territorial disputes, rebellions, and domestic policy struggles. He is credited with reforms of France's criminal justice system, including the institution of direct appeal to the king for all judgments, introducing the presumption of innocence in criminal cases, and cracking down on the crimes of blasphemy, prostitution, charging interest on loans, and gambling. Louis paid top franc for the relics of Christ's Passion, including the Crown of Thorns, and built Sainte-Chappelle in Paris to house them (I first visited the relics in their latter-day home in the apse of Notre-Dame de Paris). Louis's piety led him to personally join the Seventh Crusade in the Holy Land (remember, whatever atrocities may have been committed, the Crusades were born of the desire to recover lands that had been Christian but were overrun by Islamic armies) and this led to four years in Egyptian captivity. When that was over, he then went on the Eighth Crusade in what is now Tunisia (formerly Carthage), where he died of dysentery in 1270, never having made it to the end of the Oregon Trail. Louis is the namesake of the American city of St. Louis as well as San Luis Potosi in Mexico. Many churches are named for him worldwide, including a California mission, as well as the cathedrals of New Orleans and St. Louis. Also named for him are an island in Paris, the capital of Mauritius, and much else all over the world.

King St. Louis IX is quoted as saying,

> *"I think more of the place where I was baptized than of Reims cathedral where I was crowned. It is a greater thing to be a child of God than to be the ruler of a Kingdom. This last I shall lose at death but the other will be my passport to an everlasting glory."*

To Invade Normandy

As I tried to tear myself away from Reims cathedral, I heard in His Majesty's words the truth of the matter. As glorious as this place was, it was only a stop on the journey to heaven, a pale shadow of beauty that is the reward of a life lived seeking God's face. So I walked out the door.

> *When I walk through the shades of death,*
> *Thy presence is my stay;*
> *A word of Thy supporting breath*
> *Drives all my fears away.*
> *Thy hand, in sight of all my foes,*
> *Doth still my table spread;*
> *My cup with blessings overflows,*
> *Thine oil anoints my head.*

#

Picking up a rental car is one of my least favorite things to do as a traveler. I never really know how long it will take or how much it will actually cost or whether they'll find some reason not to accept my credit card (remember Kuwait City?) or what kind of vehicle I'll be driving or with what features it might come equipped. But there's no substitute for having a set of wheels with which to explore a particular corner of planet Earth on your own schedule, so there I was on Friday morning, an hour behind my own schedule because it took so long to tear myself out of the cathedral, at the Reims office of a major global car rental chain.

By the time another customer finished at the desk, I was getting nervous about my day's schedule. One of the tight spots was getting past Paris before the Friday afternoon rush hour traffic slowed me down so much that my fifth and sixth hours of driving might be on country roads in the dark. The representative made it clear, politely and seemingly in earnest, that she didn't speak much English, so the transaction went slowly because I had to translate it all in my head using my passable-but-rusty high school French language skills. As she took my credit card and began to process the authorization, she looked at the timing and noticed that if I waited just fifteen more minutes, I could save a day's rental charge, contingent on my returning the car at Charles de Gaulle Airport precisely at the indicated time. I thought about that aspect of my itinerary (did I mention how carefully I'd planned this trip?) and had high confidence in my return time because it was coordinated with the time of Mass at a parish near the airport…and I was looking for ways to cut expenditures. I took the lady's advice and waited fifteen more minutes in the rental office before she swiped my tarjeta and handed me the keys.

From Reims I drove south along route D951, through Épernay, the other significant city of Champagne production, past field after field of white grapes and rows of trees with the subtle colors of fall foliage, all under a crisp blue sky with a few fluffy clouds. Maybe Reims cathedral was only one of the tastes of heaven I'd experience today. At Sezanne, I picked up the N4, one of the old arterial routes built to carry traffic between Paris and the rest of France.

It was now past noon, and I was getting hungry. Using my rental car's handy-dandy built-in navigation system, I selected an Italian restaurant for lunch in a small town whose name I don't remember. The pasta dish was quite tasty, and the bread was even better. The waitstaff noticed my enthusiasm for the bread, and they put another loaf in a plastic to-go bag when they cleared my plate.

I'd been reading an actual book on the Normandy invasion while I ate, in the interest of last-minute research, but as I waited to pay, I noticed that the restaurant had Wi-Fi. So, for the first time since I'd left my Reims hotel over three hours earlier, my phone was connected to the internet. Before I had a chance to look at the forty-two or so notifications that came through, I had paid and was on my way. Getting briefly turned around on my way out the door, I still didn't look at the notifications until I'd reached my car, which was parked a couple blocks away and thus out of range of the restaurant's Wi-Fi. Among the messages were two e-mails from one of my credit card providers indicating a low-credit alert. I briefly considered going back to the restaurant to check it out, but I was behind schedule and the bank would call if they suspected fraud, so it would just have to wait until I reached my hotel that evening. Schedules, you know!

#

Within a few minutes, I parked in the free gravel lot across from Chateau de Vaux-le-Vicomte, outside the town of Melun. I'd been to Versailles on my previous visit, and while this place isn't as large or as fancy, it is still grander than any private home I've seen in America, and the gardens were as beautiful as anything. And very much unlike Versailles, there were only a few dozen visitors there.

When I paid for admission, I used the card I thought was not affected by the notice I'd just half-seen. It was declined, so I paid cash. I still wasn't worried; maybe one card was nearing its limit and by coincidence the other didn't like that I was in France. I'd figure it out later.

The Chateau was constructed between 1658 and 1661 for Nicolas Fouquet, Marquis de Belle Île, Viscount of Melun and Vaux, who served as head of the finance department under the Sun King, Louis XIV. Even though he was a bean-counter by trade, Fouquet seems to have had an excellent and innovative taste in the decorative arts, and he assembled some of the finest artists and artisans and architects of his day to create one of the finest examples of what would become the Louis XIV style. However, there was palace intrigue: a rival minister convinced the prone-to-jealousy king that Fouquet had funded the estate by embezzling royal funds, replaced Fouquet in his ministerial position, and had Fouquet arrested. The arrest took place after an extravagant party featuring the premiere of a Moliére play, so as Voltaire would put it, "On 17 August, at six in the evening Fouquet was the King of France; at two in the morning he was a nobody."

Fouquet was in prison for life, and his wife was banished from France, leaving the estate in a no-man's-land of unoccupied state control. Presently King Louis XIV, who really was the King of France, helped himself to a great many tapestries, as well as the statues and orange trees. Not content with that, he hired the same group of artists and artisans and architects who'd designed Chateau de Vaux le Vicomte and had them build a new palace at Versailles, after which His Majesty felt better about himself.

Have you noticed the difference in character between Louis IX and Louis XIV? Does it begin to make sense why people might eventually have wanted to overthrow the monarchy?

Happily, the political climate in France is now such that the Chateau has been restored to something like Fouquet's design, and is open to the public. And so I spent a happy hour or so there, traipsing through the house's dozens of rooms, visiting the unfinished attic, and noting the splendor with which the king's half of the house was outfitted. That's right: Louis XIV fell for this plot even though Fouquet had saved half the Chateau for His Majesty. Actually, this was a common practice in those days because the king tended to travel a lot; since the Howard Johnson had not yet been invented, if you had a grand-looking house it was a good idea to keep a suite of rooms at the ready in case the king dropped in unexpectedly.

I could go on about the design of the place, but I'll just mention one innovative feature: hallways. These were included to ensure the privacy of more of the house's rooms than would otherwise have been the case.

If the house is grand, the gardens want for a superlative descriptor that isn't coming to my feeble mind. The publicly-accessible area is nearly a mile long, so I spent a good hour or so exploring the paths, flora, ponds, and statues, using my camera to take hundreds of pictures that I planned to upload once I got to my hotel and connected to wi-fi. So much photography must have been taking its toll on my poor smartphone; from time to time, the screen would split or lose part of its coloring. It kept returning to normal, so I said nice things to it and went on my way.

#

Even though it was only about 4:00 in the afternoon, the itinerary in my shirt pocket told me the only remaining task was to drive to my hotel in Alençon, 143 driving miles to the west. Given the delays I'd taken earlier, I knew I would be entering the out-of-Paris traffic flow about 5:00, and that the journey would probably take a while. It did. What "should" have been a drive of less than three hours took over four, with arrival at Alençon projected for just after sunset.

And what a sunset it was, even without the assistance of stained glass. The light, puffy clouds were pink, yellow, orange, purple… the rolling farmlands… the gently-colored forests… I looked forward to visiting Monet's Giverny in a few days to understand how the landscape informed his work. I also noted the various gas stations and fast-food joints along the way. More centrally to my purpose for this trip, as I drove I reminded myself of the geography of D-Day and how the Allies managed to punch a hole in Hitler's Atlantic Wall, looking forward to exploring it over the next few days.

But first I'd have to figure out what the deal was with my credit cards and call the bank to get it fixed.

#

Alençon sits just on the edge of Normandy, but I had chosen it for its practical, rather than symbolic, value. While the town was the birthplace of Ste-Thérèse, whose Basilica my plan told me I would soon be visiting in Lisieux, I had chosen Alençon because it would position me about two hours' drive from Mont St-Michel, which would be doable in a single segment in the morning, thus allowing me to arrive in plenty of time to climb to the top for Saturday noon Mass. I'd picked a hotel outside the city center, just off the N12, with a restaurant on-premises so that I would be able to eat a decent dinner even if I arrived late (which I was), sleep a full eight hours, and then get right back on the road in the morning with a minimum of fuss.

So I parked in the hotel's gravel parking lot, opened the door, and stretched my road-weary body. I retrieved my phone, but in spite of my several attempts to wake it up, the screen remained black. I stood there for a few more minutes, trying the shutdown-and-restart procedure using physical buttons on the side of the phone. Still black. How odd, and how disconcerting.

Tonight's hotel stay was prepaid, so I didn't need to try a credit card at check-in. But as I settled into my room and my phone still wouldn't light up, I began to realize I might have a real problem. Perhaps the credit card(s) had been compromised, or perhaps there was simply a temporary system glitch, or perhaps the banks' computers suddenly decided I shouldn't be in France (past issues had led me to register as a frequent traveler with my banks so that a series of purchases far from home doesn't cause a shutdown, and instead triggers a phone call, so if they'd tried to call and couldn't get through, the cards might then have been shut down.)

Indeed my phone wasn't working, and there appeared to be no easy way around that problem. I knew from a previous experience (when I'd apparently been pickpocketed along Rome's Via della Conciliazione) that it would take up to five days to receive a new phone overseas, and I'd be a moving target that whole time if I continued according to my plan. And if I had to stay put in this one out-of-the-way location, what was the point of remaining in France for six more days?

Taking a mental survey of what I could remember of my account balances, I wasn't sure I had enough cash and credit to pay for the remaining hotel stays and anticipated costs in gas, food, tolls, parking, and admission tickets with my remaining "good" accounts. Without a phone, I wouldn't be able to monitor my account balances moment-to-moment. And even if I used a landline to reach each bank and straighten things out, it was now Friday night and any fixes likely wouldn't help me until Monday or Tuesday.

With no functioning phone, I'd have difficulty navigating outside my nav-equipped rental car; this could be important in medieval city centers and also along expansive beaches. Telling time might be a challenge.

And, worst of all, I wouldn't be able to take pictures of anything I saw. That drove it home.

Weighing the many hours I'd spent planning this mission to Normandy against the possibility of an early return, I decided there was no point in throwing in the towel until after dinner; despite the technical evidence in my pocket, I still had some hope of recovery. So I took my book with me to the restaurant, ordered a scrumptious omelette, paid for it in cash, and returned to my room. And with the phone still dead, I pulled an Apollo 13, mentally cancelling the tour of Normandy and opening the door to getting home as fast as possible with what resources remained before they, too, might go bad.

My battle plan had encountered a hostile force, and I didn't even know what it was.

#

For all I knew, I'd been the victim of identity theft and would not be able to use plastic for the foreseeable future. Happily, the resources on hand included about €90 in my wallet, enough for the partial tank of gas I'd need to get to Aeroport Charles de Gaulle and the full tank with which I'd need to return the rental car, plus a little extra just in case. So I was good to get to the airport.

I would need to change my flight reservation home to one of my airline's half-dozen or so departures to its various U.S. hubs, connecting

#justpassingthrough

from that hub (it really made no difference which one) to DCA. I had enough miles in my frequent flyer account to get the last available seat, and since it would be Saturday I figured the light load factors would give me plenty of options. Normally, the way to make such a change was to call the airline's reservation number from one's personal cell, as I'd done that morning a year earlier in Ho Chi Minh City, but since I didn't have a working personal cell, I'd need to do the exchange in person at a CDG ticket counter. I didn't have the flight schedule memorized, but I knew the earliest transatlantic flights arrived into CDG around 6:00 a.m., and that with turnaround time the earliest departures back to the fruited plain couldn't be before 8:30 or so. So I needed to get to CDG by about 7:00 a.m. to make sure I had the best possible flight options. I had to hope that the difference in taxes and fees would be in my favor, or that one credit card would allow me to pay whatever small increase there might be due to exchange rate fluctuations or changed routing (each airport may charge a slightly different user fee for international travelers to pass through its facilities), or that the ticket counter would accept a cash payment, or that a kind stranger would use his or her card if I repaid him or her in cash.

Once I got on board the plane, I would have all the food and drink I needed, and even before that there would be snacks available in the lounge, so I counted food as a €0 cost for tomorrow and moved onto the timing aspect of the drive to the airport.

Navigation to the rental car return wouldn't be a problem, since the car's satnav system had worked flawlessly thus far and was not systemically connected to any of the failed equipment. And at any rate, I would mostly be retracing my steps from yesterday afternoon's drive, so I could be assured of finding a gas station along the way.

The drive to CDG would take two and a half hours; in order to make two gas stops, return the car, and arrive at the ticket counter around 7:00 a.m., I should leave before 4:00 a.m. At least there would be no traffic congestion at that hour on a Saturday. Subtracting time for a shower and a few minutes of packing, I went to set the alarm on my phone for 3:00 a.m.

Oh, right. My phone was dead.

I reached for the bedside alarm clock, but there wasn't one.

This was no problem; I'd use the in-room phone to ask for a wakeup call. But there was no landline phone in the room.

Slipping back into my shoes and making my way back to the front desk, I momentarily took for granted that I was in France, where I know how to speak the language. There was no need for poetry or high-level metaphors or technical description tonight; basic language skills would be sufficient for what I needed to do. It didn't occur to me until later how much worse a disaster this could have been in China or Vietnam or even Brazil, where my local language skills were not so hot.

The same middle-aged woman who'd checked me in I-couldn't-tell-how-long-ago was still at the desk. Channeling my innermost Jim Lovell, I said, "Excusez-moi, madame, mais j'ai une problème. Mon telephone cellulaire ne functionne pas."

The words came out without much thought. Mlle. Zima, Mme. Zarnstorff, Mme. Serotsky, M. Millar, and Mme. Asfar would have been proud to know that the skills they'd taught me in my high school and college language classrooms were coming in handy at this critical moment. The woman behind the desk, being a service employee who faces the travelling public in a part of western Europe where they have solid historical reasons not to despise Anglophones, offered me the use of her desk phone if I needed to call anybody for assistance.

Until this moment, I hadn't occurred to me that this problem was anyone's but mine to solve, or that someone else might not mind the slight inconvenience of helping me. I asked her if there was any way someone could come knock on my door at 3:00 a.m. to wake me up so that I could return home that day. She mentioned that the room televisions have a built-in alarm function that I could try setting.

#justpassingthrough

Almost as an afterthought, I asked whether I could use her phone to make an international call. Maybe it seemed I had on hand what I needed to solve the problems I couldn't quite identify, but that was no guarantee I wouldn't need more help along the way; if it was far-fetched that I'd experienced so many failures at once, whatever was causing them might cause more failures. I called Mission Control in the form of my sister in northern Virginia, the one I'd once misplaced in the London Underground. I chose her because I had her number memorized, and I knew that because she'd be at work, her kids would be at home with the babysitter and thus she'd have her phone on. Also, she's an experienced traveler who knows the basics of several languages and the ins-and-outs of airlines and trains and so forth. She knew me and my skill set, and I knew she would take my word for it when I told her what was happening, not try to solve problems that didn't exist, and be able to understand both the gravity of the situation and the fact that I would likely be able to return home under my own power even if I couldn't be in touch as as usual along the way. As an Air Force veteran, she knew my priorities would be to "Aviate, Navigate, Communicate," in that order. Yes, my sister was the right person to have in my corner and up to speed if there were more problems.

Returning to my room, I activated the television and set an alarm for three minutes from now. On cue, the TV turned itself on; the volume was up and the light was strong. I kept the channel set to a 24-hour news station, reset the alarm for 3:00 a.m., triple-checked it, changed into my pajamas, got under the covers, curled up in a ball, and started crying like a baby. All that planning was headed down the drain and I was returning home in defeat.

#

Just like clockwork, at 3:00 a.m. the too-quiet hotel room filled with light and sound. I reached over to the nightstand to activate my cell phone.

Just as it had in the Rex Hotel in Ho Chi Minh City a year earlier, my brain's reboot function took a few seconds to remind me where I was, why I was waking up at 3:00 a.m… and that no matter how long I held down the power button, my phone's screen was going to stay black.

Taking a deep breath and stepping on the floor that I was just shaken enough to believe might not be there, I recited "Glory be…" with bitter irony.

It's amazing how much you can accomplish when you're not stopping to look at your phone every fourteen seconds. I took my shower, combed my hair, brushed my dents, shaved, dressed, packed, loaded my luggage – UGH! – in the back of the car, and when I turned the ignition key and saw the time, it was 3:35 a.m.

#

My new plan failed to account for the weather. You might ask how the weather could possibly be a major problem in France in mid-October, but in the couple hours I'd actually been asleep a dense fog had rolled in. If this were a fiction novel, the fog be majorly symbolic of something, but in reality I had to treat it as just another one of Moltke's hostile forces requiring me to alter my plan of battle.

The thing about driving in the fog is that you just have to match the speed of other traffic. The thing about driving in the fog in the middle of the night in the middle of nowhere is that there is no other traffic, no other source of light, no way to gauge yourself against the collected wisdom of others who are facing the same challenge. I thought of that night fifteen years earlier when I'd merged onto I-95 in South Carolina in pouring rain and the speeding pickup truck had to swerve around me. Conditions were ripe for a speeding vehicle not to be able to swerve around me, but there was certainly some kind of wildlife in these woods, so I didn't dare go full speed. Either way, I didn't need to add a car crash in a foreign country to my list of problems just now.

Inching eastward along the N12 at half or two-thirds the normal speed, my gas gauge was now below a quarter of a tank. I saw one of those highway oases with a gas station and a McDonald's (yes, even in France!) and pulled in. Unfortunately, there was no human working there at this hour and therefore no way to pay with cash. I pulled out my wallet and retrieved my debit card, which had not been affected by the problem yesterday, and put it in the machine. It was declined.

I'd love to tell you that I said a "Hail, Mary" at this point, but my fuzzy memory tells me I probably said something less holy. Here I was alone at a gas station in the middle of nowhere in the middle of the night, without enough gas to get to Paris, and no way to pay for gas. Briefly, I considered waiting for another motorist to come along and offer cash for the use of their plastic in my pump. It's probably for the best that I abandoned that plan because there was nobody else out driving in these parts. Such an interaction might not have ended well, anyway.

Seeing no other choice, still encased in heavy fog, and watching the clock tick faster per mile than I had anticipated, I kept driving, hoping to be able to make it to another gas station before the tank ran dry. About twenty minutes later I pulled into another unattended gas station and attempted to use one credit card: Declined. Another credit card: Declined. The debit card: Approved this time.

And when I got back in the driver's seat, I noticed the plastic bag still sitting on the passenger seat from yesterday's Italian lunch restaurant. How many times had I prayed for daily bread? Here was a nice, reasonably fresh supply I could munch on.

As I drove eastward, the fog thinned to "somewhat foggy" and the road widened to "multiple lanes" and the traffic picked up to "very light". Pretty soon I found myself gliding past Versailles for the second time in

12 hours, around part of the Paris Périphérique, and up the Autoroute toward Charles de Gaulle.

After stopping to top up the fuel supply at the same place I'd used for the same purpose three years earlier, I turned in the rental car. This was a logistical step, sure, but also a psychological one. Now that I no longer had wheels, I was no longer roaming about France but heading home. And whether or not turning in the car would help the state of my credit card accounts, it certainly couldn't hurt. Reims seemed like a memory from another lifetime (a sign, in retrospect, of trauma), but I'd had the car for less than one full day.

#

The most hostile force I encountered on my third lifetime visit to France was not the train blocking the Chunnel, nor the fog, nor even the loss of phone functionality and purchasing power. The most hostile force I encountered was the woman working at the airline ticket counter.

It was just past 7:30 a.m. when I got to her. After she greeted me in English (de rigueur, as she was in the employ of an American company), I told her I held a miles-based ticket for departure on another date and needed to change to a flight today. She curtly informed me that I needed to call reservations to take care of that and attempted to brush me aside to help a more deserving customer. I stood my ground and gave her a look, to which she replied, "It is not possible."

My French training kicked in. "Oui, c'est possible." She froze. Until that moment, I'd been a dumb American challenging her plan not to do any work at work today. Now I was a hostile force who could speak French. Within moments, she pulled up my existing reservation and used her landline desk phone to call the airline's reservation number. I spent fifteen precious minutes on hold before reaching an operator, several more minutes explaining where I was and where I needed to go as soon as possible, and about three point two more seconds listening to her tell me there was no way to do that. I guess the phone agent could see the look on my sleep-deprived face through her phone, because suddenly there was a way to do the impossible. Several ways, in fact, as long as I didn't mind flying Economy; willing to stomach that for a daylight flight, I could choose between Charlotte and JFK for connection points, as well as Miami. My first inclination was to pick JFK because it's closest to DCA, but I hadn't been able to see a weather forecast for the northeastern USA (I'd had no reason to look at one before my phone went black, and no way to look at one afterward) and didn't want to risk getting stuck. And then I remembered which planes my airline tends to assign to each hub and decided Charlotte was going to be my most comfortable bet on that front, not to mention the weather there is rarely bad enough to cause big problems in October.

#

Flying from Paris to Charlotte was an opportunity to rest after the short night's sleep, the foggy drive, the confrontation at the ticket counter. For nearly nine hours, I was seated next to a woman who was experiencing even more shock, having started from Bahrain the night before. I hadn't flown long-haul Economy in nearly three years, and once the meal service was over, I had plenty of time to contemplate the situation at hand.

Yes, I mourned that I was throwing away all that planning, to say nothing of all those prepaid hotel rooms. I'd dreamt of climbing Mont St-Michel for over half my life, and had always wanted to see where the Greatest Generation saved what was left of old Europe from total oblivion under Hitler.

As the flight wore on, I began to count the little things, bitter and overtired: I was returning home with the tattered old shirt I hadn't worn and thus hadn't thrown out. I hadn't had time to pick up any souvenirs for myself or for others.

To Invade Normandy

A number of friends had asked me to pray for specific intentions; while I'd been able to do so at Westminster Cathedral and Sacré-Coeur and St. Remi and Reims Cathedral, what about the needy people I'd meant to pray for at Mont-St-Michel, Lisieux, the Normandy beaches, and St-Étienne-du-Rouvray (where, the previous year, Fr. Jacques Hamel had been martyred by ISIS militants while he said Mass)?

And then, somewhere southeast of Nova Scotia, I reached into my pocket and found the cheap rosary I'd purchased at Reims two days earlier. Aside from pictures posted to Facebook and a few sales receipts and a couple passport stamps, this would my only physical reminder of the aborted journey, the pilgrimage gone wrong. So now, every day when I pray the rosary, I'm reminded of my visit to Reims as a foretaste of heaven, and of the sudden death of my travel plans, and of the way I had just enough resources to make it home.

Holding the rosary tighter, I dwelt on that word, "pilgrimage". I began to remember what pilgrimage is for: pilgrimage isn't about arriving on your schedule at your chosen waypoints and having your pre-planned experiences; pilgrimage is the journey of life in microcosm. Sometimes life looks full and you check all the boxes: First day of school, graduation, career, marriage, kids, grandkids, retirement. Sometimes, there are hostile forces that prevent or delay big milestones and medium-size plans: disease, economic disaster, family strife. The pilgrimage changes the pilgrim. And, no matter what, it's all followed by death and judgment. What did you do with what you were given?

But even death is not the end. It is only a step on the pilgrim journey toward heaven. Heaven is the goal, heaven is home, home is the goal.

It would take me many weeks of purgatory to pick up the pieces of this mess. I never did quite get to the bottom of the credit card problem, but my best theory is that the non-Anglophone car rental agent at Reims took an authorization based on my planned rental period, and then another when I accepted her suggestion to wait fifteen minutes and save a day's charge. Phones are human-made machines; I'd worked mine hard,

#just passingthrough

and it broke. That's the closest I can come to saying what was the proximate cause of this failed mission.

#

On landing in Charlotte, back in my native land, I thought I was done with hostile forces. Ha.

At immigration, the computer flagged my passport as suspicious, setting off an alarm when I scanned it. That could have made for another interesting chapter, but the nice USCBP agent eyed my passport photo, said, "Looks like you to me," rolled her eyes, and welcomed me home. What a day I was having... a USCBP agent had used common sense.

Next came the Blueshirts. It took nearly a half hour to get to the metal detector, but not because there were thousands of people to be screened. The TSA had just installed new screening software on its computers, and roughly 50% of the bags were being flagged for hand screening. Unfortunately, the TSA's staffing protocols hadn't changed, and only one Blueshirt was performing the manual inspections. Well, the line of bags backed up as far as it could, and nobody was moving through the line. Meanwhile, several more agents were yelling at the people in line to follow instructions and remove the things that got a bag flagged for hand-screening. One righteously obnoxious fellow traveler asked, "What things are those?" The Blueshirt, perhaps not accustomed to being challenged, appeared to get even angrier and said, "Read the sign". Another traveler said "What sign?" I half-expected the Blueshirt to say it's as plain as the nose on his face... but there was no sign.

At great length, I walked through the scanner, only to see that my larger – ugh! – bag had been flagged for extra screening. After waiting another fifteen minutes for my turn (I found the clock on the wall) the Blueshirt opened my bag and removed the offending item, asking me to identify it. It was my travel carrier of Compact Discs. He laughed. I wasn't sure whether his derision was directed toward the idiotic system that flagged this item as dangerous only on the 43rd time I'd traveled with it, or at the stone-age traveler who carried CDs around with him in 2017.

#

It still wasn't over.

Three of my adorable niblings (one of whom had been born since my return from Vietnam the previous fall) and their parents (one of whom is my sister, who I'd called from Alençon the previous day) met me at DCA. I've not yet had the experience of being welcomed into paradise by angels, but seeing those little people so happy to see me was enough welcome to turn all kinds of weeping into joy. Their parents bought me Chick-Fil-A for dinner, which was appreciated because I had no idea whether or when I'd be able to pay for food.

After we finished eating, I turned down their repeated offers of a ride home. I'd refilled my Metro card with fare money before flying away on Monday afternoon, so I'd be good to go. I hugged everyone goodbye, thanked them for dinner, and proceeded to the Metro station.

Which was closed for track work all weekend.

So it was off to a free bus ride for me, and then two train rides, then dragging my luggage four blocks to my front door. Of course, entry to my apartment building requires the use of my phone, so I had to wait outside for about ten minutes on this beautiful evening for someone else to come by and let me in. I thought of all the sacrifices people make so that the holy souls in purgatory can get home to heaven, and realized the importance of making more of those each day: Charity, charity, charity.

And my refrigerator had broken while I was away, but lumped in with the ridiculousness of trying to replace a broken phone without credit cards and trying to revive credit cards with no phone, it was just more fodder for the book people kept telling me I should write.

But all that could wait until morning. Once again, I'd been helped on my journey home by a mix of human kindness and the skills and

#justpassingthrough

knowledge I'd acquired on my pilgrimage through this strange world. Despite the array of hostile forces working against me, by the prayers and sacrifices of others along the way, I had made it. I'd had to give up the path I'd so carefully chosen, and instead follow the way I knew would lead me home. Ultimately, my help had come from the Lord, the maker of heaven and earth, who hadn't allowed my foot to stumble, but brought me home rejoicing.

The sure provisions of my God
Attend me all my days;
O may Thy house be my abode,
And all my work be praise!
There would I find a settled rest,
While others go and come;
No more a stranger, nor a guest,
But like a child at home.
(Isaac Watts)

Denouement

The world doesn't stay the same for long, does it? I'm reminded of that reality each time I drop into London on an extended layover. On my first visit in 1994, we struggled to complete a transatlantic phone call. On my next visit in 2004, I carried a rented cellphone which successfully received calls forwarded from my number about 2/3 of the time, but it was of no help when I briefly lost my teenage sister in the Underground because she didn't have a phone of her own. Now, I can be walking through Hyde Park and answer calls and texts and emails about work just as easily as I can from home. Supposedly that's a positive development.

I began writing in November of 2017, a few weeks after that abrupt return from France, and continued through October of 2018, with publication slated for the end of 2019. Even in that short time, the world has changed a fair amount. Rather than going back to update the prose of the affected sections – a task that could quickly turn me into the dog that chases its tail all day – I decided to leave my descriptions as they were written in 2017-18, and to provide a few updates here.

#

My visit to the Persian Gulf (ahem, Arabian Gulf, or Sinus Persicus) region in early 2014 turns out to have been in a peaceful lull for that troubled Sandbox. I visited after most American troops had withdrawn from Iraq, and just before ISIS, or ISIL, or IS, or whatever it's called this week, began to terrorize Iraq and Syria and persecute Christians there. That said, Highway 80 is still open from Kuwait City to the Iraqi border near Basra, and they're still not widely using the "Highway of Death" moniker on the guide signs.

#justpassingthrough

\#

Brazil got a taste of increased inbound traffic from the USA during the Olympic-time visa waiver period, and decided to allow tourists to visit without a visa on a more regular basis.

\#

As expected, Archbishop Alexander Sample released a fine pastoral letter on sacred music for the Archdiocese of Portland in early 2019. I commend it to anyone interested in the topic.

\#

Georgetown, Guyana is now home to a Marriott hotel with an oscillating navigation light on top. The opening of the 197-room luxury hotel in such a small market had other effects, though: the Halito Hotel folded in 2016, and is now the location of a jewelry dealer.

\#

After a wave of mergers in the U.S. airline industry, the new mega-airlines are using the reduced competition as an opportunity to turn their frequent-flyer programs into big-spender programs. This has not quite eliminated the mileage run (a technique of travel that led to several of the journeys chronicled in this book), but it has limited the use of that technique to a relatively few specific situations.

\#

This latter part of 2019 has seen an increase in protests and violence in Hong Kong, as the Chinese government meets resistance in its efforts

Postscript

to exert more control in the Special Administrative Region. The ongoing strife has depressed demand for travel to and from Hong Kong, leading some airlines to reduce flight schedules and/or use smaller planes.

#

The situation of Catholics in mainland China has gotten even worse since my visit at Easter 2015. In 2018, the Vatican and the Chinese government announced an accord whereby Beijing would be allowed to appoint Catholic bishops, supposedly ending the need for Catholics in China to remain underground. (Can you imagine anyone thinking it kosher to allow U.S. bishops to be appointed by Donald Trump or Bernie Sanders?) The real effect has been disastrous: the Chinese government has been demanding that the Ten Commandments be removed from churches and be replaced with the sayings of Chairman Mao. Stories have emerged to the effect that Chinese Catholics have barricaded themselves inside churches to save those buildings from planned destruction by the government.

The best one can say for the Vatican is that it seems to have reached this accord with a great deal of naïveté. The matter remains a huge question mark on the record of Pope Francis, not least because of informed speculation that the former Theodore Cardinal McCarrick may have been involved in negotiating the deal.

#

Closer to home, the summer of 2018 was a rough one in Catholic circles. I was at weekday Mass here in Washington when the priest told us about the news of Mr. McCarrick's history of abusing kids and harassing seminarians under his care. This came along with revelations about the related coverups that seemed to have reached the very highest levels of the Church hierarchy and enabled McCarrick to become Archbishop of

Washington. Shortly after the McCarrick story finally came into the light of day, a Pennsylvania grand jury released a report into decades of clerical abuse and its coverup in the dioceses of the Keystone State. Similar reports were soon issued in other jurisdictions. Both Catholic journalists and the secular press became more aggressive in reporting these kinds of corruption.

As part of my own disgusted and horrified reaction, I elected to share the bad news on social media without whitewashing, to join my voice with those faithful laity and clergy demanding that predators be prosecuted where possible and that enablers be removed from positions of authority they demonstrably can't handle, and to call for prayerful solidarity with the victims of these destructive acts. Along the way, about a dozen people I know have identified themselves to me (or been identified to me by others) as adult victims of clerical abuse and/or harassment, most of the incidents occurring within the last decade. As of November 2019, some of those perpetrators have been sidelined while others have yet to meet anything like justice for what they've done. Abuse of the faithful by the clergy is not just abuse of the abuser's authority and of the victim's physical body, but a diabolical attempt to murder the victim's soul; if the victims can't trust the clergy who are ordained to help them on the journey to heaven, how can we even expect them to want to get to heaven at all?

I see in this crisis a situation very much like what Jesus describes in the Good Samaritan parable: a traveler has been robbed, beaten, and left to die (in this case spiritually) by the road. Too many of the 'good' people who'd never attack anyone are passing on the other side because they don't want to be inconvenienced or have their reputations tarnished by being associated with someone whose experience seems to discredit them or their peers. Abuse victims need to be believed and have their physical and spiritual needs met, both in the immediate aftermath and in the longer term. Their attackers need to be removed from positions where they can harm others and called to repentance for the good of their own souls.

Postscript

This book is dedicated to my friends and coworkers who've been abused by wolves in shepherds' – pastors' – clothing, and to all victims of clerical abuse. These ordinary men and women have encountered a hostile force on their life pilgrimage that nobody should have to encounter. In union with so many faithful clergy and laity, I express my solidarity with those survivors and recognize the immense cost they will pay for the rest of their lives. I call for increased and continued efforts at removing predators from "ministry". My neighborly prayer is that, by God's grace and with our help, they, too, may make it safely home.

#

Being a first-time author is daunting enough in itself. In preparing to self-publish this book via Amazon's Kindle Direct Publishing, I was forced also to become a graphic designer, advertising designer, and marketing agent. One small task – yet enormously important – was designing the cover. After wrestling with the design for a while, I decided to use an image of my own as the background for the cover. It's taken along the D951 heading from Reims toward Épernay, when I was heading from Reims Cathedral to Chateau de Vaux-le-Vincomte just a few hours before aborting my tour of Normandy.

The image is not of the clear quality you would normally expect on a book cover; that's what happens when you take a picture through the windshield of a car on the road, upload it to Facebook, download it to your laptop two years later, upload it to a photo editor program, crop it, increase its size, and then put it on the cover of a book. I stuck with it because its very existence captures something of what I've been trying to say with this book – something about making the most of every moment along the way toward a destination we can't quite see.

#justpassingthrough

On Easter Day of 2019, arriving home from a long day (and week) of liturgical music, I reached into my pocket intending to pull out the Reims rosary and pray. It was missing, and I never found it.

#

The abandoned plan to tour Normandy was raised from its premature grave and tried again with more success. But you'll have to wait until I write my next book to read more about that second attempt, including how I made a big mess of things by falling off one of Hitler's guns.

Friday, November 22, 2019
The Memorial of St. Cecilia, Virgin, Martyr, and Patroness of Music and Musicians
Washington, District of Columbia